*Chairman Mao Would Not Be Amused*

# Chairman Mao Would Not Be Amused

## FICTION FROM TODAY'S CHINA

### Edited by Howard Goldblatt

GROVE PRESS

NEW YORK

Portions of the Introduction first appeared, in slightly different form, in the *Los Angeles Times*. Reprinted by permission.

*Published simultaneously in Canada*
*Printed in the United States of America*

FIRST EDITION

Library of Congress Cataloging-in-Publication Data

Chairman Mao would not be amused: fiction from today's China / edited
    by Howard Goldblatt.
        ISBN 0-8021-1573-X
        1. Chinese fiction—20th century—Translations into English.
    I. Goldblatt, Howard, 1939-
    PL2658.E8bC43    1995      895.1'35208—dc20      95-1931

Grove Press
841 Broadway
New York, NY 10003

10 9 8 7 6 5 4 3 2 1

# Contents

# Introduction

## 1

I sometimes wonder what Chairman Mao, who almost single-handedly launched, then single-mindedly derailed, the Chinese Revolution, might have thought of the literature published since his death in 1976. Taking the long view, I think he would have approved of "scar literature," a cathartic body of writing that voices the sufferings of the Cultural Revolution, for its success in pacifying the people at a difficult historical moment; after all, if, for the time being, they could not be united under the banner of permanent, violent revolution, why not keep them busy airing their collective discontent, mainly with one another? Mao knew the value and limitations of literature and writers, and he trusted neither. Yet he knew how to harness their power; over the years, he had used literature and the arts both to bring down his enemies—most of them erstwhile friends—and to keep the people's attention focused on his political agenda. If national events and socialist behavior remained the raison d'être of the writing, it served his purposes. The fiction that began appearing shortly after his death was, by any reasonable literary standard, rather badly written; but that would not have concerned Mao, for in his earliest pronouncements on literature, back in the Yan'an caves in the 1940s, he had said, "Literature and art are subordinate to politics, but in their turn exert a great influence on politics." By focusing on the evils wrought by the renegade

Gang of Four, and thus deflecting charges of responsibility away from the Party and the current government, this generally amateurish writing played a significant political role in the days immediately following the Cultural Revolution.

"Scar literature" gave way in the late 1970s and early 1980s to "introspective writing" and "root-seeking literature," both of which would have fit nicely into Mao's plans to keep the socialist pot boiling. The questions posed in the fiction of this period—like, Why are we the way we are? and What are the origins of our Chineseness?—are just the sort of questions Mao would have wanted people to ask, since he could have been counted on to provide the answers. And if the writers went a bit far afield, or strayed into one form of heresy or another, then they would become grist for his mill, a mill that produced exemplars for the next generation. Indeed, there were some anxious moments, as when the avant-garde versifiers known as "misty poets" renounced a collective mentality with their imagistic, impenetrable poems; but who reads poetry anyway? Mao would have merely swatted them away with one of his famed waves of the hand, a superior smile on his face, smug with the knowledge that the "neo-realistic" prose then capturing the imagination of readers in China and in the West was highly politicized, making it one more potential weapon to be used by those in power to retain that power.

The literary scene in the mid-1980s was charged, as large numbers of readers were won over by the passion of writers hewing to the role of social reformer. Finally, people assumed, a literature of dissent worthy of the name was emerging: stories revealing the ugly side of the revolution, poems that sang the praises of romantic love, dramas that acted out some of the dangers facing the Chinese nation, even films portraying the betrayal of the revolution by people *within* the Communist Party and the government itself! But Mao, I think, would not have been concerned, knowing it was only a matter of time before someone went too far and the orthodoxy of power could reassert itself. Mao must have known that the only truly dangerous writing in a totalitarian society is that which ignores politics

altogether, literature that serves art, not society. Anti-Party dia-
tribes? They would play right into his hands. Lurid sex and gratui-
tous violence? He certainly had nothing against either of those in
real life. Utopian pie in the sky? What, after all, is Marxism?

But then China's new leaders turned their guns on their own
students and workers, and the ensuing loss of faith, coupled with
the supremely individualistic desire to get rich quick, changed almost everything in China, including its literature. I suspect that
even the chairman's confidence would have been shaken by reactions to events of June 1989. The writers responded to the new
realities by staking out territory independent of societal and political pressures; they were now more interested in mocking the government and socialist society than in trying to reform them, more
concerned with the reception of their work by the international
community than with their status in China. If Mao were still
around and running the show, I'll bet that few, if any, of the stories
in the present collection would have pleased him. At best he might
have asked, "What's the point?" At worst . . . well, we mustn't get
carried away. Most troubling to him, I suspect, would have been the
artistry—the playfulness of some of the pieces, the angst-ridden in-
trospection of others, and the layered possibilities of most; that, of
course, and their lack of utility, something no socialist revolutionary could abide. No, if confronted by the literary offerings of the
twenty men and women represented here, Chairman Mao would
certainly not be amused.


# 2

Of the writers included here, only one, Wang Meng, was born
before the creation of the People's Republic in 1949, and only he
published works of fiction prior to the Cultural Revolution, a ten-
year period (1966–1976) of unprecedented cultural sterility and political upheaval. In post-Mao China, writing got off to a slow start,
as long-stagnant waters were tested with extreme caution. Writers
came and went, and before long the process of generational transi-

tion had accelerated to the point where novelists and poets sometimes found themselves out of favor with a fickle and volatile readership within months of breaking new ground or of being lionized
as the latest literary superstars. Many had spent all or part of the
Cultural Revolution either as Red Guards or as their victims, and
most had been sent to the countryside to "learn from the peasants"
(and to be kept a safe distance from the real seats of power). Their
experiences (as in the cases of Li Xiao and Kong Jiesheng) or their
newly acquired understanding of China's peasantry (as with Yang
Zhengguang and Li Rui) formed the foundation of their literary
output. Rural China—enigmatic, cruel, simple, and wretchedly
poor—also informs the works of writers like Mo Yan, Cao
Naiqian, and Wang Xiangfu; artistically superior to most of what
had gone before, their fiction remains invested with a conscience
but is no longer at the service of external interests.

As the decade ended, the Tiananmen massacre caused an artistic and philosophical rupture of unprecedented significance, and
that has produced a generation of novelists who describe in graphic
and revealing prose a place where surface stability uneasily masks a
society in turmoil, whose work probes the darker aspects of life and
human behavior. These writers, generally in their thirties, although
some are younger, have gained unprecedented notoriety and ac-
ceptance in the West, if not always in their own country, where
their work sometimes does not see the light of day until it is first
published in Taiwan or Hong Kong. No longer interested in being
seen as state-supported "literary workers," writers like Su Tong,
Yu Hua, and Ge Fei have proclaimed independence from the literary establishment, often publishing abroad to escape ideological and
financial pressures, and confidently asserting their artistic freedom.
While stretching the limits of "taste" in their writing, they simultaneously demonstrate a heightened interest in China's past; for them
history is neither circular nor linear, but random and shifting, until
the boundaries between past and present blur into obscurity. By de-
nying history its traditional authority, they raise fundamental questions about contemporary life, politics, and values. Visions of the

future, as a result, run from murky to apocalyptic. Unthinkable acts and ideas—from cannibalism to perverted sex—have become trademarks of the most conspicuous among them. Once a refuge for writers intent on buttressing or criticizing specific politics or ideologies, historical fiction has now become a showcase of human nature, often at its most despicable. Additionally, the more daring among these writers, such as Duo Duo and Can Xue, have created dialogues with their own texts and with their readers that challenge and subvert the very way we approach and interpret fiction.

Throughout most of the history of the People's Republic, women writers have played a significant and pioneering role in literary developments. The issue of sexuality is of particular concern to novelists like Hong Ying, Ai Bei, Chi Li, and Chen Ran, whose experiments in narrative and linguistic style have earned them praise from readers and critics both in China and in the West.

Concurrent with recent changes in the way novelists are writing these days are changes in the way these fin-de-siècle writers view their role as artists. No longer interested in placing their pens in the service of society, which seems to be unraveling in the midst of economic reforms intended to fulfill the national dream of becoming rich and powerful, they view the xenophobic zeal of their parents' generation with skepticism at best, contempt at worst. They see themselves as independent artists whose works can, and will, appeal to readers and viewers all over the world. Frequently attacked for pandering to Western tastes rather than writing for their countrymen, they are, if anything, becoming more defiant and self-assured. In their truth-telling about contemporary and historical China, they present a picture of a nation that is turning away from its past and demanding new paths to an urbanized, entrepreneurial, less static future; it may turn out that, like Yukio Mishima, Aleksandr Solzhenitsyn, and Nadine Gordimer before them, they are appreciated less in their own country than elsewhere.

In fact, these young writers speak to the rest of the world precisely because they no longer care to speak *for* China. The common thread of misanthropy running through much of their work and the emphasis on skewed, anti-Confucian family relations, including incest, rape, murder, voyeurism, and more, underscore a belief that they are no more responsible for social instability in their country than are entrepreneurs who want only to get rich, students who want only to leave, or petty bureaucrats who want only to get by. Whether their pessimistic views of China turn out to be prophetic, mimetic, or even wrong, it is now as hard to make arguments for a benign Chinese exoticism as it was to evoke visions of a genteel, kimono-clad Japan in the wake of novels by Kenzaburō Ōe, Murakami Ryu, even the trendy Banana Yoshimoto.

In the urban centers of China, where images have eroded the power of ideas and where the pace and nature of daily life are changing rapidly under the influence of MTV, rock concerts, and soap operas, darkly cinematic writings by Shi Tiesheng, Chen Cun, and Bi Feiyu are winning over a materialistic and cynical readership that is caught up in a rush to embrace capitalist consumerism and experience as much decadence as they can squeeze into their young lives.

All this recent activity, it seems, is but the beginning. A stream of literary offerings by these and other, even younger, writers will surely establish a Chinese presence in international literary circles, just as Chinese films already have in Japan and the West; in their desire to experiment, to shock, and, in the words of one hip novelist, "to be famous till I'm dizzy, without worrying about the consequences," they will, by the very nature of their writing, continue to question the official version of the truth for an increasingly alienated populace. "The wisdom of the novel," Milan Kundera reminds us, "comes from having a question for everything." We readers are being supplied with a rich source of material from which we can seek answers.

## 3

The concept of sparseness does not easily enter the consciousness of anthologizers. There is, it seems, always one more story, one hot new author, one last category demanding inclusion. And the questions one asks oneself: Is there adequate balance between established writers and future stars? Is the range of ages dealt with fairly? Are there enough women represented? But stop one must, for not to do so would deprive too many authors and readers of the opportunity to meet.

Space alone has kept some writers out of these pages. That includes Wang Shuo, whose "punk-cool" patois and contemporary settings have captured a large urban readership with irreverent tales of hedonistic life among China's restless, often aimless, urban youth. Or Wang Anyi, a middle-aged novelist who writes of her less "hip" generation of city dwellers, probing internalized worlds as they strive to break free of stultifying tradition. They and other novelists who are expanding the parameters of contemporary fiction, thematically, linguistically, and philosophically, are given to writing "big" books—stories running to well over a hundred pages and novels of nearly half a million words.

All the selections in this anthology were written or first published in China proper; the earliest pieces appeared in 1985, the most recent in late 1993. Novelists who left China more than a decade ago, those who have moved on to other pursuits (most, in contemporary terms, to take the plunge—that is, become entrepreneurs), and those from other Chinese communities—Taiwan, Hong Kong, Southeast Asia, the West—are not represented here; their work can be found in translation elsewhere.

Many people have graciously contributed to this anthology: Colin Dickerman, who suggested the project; Shelley Wing Chan, who performed many important tasks for me as the project built up steam; friends and colleagues who either commented upon the growing list of authors and stories or made recommendations of their own; and, of course, the accomplished translators, who maintained their composure and humor even when I could not. On behalf of the authors whose work graces the pages that follow, I thank them all.

H.G.

# First Person

## SHI TIESHENG

That year, in the fall, I was assigned housing. It wasn't a bad apartment, just too high up, on the twenty-first story, and a long way from downtown. I took half a day off work to go have a look. The trip took almost two hours by bus, and by the time I got there, it was already after four o'clock. I saw it right away. Just as I had been told, it was the only building for about a mile around. It was white and surrounded by a green brick wall. The area was pleasant, with trees on three sides and a river to the south. The river flowed west to east, just as I had been told. The wall ran right up against the riverbank, and a small bridge led to the courtyard gate.

Even so, as I walked through the gate, I was thinking I should make sure I'd come to the right place. Near the western wall stood a huge parasol tree; a young woman was sitting against its trunk in the quiet, concentrated shade. I walked over and asked her if this was the building I was looking for. I didn't think I was speaking too quietly. She lifted her head, seemed to glance at me, and then settled back down as before, looking with lowered eyes at the shifting dots of light that the autumn sun was sprinkling down through the shade. It was as if I no longer existed. I stood waiting for a while, and then I heard her murmur, "Go with the flow." Her voice was quite soft, but she spoke each word slowly and distinctly. I nodded. I was positive I no longer existed. Her thoughts were off in a fantasy land. Some vulgar noise had disturbed her for a minute, that was all. I felt a little apologetic and a little abashed, so I stepped back, turned away, and walked straight for the front door of the apartment building, thinking that this had to be the place.

The building appeared empty; people hadn't started moving in yet. No one was there to run the elevators, which were all locked. I have heart trouble, but since I'd come so far, I couldn't just leave after one look at the stairs. I figured that as long as I didn't try to go fast, I wouldn't have much of a problem climbing to the twenty-first floor. "Go with the flow" was what the girl said. That seemed to be sincere, appropriate advice, so I took a few deep breaths and started to climb. When I reached the third floor, I stopped to catch my breath. I leaned out the window and caught sight of the girl. She was still sitting there in a trance, her head slightly lowered, her hands resting casually on her knees. On her simple, elegant skirt, dots of sunlight and shade silently divided and then combined, gathered together and fell apart again. "Go with the flow" was what she said. Actually, when she said it, she didn't see me and didn't hear any vulgar noise. She didn't see anything and didn't hear anything. She was a thousand miles away. I couldn't see her face, but I could sense her tranquillity and enchantment. The autumn wind swept invisibly past the huge parasol tree, making a soft, dignified sound.

On a fall evening, when the sun was about to set, she left home alone, locking the gradually gathering twilight in her room. She walked where she pleased along paths through the fields. She followed the smells of the grasses and the earth as she walked where she pleased. Who was she? She walked to a remote, quiet place and sat down facing a tall, empty building. She leaned against an ancient tree. She sat in its deep, swaying shade, sat in the low, chanting sound it made. She made the place her own. Who was she? She thought about things near and distant, about things real and illusory. Her mind and body slipped into a natural, mysterious realm. . . . A woman like that, who could she be? A woman to be admired.

But I had to keep climbing my stairs. I didn't know what had been arranged for me by nature's mysteries. Take, for example,

climbing stairs; take, for example, the fact that there was an apartment on the twenty-first floor that would belong to me. When had
this been determined? How had it been determined? Fourth floor,
fifth floor. I had to rest again. To tell the truth, resting was of sec-
ondary importance. As I climbed, I didn't stop thinking about the
girl, even for a minute. I had no bad intentions, I just wanted to
look at her again and was afraid she had already left. I just wanted
to have another look at her, another look at the contented noncha-
lance with which she sat alone under that big tree, quietly lost in
thought. I looked down. She hadn't left. She was still sitting there
by herself, still sitting the same way. But now I saw someone else.

There was a man walking back and forth along the outside of
the western wall. I hadn't noticed him before. The wall had
blocked my view, and I couldn't see him. The wall was quite high.
By this time, I was on the fifth floor; yet even so, I could see only his
head and shoulders. He paced back and forth as if caged. He
walked for a while, then stopped, looked into the distance, and
puffed repeatedly on a cigarette. Then he started walking back and
forth again, then stopped again, and smoked furiously as he peered
toward the distant woods. I could hear his footsteps; they sounded
irritated, restless. I heard the snap of each match he struck; he
broke match after match. The spot where he stopped was also in
the shade of the parasol tree; only the wall separated him from the
girl. Along with the appearance of this man, I noticed that not far
from him and the girl, in the northwest corner of the wall, there
was a small gate. It had been there all along, of course. I had just
overlooked it. Now it was especially obvious. Who was the man?
What was he to her? One was inside the gate, the other was outside.
There was no one else around, no one else in the vicinity. What was
going on? The man was terribly upset and anxious, and the woman
was in an absolutely silent trance. What had happened? What had
happened between them? A slanting beam of sunlight came
through the gap between the doors of the small gate and settled in
the damp shadow at the base of the wall; it was bright and sadly
beautiful.

"Go with the flow" was what the girl said, but what did she mean? To what did "Go with the flow" refer? Was she forced to leave him? Did she have no choice but to leave him? Yes, yes. If she had no choice but to leave him, then all she could do was go with the flow. No choice but to leave him. That meant she still loved him, but there was nothing she could do. "Go with the flow." Wasn't that the truth? When she said it, her voice was hollow, her eyes dazed. She didn't see me at all and, of course, couldn't hear what I asked her. She was overcome with sadness; all she could think of was the happiness and the bitterness of the past. But finally there was nothing she could do. And the man outside the wall? He was madly in love with her and wanted to make her happy. How he hoped she would be happier because of him. It never occurred to him that he would drive her to such suffering. It never occurred to him that things could end up like this. He had thought it was enough that he loved her and that she loved him, too. It never occurred to him that the world was so large or that everything in life was connected in so many ways.

"As long as you're happy, it's OK." Maybe that's what he said finally.

The woman sat under the tree with her head lowered. Restlessly, the man walked to her side, around her, in front of her.

"As long as you're happy, I'll be OK whatever happens," he said to her.

"But if you'll just not be afraid, if you'll just have a little courage.

"Will you say something? After so long, you must give me a definite answer."

The woman couldn't speak. Yes or no. The logic of it wasn't so simple.

The man said, "I'm waiting for you to say the word. Yes or no."

The man said, "What's important is what you want. What's important is what you think will make you happy."

The man said, "It's not that I want you to make a decision right away, but I have to know what you think is best."

The woman couldn't speak at all. What would be best? Maybe it would have been best if you and I had never met. Maybe it would be best if people didn't fall in love, if there were never such a person as you, never such an autumn as this, never such hollow afternoon light, and never such an expanse of shade. She didn't want any of it. Such long, slender, restless legs, such delicate, nimble feet crushing fallen leaves. She didn't want any of it. And the long, drawn-out sound of leaves ripping into pieces. She didn't want it. She had never wanted it.

"Are you going to say something?" the man asked. "I don't know what it means that you won't say anything.

"I don't understand why it's so hard to answer my questions.

"I don't know what else I can say. I don't know what to do.

"OK, OK, maybe I shouldn't pester you like this. Maybe I should be sensible and just walk away.

"OK, I'll go. I never thought I could make things so difficult for you. I'll just say one more thing. As long as you're happy, it's OK with me whatever happens."

He turned and walked out through the small gate. She didn't stop him. She really no longer had the strength to stop him. She heard him walk through the gate, listening with despair to the sound of his departing footsteps. She held her breath and listened, listened. The familiar sound didn't travel far, and she sighed in relief. Or maybe it was the opposite. Her despair deepened. She heard him walking back and forth outside the wall, heard him smoking, heard him sighing, heard him crying his heart out. She could fully imagine his pain, but she had no idea what she should do. The only answer left to her was "Go with the flow." The wind blew between the dense, broad leaves of the parasol tree and through the surrounding woods; it sounded like water, like splashing oars, like waves someplace off in the distance. Why? Were their parents opposed? What other reason could there be? It was better to keep climbing my stairs. I came to look at my apartment. All I could do was get myself up to the twenty-first floor.

Then again, maybe she didn't love him. Or once loved him but didn't anymore. "But why?" the man asked. "I don't want to pressure you, but I have to know why this is happening." It wasn't that she didn't want to tell him, but she truly didn't know what to say. There seemed to be many reasons, but when she tried to speak, she couldn't make any of them clear. There really were many reasons, but when she spoke, she couldn't find any of them. "Go with the flow" was what she said. It was what she always said to him. In her mind, she was still saying it to him and to herself. There was no way to prove or disprove love; all one could do was go with the flow. The man went around to the other side of the wall. Maybe he was grieved; maybe he was angry. He just turned and walked out through the small gate. Maybe it was love; maybe it was hatred. Not wanting to say anything more, he walked out through the small gate. But he couldn't leave her. He didn't want to leave her. He was upset and anxious and didn't know what to do; he stood looking around helplessly. The sun had neared the woods. Gray magpies called back and forth. Inside the wall, the woman listened worriedly to the man's movements. She couldn't leave either. She was afraid he might be capable of anything. But what should she do? There was absolutely nothing she *could* do except go with the flow. That and pray quietly. It was the only wise thing to do, the right thing.

I reached the seventh floor. When I looked down, I could see over the dense treetops nearby. I saw a gravestone among the trees. First one, then two, then three. When I looked carefully, I saw they were all over, like stars in the sky or men on a chessboard, and I realized it was a cemetery. So *that's* what was going on. All along, the man had been gazing at the cemetery. That's what was going on. That's why the woman was dressed so plainly and neatly. Maybe it was the anniversary of someone's death, and they had come together to visit the grave.

Death has always been the most mysterious of affairs. A living, breathing person is gone. A living soul, someone who could think, could speak, could laugh, could love . . . suddenly is gone. You and he were once so intimate. You could see him whenever you wanted.

You could say to him whatever you wanted to say. But he died, and you'll never see him again. If there's something you forgot to tell him, it's too late now. But even after many years, when the woman came to the dead man's grave, she still couldn't accept this fact. She placed a handful of earth on the grave, sprinkled a little wine on it, and set down a bouquet of wildflowers. But the deceased? He was dead, gone, couldn't be found, couldn't be found anywhere, would never be found. The woman sat by the grave and felt chills run through her body and her heart, too.

The man pleaded with her. "This is the natural way of things. You've got to understand that this is the inevitable resting place for us all."

Looking at the irrefutable grave, she still could not believe death was so cruel.

"Don't be this way, OK? Don't be like this." He pleaded with her in a gentle, humble tone, as if it were all his fault.

"To live, you've got to learn to forget," the man said.

Looking at the grave, the woman also saw the dead man's likeness, smiling and very real. She still could not imagine what dying was.

The man said, "You have to keep thinking that he's gone, that he's been released. You have to keep thinking that we are alive.

"You and me," the man said, "we're together. I'm here with you."

After a long time, the woman left the graveside and walked blindly through the woods. Her long skirt drifted in the air like a ghost. She walked out of the woods. There was a white apartment building surrounded by a long, green brick wall. She walked through the small gate. It was a good place, with a big, lonely tree that calmed one down a little and gave one something to lean on. "Let me be alone for a while, just be by myself, OK?" she said. She didn't have to look back to know the man was right behind her. Obediently, he turned and walked back through the gate. She sat down against the tree. It was a little better here, by the vacant building. Unfamiliar places help one forget the past. The gently sliding shadow of the tree and the softly falling leaves made just the place for a grieving heart. Go with the flow, just go with the flow, she thought. Really, he was right—death didn't have to be so scary. "Go with the flow," she said quietly. Maybe she thought the man had come back inside the courtyard, or maybe she was speaking to whomever it was who had died. She didn't see clearly who I was, didn't understand at all what I was asking. The man kept watch outside the gate. The woman's persistent heartache often left him at a loss. He didn't know if he respected the dead man or was jealous of him; maybe he even hated him a little. At such times, he couldn't say if he himself was decent or base and mean. He had come here with her, he had agreed to come every year. He knew he would live up to his word, but he also knew, and only he knew, that he truly wished that she would forget that man, forget him forever. He looked toward the woods and the grave they surrounded. He prayed to heaven either to bless and protect him or forgive him: let that man die for good, and let the two of them never come here again, never return to this place.

The ninth floor. It was evening, and the autumn breeze had stiffened. If there was a strong wind that night, by the next day most of the leaves on the trees would be down. By now, the rays of the setting sun seemed to be coming in on the horizontal. I could see that the man outside the wall was shading his eyes with his hand and staring at the woods, in the same direction in which he had been looking so expectantly before—toward the setting sun. In that direction, through the trees, I could see two roads that intersected. Where struck by sunlight, the roads' pale surface was dazzling. One of the roads ran east-west, the other north-south. At the far end of the east-west road—the west end—I could see a stop sign for a suburban bus. A bus was pulling in just then, and a few people got off. The man was looking in that direction. He remained absolutely still as he watched the people. He seemed to be waiting for some- one. Then the bus pulled away, and the people dispersed. They had probably come to visit graves. Some carried fresh flowers. The man's hand came down slowly, fished out a cigarette, and placed it between his lips. As he lit the cigarette, he began to pace back and forth. But now he seemed to notice something else. He raised his hand to shade his eyes and looked off in the same direction again: a woman was walking this way. She had probably taken the wrong road; she turned around and headed back this way. Her snow-white windbreaker was striking as it appeared and disappeared among the trees. The man's head turned slowly as he followed the woman with his eyes. But she stopped, looked around for a minute, then turned, and headed north. The white windbreaker disappeared among the trees to the north. At this, the man finally took a drag from his cigarette. He was definitely waiting for someone. Who? A woman? So that's what was going on. He was waiting for another woman. They had agreed to meet below the empty building east of the woods.

"The building is white and has a green brick wall around it. After you get off the bus, go east. Pass through a grove of trees and a cemetery."

"A cemetery?"

"Yes, I'll wait for you there."

Maybe it was at the entrance to an alley. Maybe it was while they were both rushing to work. Maybe the streets were already full with a crashing flood of cars and people. Or maybe there was only a handful of pedestrians on the sidewalk, and the city was still a pale blue.

"What did you say, there's a cemetery there?"

"Don't worry about it, don't worry. It isn't scary in the least."

Maybe it was a Saturday or a Sunday evening, at a bus stop near her dormitory, the last time they said good-bye. The sky was already very dark, and it was about to rain. The wind came in swift, violent gusts; dampness spread out through the black night. Or maybe it was after the rain, and everything was quiet, not a single person in sight. The streetlamps shone on the wet street, which was like a river reflecting festival lights.

"Honest, it's not scary. It's a pretty cemetery."

"Go east? Is it far?"

"No, not far. You'll be able to see it as soon as you get off the bus. It's a very tall building."

Maybe it was close to midnight, in a gloomy corner of a diner. The occasional sound of lonely whistling from someone walking came from the street. The little diner was about to close.

"The building is twenty-one stories. It's white."

"A green brick wall?"

"Right, I'll wait for you there."

But what about the woman inside the wall? Who was she? What was she doing here? Maybe she and the man outside the wall had absolutely no connection to each other. But did they really have no connection? She was sitting beneath the big tree, not making a sound. Behind it, actually. If you looked carefully, you would notice that she, the big tree, and the small gate all happened to line up perfectly. If you looked in through the crack between the doors of the gate, you wouldn't be able to see her. Why should this be? The man couldn't see her, but she could hear everything outside the wall. And why didn't the man go to the bus stop to wait for his friend? Why did he hide over here and waste all that energy peering into the distance? "Go with the flow" was what the woman said. If her husband had fallen in love with another woman and if she had found out, what could she do? Suffer, yes, she would suffer. She would cry, argue, throw a fit, but in the end what good would that do?

"Nothing like it, nothing at all," the man said. "There just isn't anything like that going on."

But after he said this, she knew that if he continued to see the woman, there would be little she could do. "No! No!" She would cry and shout. "No, this won't do! It won't do . . ."

"How can you be so vulgar?" the man said. "How can you be so petty?"

The man said, "I never thought you'd act like this. She's just a friend, an ordinary friend."

But he spent far more time with his ordinary friend than he spent with her. When he was with his ordinary friend, he laughed and talked excitedly, but when he was with her, he had less and less to say, and he grew more and more withdrawn. What could she do?

"For the children," she said to him. She didn't want to argue anymore, and she didn't have the strength to cry anymore.

She said, "You don't have a thought for me, but you must think of the children."

"OK, OK," the man said. "Since you refuse to believe me, I won't have any more to do with her."

But after he said this, he kept seeing the other woman behind his wife's back. If that was how things were, what could she do? She could take him to court. She could cause a scandal, raise such a fuss that everyone in the neighborhood would know. She could walk away. She could leave him. But she loved him. Love was as difficult to explain as death. She didn't want to hurt him, and she didn't want to leave him. What should she do? Obsessed, she followed him here. She watched him walk back and forth along the outside of the wall, anxiously waiting for that ordinary friend of his. Quietly, she went around to the other side of the vacant building, crossed the little bridge, and came in through the main gate. She walked over beneath the big parasol tree and listened for a while. She could hear that he was still outside the wall. Not wanting him to discover her, she hid behind the thick trunk of the parasol tree. She wondered what it was she thought she was going to do. Make her existence known to the other woman? Talk face to face with her? Expose the man's lies there and then? But what good would any of that do? What would be the point? If he had already fallen out of love with you, if he longed for another woman, what more hope could you have in him? All you could do was go with the flow. Let him go, all you could do was let him go. "Go with the flow." When she said this, her heart was like a cemetery. She was unaware that somebody had walked over to her, unaware that somebody had asked her a question. The sun had sunk completely behind the trees. The evening breeze was stronger with each gust. It grew gloomy and lonesome beneath the tall tree. The shadow of the tree and the dots of light that had swayed and pulsated were the same as the past, the same as yesterday; they passed away quietly, unnoticed. Of course, tomorrow they would do it all over again in the same place. Let's go, but where? Let's go home, but what is home? Were you just going to wait? Wait until when? You didn't care? You were indifferent? OK, OK, go with the flow. But I had to be on my way, for I still had a dozen more floors to climb.

As I'd expected, my new apartment wasn't bad. Two bedrooms and a living room. The bigger bedroom was close to 180 square feet, sixteen feet long and eleven feet wide. The smaller bedroom was sixteen feet long and eight feet wide, 128 square feet. It was a miracle for a bachelor like me to have an apartment like this. The living room was 75 square feet. The kitchen was only 54 square feet, but there would just be me cooking and me eating, so it was big enough. To my surprise, the toilet was in a different room from the shower. I hadn't expected that. The closet was so large I could sleep in it. The balcony? Four feet by seven feet. (How many square feet would that be?) From it, I could look down to the woods.

Under an unfathomable autumn sky, the trees were a riot of color. The maple leaves were already red, the ginkgoes were completely golden, the pines and cypresses were so green they were almost black, and numerous white tombstones ornamented the spaces between the trees. I wondered if in the future I would want a gravestone. If I did, where would it stand? Would I want words engraved on it? What should I have engraved? Over the years, a number of people are likely to come to my grave, on rainy days, on windy days, on snowy days, on clear days. They will pass by my grave, read the words on the gravestone, and then walk away. Who will they be? Will they wonder who the person buried in the grave might be or wonder about the experiences he might have had? Will it occur to them that the person in the grave once imagined their coming? Perhaps some of the people destined to walk by my grave have already been born and are walking toward my gravestone. Of course, they have a long way to go, and many things have to happen in their proper sequence. There is no way to predict which road they will take to get to my grave, because I have yet to die. There is no way yet to determine the place and time, but this sort of thing is certain to occur. Someone who is certain to pass by my grave has already begun his trip. Maybe he is in Africa, or maybe he is within my field of vision. As I was thinking about all of this, I suddenly noticed a child in the woods.

It was a baby. You could see him only from the twenty-first floor. He was lying behind a gravestone in the pale red light of the setting sun. There was a baby carriage beside him, filled with many colorful toys. He was wrapped in a pink woolen blanket so that only his little face showed. He was sleeping soundly and peacefully, as if nothing could disturb him. Who was he? Whose child was he? Where were the adults? Where had his mother and father gone? Why had they stayed away so long? There was no one else around; I could see clearly from the twenty-first floor that there was no one else anywhere in sight. Why wasn't the child in the baby carriage; why was he sleeping on the ground? Heavens! I understood: an abandoned infant! In a flash, I realized what was going on. The man outside the wall! And the woman inside the wall! The man was gazing steadily in the direction of his child. He paced back and forth beyond the wall, looking off into the distance at his child. He watched the bus stop to see who would come take the baby away. He had no choice but to abandon his child, but he was uneasy; he wanted to see with his own eyes what sort of person would take the boy. Why are you doing this, young father? And you, the mother, why are you doing this? She couldn't bear to watch, so she hid. After walking in through the small gate, she no longer had the strength to stand, and so she sat down beneath the big tree as if at the center of a nightmare. She listened to hear if the child was crying or not. She wondered if she had brought along enough toys. She listened for any movement from the distant woods. She wondered what sort of fate was in store for the child. Yes, when she looked at me, her eyes were full of alarm. It never occurred to her that someone might come in through the main gate to the south. "Go with the flow," she said in a voice heavy with despair. Maybe I look reasonably honest and decent, but I didn't go toward the small gate, and she couldn't say to me, "Go into the woods. Thank you. Please take care of the child for us." She thought with resignation, Go with the flow, just go with the flow. The sky grew darker and darker, but the child was still lost in his sweet dreams. Did he dream? What did he dream of? No, no! This could not be! No matter what had happened, they could not do this. I went down the stairs. I have a little heart trouble, but going down stairs is always easier than going up. I rested on the fourteenth floor and again on the seventh. When I reached the bottom, it seemed that other than the fact that my heart was beating a little faster than usual, nothing was amiss.

The woman was still there. Her hands were on her knees, palms up. She was sitting with her eyes closed, beneath the big parasol tree, absolutely motionless. I stood beside her for a while, but she seemed oblivious to my presence. It occurred to me that as a man, I should go talk with the man. I walked over to the small gate and pushed it, but it didn't open. I pulled it, and it still didn't open. It was locked; there was a great big lock on the outside. Strange. Then how did the woman get inside? My head, like my heart, is not particularly good. I thought for a minute before recalling how I myself got inside. I ran over toward the south gate, planning on circling around to the west side of the building. It would be best to first go have a look at the child. It was late and getting cold. The child had to be kept from getting sick. I would go have a talk with the young father and then maybe speak to the child's mother also.

What is it you're doing? Just what are you doing? What calamity has occurred? You're not married? If you're not married, then hurry up and get married. There's still time. You simply cannot do this. You were pretty daring in the beginning, so what are you afraid of now? There's no need to be afraid of anything. Let people talk. "Go your own way and let others talk." An important person said that, so it can't be wrong. Look, you two, this is a wonderful child, so well behaved. Illegitimate children are all smart. He could grow up to be a great man. Great men shouldn't just be tossed aside in some cemetery.

But, but! There was a river in front of the main gate on the south side. I had all but forgotten it. The river flowed right up against the green brick wall; there was virtually no space between them. The bridge could take one only to the south bank, and there was absolutely no way to circle around to the west side of the wall. I crossed the little bridge and walked west a long way but didn't find any place where I could cross the river. Then I followed the riverbank east. I walked a long way, but there was still no place to cross. Now what was going on? The wall around the compound was so high that the man would have had a hard time jumping over it, let alone the woman. I continued on, figuring that sooner or later there had to be a place where I could cross the river. By the time I'd gone another considerable distance, it was deeper into the twilight, and still I hadn't found a place to cross. If there were such place, I reasoned, it had to be on the west side; so I turned and headed back. After I had walked for a while, I met up with a woman.

"Excuse me," I said, "where can I cross the river?"

"Cross the river?" She glanced all around. I realized she was the woman who had been sitting beneath the tree.

"Go west. After about five hundred yards, more or less, there's a big bridge," she said.

"Where are you going?" I asked.

She looked at me for a moment with suspicion. "I'm going home."

"Well, what about him?"

"Who?"

"Who's that man on the other side of the wall?"

"What? What man? What do you want?"

"OK, we won't talk about that," I said. "But what about the child?"

"Child? What child?"

"The child in the woods to the west."

She laughed. "You're not feeling well, perhaps?" She turned and was about to leave.

"There's an abandoned child over there! Listen, no matter

what, it's getting late, and we have to get that child and take it home. Tell me again, where is the bridge?"

Events proved my heart was OK, for I jogged all the way to the woods, and it kept working normally. I found the gravestone. I was positive it was the one. I could swear my eyes hadn't deceived me. I couldn't have been wrong. But there was nothing in front of the gravestone—no child and no baby carriage. I hurried off to find the man. He was still outside the western wall. He was just then in the process of tidying up a pile of painter's things. Brushes, portfolios, paints, bottles, and jars were spread out at the base of the wall, and a finished painting titled *Cemetery in the Woods* stood to one side.

I walked up and asked him, "Did you happen to see a child in the woods?"

"A child? What sort of child? How old?"

"Very small, a couple of months."

"Good Lord, aren't you a case? How could you lose such a small child? He couldn't run away by himself, could he?"

We looked off toward the woods simultaneously. I walked back and forth along the green brick wall, from south to north and north to south. I couldn't see it; from there, I couldn't see the gravestone at all. Then the woman showed up. I described for them everything I had seen.

"Please believe me, my eyes work better than anything else in my body," I said to them. "Please don't look at me like that, like there's something wrong with me."

I said to them, "If we spent some time together, you'd realize that I'm quite normal."

I said, "Will you go with me to have another look?"

The man said, "I don't doubt your sincerity, but how can you guarantee you saw everything there was to see? As for me, I'm sorry, I have to go home."

The woman said to me, "All right, I'll go with you." I could tell she said this only because she wasn't entirely satisfied that I was OK.

We went into the woods and walked to the gravestone. Sure

enough, nothing. There was nothing there at all. I sat down beside the grave. I said, "Go on home. Weren't you on your way home? Go on." She sat down beside me. I said, "Don't worry. You don't have to worry about me. I'm a little tired. I think I'll rest here for a while." She reached out and felt my pulse.

I said, "Maybe the painter was right, maybe the child's parents were nearby."

I said, "But maybe I wasn't wrong, and someone took the child away while I was looking for the bridge."

I said, "Shall we take another look around?"

We walked through the woods together. We walked until the sky was completely dark.

I said, "What sort of person do you think took him away?"

I said, "I think it was a good person who took him away. What do you think?"

I said, "What do you think that child's fate is going to be?"

She said, "Go with the flow."

And that's how we met. Who would have expected it? Two years later, she became my wife; three years later, the mother of my son.

TRANSLATED BY THOMAS MORAN

# The Field

## HONG YING

Only at daybreak did the gunfire finally stop, if ever so reluctantly. Li Jiming heard the distant rumbling of a tank. He crawled up to the rim of the crater, hoping to get a look, but heard only the sorrowful cries of the wounded. Though no snow had fallen during the night, a bitter wind swept across the field, blowing about bits of frost that resembled gunpowder smoke.

At the base of the crater, Junni rolled over. She murmured, then slept again, knocking off in the process one of three field coats that covered her. Li Jiming slid back down the slope and replaced it.

"I dreamed about Chinese New Year." Junni did not open her eyes. "The crowd at the Daweiwu opera was going wild, and the fireworks were so bright they hurt your eyes." She smiled. "Jiming, did your dad let you go that year?"

"What year was that?"

"What do you mean, what year? When did my dad come back with the militia?"

Li Jiming was about to answer when a muffled voice called out, "Big Brother." A man holding a rifle appeared at the rim of the crater and came slithering down. Junni sat up. "You're wounded. Where were you hit?"

Sonny felt his face, his hand sticky with blood. "Fuck, this smells." He took off his large, blood-soaked coat. "It's not my blood. This coat is completely ruined."

He pulled something battered looking from his pocket. "These are all I could get. It's motherfucking incredible—people getting killed right and left for a few measly crackers."

Junni picked a coat up off the ground and draped it over his shoulders. "What's wrong? We'll be going back soon."

"No way to cut through." Sonny looked over to where the shells continued to explode and shook his head. "I don't think there's a single man left from the Thirty-fourth." He turned to Jiming. "Give me some water to wash down these crackers."

As Junni searched through the heap of coats for the canteen, Jiming said, "Look, don't worry about me and Junni—get to a village, dress up like a native, dump the rifle, and make a break for it when you can."

Sonny smiled. "In all these years, I've never known you to give up like this." But the enemy lines were in fact closing in, and the few villages in the area had long ago fallen to the regular forces. Militia stragglers had little choice but to tuck themselves away in a shell hole like the one that sheltered them now.

Jiming lowered his head. "If I'd known this was going to happen, I'd never have left Xuzhou with the Nationalist retreat. Let's wait till the regiment has gone by, then watch for a chance to run."

"And go where?"

"Back home."

"Too risky," Junni said. "The tenant farmers are out of control these days; if we get caught, they'll cut us to pieces. You want us to get our heads chopped off like our dads did?"

She walked over to the two men. "Don't be so depressed. Why do we have to go anywhere? Isn't it nice here, all of us together?" Making a bed out of the coats, she said, "Sonny, why don't you stretch out for a little while; you haven't slept all night."

Sonny lost no time lying down and was soon buried in the pile of coats. "Head or no head, I need to get some fucking sleep."

"How about you, Jiming? You haven't slept a wink either."

Jiming squatted down, holding his head in his hands. He was silent. Junni walked over to rub his scalp. His bandage was caked with dirt and crusty blood. Never before had the two been so close.

Jiming looked up at her. "If I'd known, I never would have sent Sonny to Xuzhou to rescue you from the whorehouse. At least in that hellhole, you'd still be alive."

"Don't go on about what could have been. My uncle was just trying to help me survive. What with all the fighting in the village and the bad blood, I couldn't stay near those people. He said that an orphan girl without a name was bound to run into a kind man eventually, and that way I wouldn't starve."

"Yeah, right, so look where you ended up! Here—with us—at the mercy of your fellow villagers' evil spirits after all." He forced a smile, looking straight at Junni. "I always thought there'd be a day with banging gongs and a big red sedan chair, when I could marry you the proper way."

"Oh, Jiming," she sighed, lowering her gaze. "I got myself dirty a long time ago."

"Nobody at home knows that."

"Nobody at home, maybe, but heaven and earth know." She pressed his head to her breast. The cold wind carried the smell of death in their direction, wave after wave of air so thick that it was impossible to breathe. Jiming pushed her away gently and, with his hand on his head wound, lay down on the ground, sinking into the heap of overcoats rank with blood and smelly shoes. Before he dozed off, he heard what sounded like Junni urinating and buried his head even deeper.

On January 7, 1949, the thirty-eighth year of the republic, snowy winds whipped across the plains of Xuhuai. At about three-thirty in the afternoon, the frozen and hungry militia camped between Chenguanzhuang and the Lu River awoke, stunned by sudden attack.*

As artillery shells whined overhead, Jiming tossed aside the coat covering him and jumped up but fell right back to the ground.

---

*The Huai-Hai Campaign, stretching from November 6, 1948, to January 10, 1949, was the second of three decisive battles contributing to the ultimate defeat of the Nationalists by the Communists.

The bombing grew louder, as if the shells were about to drop on their heads. It was a gray, wintry day, and evening had set in imperceptibly, the low clouds illuminated only by the explosions. Out on the field, voices called out, soft and feeble. It seemed almost that several hundred thousand soldiers had all perished, leaving behind only these three civilians.

"There's no fucking way out tonight," said Jiming.

Sonny lay on his back, inert, lifting his head from time to time to watch the bursts of light. He knew in his heart what the others were thinking: "Don't run; there's no point."

"It'll be a lot worse for us if we get taken back to Daweiwu by the Communists."

"Who can say what will happen? Let's wait and see."

All three lay there, at the bottom of the crater, no longer speaking. The sound of shelling moved slowly eastward; the sky, red and black, smoked and suffocated till it could no longer support itself. Perhaps it would come crashing down and crush everything beneath it.

Softly, as if to herself, Junni said, "When I first got to the whorehouse, all I could think about was murdering somebody. Then I was going to hang myself."

The others did not reply. Sonny began to sob silently.

"But then I thought, What am I doing? They were soldiers far away from home, so lonely and sad, without very much time to live. Why should I go around killing people—why not give a little pleasure?"

Li Jiming sat up suddenly and turned to Junni. "Huh? Is that what you think? You were better off at the whorehouse? Where there's pleasure!"

Junni pushed herself up to her feet and, forming her words slowly, said, "Don't get all worked up. Look, if we're going to die, why not die happy?" She pulled at Li Jiming. "Come on, Big Brother. You first."

Jiming jumped up from the pile of clothes. "What are you saying? 'Me first!' You stinking whore!" He ran over to the far side of the crater and, opening the pocket of one of the coats, pulled out a hand grenade. "Goddamn it, I went through hell to save a fucking whore like you!"

In no time, Sonny was on his feet, too. "Just calm down; let's talk things over. Don't be messing with a fucking grenade." He was trembling.

"Slow down, Sonny. Your brother didn't mean anything," Junni said.

Sonny walked over to try to take the grenade away, but Jiming wouldn't let go. The two of them rolled around against the wall of the crater, covering themselves with snow and mud.

When the grenade rolled to the ground, Junni picked it up and put it to the side. "What the hell are you boys doing? That's not how brothers act!"

Jiming, weakened by his injury, was soon pinned beneath Sonny, who bound his brother's hands behind his back with one of the coats. Jiming cursed between gasps for air. But the two stopped suddenly at the sight of Junni, who had begun to undo her buttons. They watched her remove the soiled jacket, the flashes far in the distance irradiating her breasts, fine and white. It was as if her body did not belong to this blood-spattered field.

"Don't let the fact that I'm a little dirty bother you. Let me take good care of you one last time." She leaned over, straightened the coats the men had scattered during their scuffle, and then sat down, covering her lower half with an old quilted jacket. "Jiming, come lie down next to me."

Li Jiming's mouth dropped. After a moment, he stammered, "I wanted you to be my fucking wife."

Junni smiled. "I never said I'd marry you. What's the point of bringing that up again. Now is now." She turned around and pulled at Sonny's leg. "Sonny, I'll take care of you first. You've been to a whorehouse before, right? You're not an old hen like your brother."

Sonny nervously turned to look at Li Jiming, then quickly unbuttoned his tattered shirt, revealing his smooth, slight frame. He crawled under the pile of clothing.

A sudden burst of fire; the action was getting closer by the minute. Li Jiming, who had wrestled himself free of the coat, leaned against the crater wall, dully looking in the direction of the clothes. Occasionally a leg appeared, or an arm, and then he heard a rapid panting and Junni's voice: "All right, Sonny, go get your brother. It's his turn."

Sonny was silent. Junni emerged from under the pile and walked over to Li Jiming. "Stop standing around in your underwear, torturing yourself. Come on, I can take care of you both."

As her warm body clung to his, Li Jiming smelled a woman's sweat, something that he had never noticed on her before. He followed Junni to the ground.

A shell landed very near, stirring up clouds of dust. Two or three people screamed at the top of their lungs, a sound terrible and numbing.

After a long while, Junni said, "Sonny, was it OK for you?"

"It sure was."

"Jiming, are you content?"

"Hmm," said Li Jiming, still catching his breath. He felt a warmth he had never known boring up through his body all the way to his head, making him dizzy, as if he were about to melt.

"All right, then," Junni said. "I'm feeling really good, too. We're all content."

She reached over for the ice-cold grenade and held it tightly.

Neither the troops retreating across the fields of Chenguan-zhuang nor the troops advancing in the same direction paid any attention to the shell hole. Three days later, after the sulfurous smoke had dissipated, the corpses littering the field began to emit a stench that could not be ignored, and a civilian clean-up crew moved in. What they found in the hole was not easy to collect—all severed limbs and pieces of flesh—so a decision was made to dump in the frozen bodies from the surrounding area. Before long, the hole was full.

When it was dark, the crew wiped their hands on clods of dirt and, on the newly flattened earth, proceeded to build a fire and prepare dinner.

TRANSLATED BY SUSAN MCFADDEN

# The Brothers Shu

## SU TONG

The story of Fragrant Cedar Street is legendary among people in my hometown. In the south of China, there are lots of streets just like it: narrow, dirty, the cobblestones forming a network of potholes. When you look out your window at the street or at the river's edge, you can see dried meat and drying laundry hanging from eaves, and you can see inside houses, where people are at the dinner table or engaged in a whole range of daily activities. What I am about to give you isn't so much a story as it is a word picture of life down south, and little more.

The brothers Shu Gong and Shu Nong lived on that particular street.

So did the Lin sisters, Hanli and Hanzhen.

They shared a building: 18 Fragrant Cedar Street, a blackened two-story structure, where the Shu family lived downstairs and the Lins above them. They were neighbors. Black sheet metal covered the flat roof of number 18, and as I stood at the bridgehead, I saw a cat crouching up there. At least that's how I remember it, fifteen years later.

And I remember the river, which intersected Fragrant Cedar Street a scant three or four feet from number 18. This river will make several appearances in my narration, with dubious distinction, for as I indicated earlier, I can only give impressions.

Shu Gong was the elder son, Shu Nong his younger brother.

Hanli was the elder daughter, Hanzhen her younger sister.

The ages of the Shu brothers and Lin sisters can be likened to the fingers of your hand: if Shu Nong was fourteen, then Hanzhen was fifteen, Shu Gong sixteen, and Hanli seventeen. A hand with four fingers lined up so tightly you can't pry them apart. Four fingers on the same hand. But where is the thumb?

Shu Nong was a timid, sallow-faced little devil. In the crude and simple classroom of Fragrant Cedar Middle School, he was the boy sitting up front in the middle row, dressed in a gray school uniform, neatly patched at the elbows, over a threadbare hand-me-down shirt with a grimy blue collar. The teachers at Fragrant Cedar Middle School all disliked Shu Nong, mainly because of the way he sprawled across his desk and picked his nose as he stared up at them. Experienced teachers knew he wasn't listening, and if they smacked him over the head with a pointer, he shrieked like splintered glass and complained, "I wasn't talking!" So while he wasn't the naughtiest child in class, his teachers pretty much ignored him, having taken all the gloomy stares from his old-man's eyes they could bear. To them, he was "a little schemer." Plus he usually smelled like he had just peed his pants.

Shu Nong was still wetting the bed at fourteen. And that was one of his secrets.

At first, we weren't aware of this secret. It was Hanzhen who let the cat out of the bag. Devoted to the act of eating, Hanzhen had such a greedy little mouth she even stole from her parents to buy snacks. One day when there was nothing to steal and she was standing outside the sweetshop looking depressed, Shu Nong happened by, dragging his schoolbag behind him. She stopped him: "I need twenty fen." He tried to walk around her, but she grabbed the strap of his bag and wouldn't let him pass. "Are you going to lend it to me or not, you little miser?" she demanded.

Shu Nong replied, "All I've got on me is two fen."

Hanzhen frowned and casually slapped him with his own strap. Then, jamming her fists onto her hips, she said, "Don't you kids play with him. He wets the bed. His sheets are hung out to dry every day!"

I watched her spin around and take off toward school, leaving Shu Nong standing motionless and gloomy, holding his face in his hands as he followed her pudgy figure with his eyes. Then he looked at me—gloom filled his eyes. I can still see that fearful look on his fourteen-year-old face, best described as that of a young criminal genius. "Let's go," I said. "I won't tell anybody."

He shook his head, jammed his finger up his nose, and dug around a bit. "You go ahead. I'm skipping school today."

Shu Nong played hooky a lot, so that was no big deal. And I assumed he was already cooking up a way to get even with Hanzhen, which also was no big deal since he had a reputation for settling scores.

On the very next day, Hanzhen came into the office to report Shu Nong for putting five dead rats, some twisted wire, and a dozen or more thumbtacks in her bed. The teachers promised to punish him, but he played hooky that day, too. On the day after that, Hanzhen's mother, Qiu Yumei, came to school with a bowl of rice and asked the principal to smell it. He asked what was going on. Qiu Yumei accused Shu Nong of peeing in her rice pot. A crowd was gathering outside the office when the gym teacher dragged in Shu Nong, who had sauntered in to school only moments earlier and flung him into the corner.

"Here he is," the principal said. "Now what do you want me to do?"

"That's easy," Qiu Yumei replied. "Make him eat the rice, and he'll think twice about doing that again."

After mulling the suggestion over for a few seconds, the principal carried the offending bowl of rice over to Shu Nong. "Eat up," he said, "and taste the fruit of your labors."

Shu Nong stood there with his head down, hands jammed into his pockets as he nonchalantly fiddled with a key ring. The sound of keys jangling in the boy's grimy pocket clearly angered the principal, who in plain view of everyone, forced Shu Nong's head down over the rice. Shu Nong licked it almost instinctively, then yelped like a puppy, and spat the stuff out. Deathly pale, he ran out of the office, a single kernel of rice stuck to the corner of his mouth. The bystanders roared with laughter.

That evening, I spotted Shu Nong at the limestone quarry, wobbling across the rocky ground, dragging his schoolbag behind him. He picked an old tree limb out of a pile of rubbish and began kicking it ahead of him. He looked as gloomy and dejected as always. I thought I heard him announce, "I'll screw the shit out of Lin Hanzhen." His voice was high-pitched and shrill but as flat and emotionless as a girl saying to a clerk in a sweetshop, I'd like a candy figurine, please. "And I'll screw the shit out of Qiu Yumei!" he added.

A male figure climbed onto the roof of number 18. From a distance, it looked like a repairman. It was Shu Nong's father. Since the neighbors all called him Old Shu, that's what we'll call him here. To members of my family, Old Shu was special. I remember him as a short, stocky man who was either a construction worker or a pipe fitter. Whichever, he was good with his hands. If someone's plumbing leaked or the electric meter was broken, the lady of the house would say, "Go find Old Shu." He wasn't much to look at, but the women on Fragrant Cedar Street liked him. In retrospect, I'd have to say Old Shu was a ladies' man, of which Fragrant Cedar Street boasted several, one of whom, as I say, was Old Shu. That's how I see it, anyhow.

Let's say that some women doing their knitting see Old Shu on the roof of number 18. They start gossiping about his amorous escapades, mostly about how he and Qiu Yumei do this, that, and the other. I recall going into a condiments shop once and overhearing the soy sauce lady tell the woman who sold pickled vegetables, "Old Shu is the father of the two Lin girls! And look how that trashy Qiu Yumei struts around!" The condiments shop was often the source of shocking talk like that. Qiu Yumei was walking past just then but didn't hear them.

If you believed the women's brassy gossip, one look at Lin Hanzhen's father would strengthen your conviction. What did Old Lin do for a living? you ask. Let's say it's a summer day at sunset, and a man is playing chess in the doorway of the handkerchief maker's. That will be Old Lin, who plays there every day. Sometimes Hanzhen or Hanli brings his dinner and lays it next to the chessboard. Old Lin wears thick glasses for his nearsightedness. He has no special talents, but once after losing a chess game, he popped the cannon piece into his mouth and would have swallowed it if Hanli hadn't pried open his mouth and plucked it out. She knocked over the chessboard, earning herself a slap in the face. "You want to keep playing?" she complained tearfully with a stomp of her foot. "I should have let you swallow that piece!"

Old Lin retorted, "I'll swallow whatever I want to swallow, and you can just butt out!"

People watching the game laughed. They got a kick out of Old Lin's temper. They also got a kick out of Hanli, because she was so pretty and had such a good heart. The neighbors were unanimous in their appraisal of the sisters: they liked Hanli and disliked Hanzhen.

Now all the players in our drama have made an appearance, all but Shu Gong and his mother, that is. There isn't much to be said about the woman in the Shu family. Craven and easily intimidated, she padded like a mouse around the downstairs of number 18, cooking meals and washing clothes, and I have virtually no recollection of her. Shu Gong, on the other hand, is very important, since for a time he was an object of veneration among young people on Fragrant Cedar Street.

Shu Gong had a black mustache, an upside-down V sort of like Stalin's.

Shu Gong had delicate features and always wore a pair of white Shanghai-made high-top sneakers.

Shu Gong had been in a gang fight at the limestone quarry with some kids from the west side, and he had had a love affair. Guess who he had the affair with.

Hanli.

In retrospect, I can see that the two families at number 18 had a very interesting relationship.

Shu Gong and Shu Nong shared a bed at first and fought night after night. Shu Gong would come roaring out of a sound sleep and kick Shu Nong: "You wet the bed again, you wet the goddamned bed!" Shu Nong would lie there not making a sound, eyes open as he listened for the prowling steps and night screeches of the cat on the roof. He got used to being kicked and slugged by his brother since he knew he had it coming. He always wet the bed, and Shu Gong's side was always clean as a whistle. Besides, he was no match for Shu Gong in a fight. Knowing how reckless it would be to stand up to his brother, Shu Nong let strategy be his watchword. He recalled the wise comment someone made after being beaten up one day on the stone bridge: a true gentleman gets revenge, even if it takes ten years. Shu Nong understood exactly what that meant. So one night after Shu Gong had kicked and slugged him again, he said very deliberately, "A true gentleman gets revenge, even if it takes ten years."

"What did you say?" Shu Gong, who thought he was hearing things, crawled over and patted Shu Nong's face. "Did you say something about revenge?" He smirked. "You little shit, what do you know about revenge?"

His brother's lips flashed in the darkness like two squirming maggots. He repeated the comment.

Shu Gong clapped his hand over his brother's mouth. "Shut that stinky mouth of yours, and go to sleep," he said, then found a dry spot in bed and lay back down.

Shu Nong was still mumbling. He was saying, "Shu Gong, I'm going to kill you."

Shu Gong had another chuckle over that. "Want me to go get the cleaver?"

"Not now," Shu Nong replied. "Some other day. Just don't turn your back."

Years later, Shu Gong could still see Shu Nong's pale lips flashing in the dark like a couple of squirming maggots. But back then, he could no longer endure sharing a bed with Shu Nong, so he told his parents, "Buy me a bed of my own, or I'll stay with a friend and forget about coming home."

Old Shu was momentarily speechless. "I see you've grown up," he said as he lifted his son's arm to look at his armpit. "OK, it's starting to grow. I'll buy you a real spring bed tomorrow."

After that, Shu Nong slept alone. He was still fourteen.

At the age of fourteen, Shu Nong began sleeping alone. He vowed on his first night away from his brother never to wet the bed again. Let's say that it's an autumn night forgotten by all concerned and that Shu Nong's dejection is like a floating leaf somewhere down south. He lies wide awake in the darkness, listening to the surpassing stillness outside his window on Fragrant Cedar Street, broken occasionally by a truck rumbling down the street, which makes his bed shake slightly. It's a boring street, Shu Nong thinks, and growing up on it is even more so. His thoughts fly all over the place until he gets sleepy, but as he curls up for the night, Shu Gong's bed begins to creak and keeps on creaking for a long time. "What are you doing?"

"None of your business. Go to sleep, so you can wet your bed," Shu Gong snaps back spitefully.

"I'm not wetting my bed anymore." Shu Nong sits up straight. "I can't wet it if I don't sleep!"

No response from Shu Gong, who is by now snoring loudly. The sound disgusts Shu Nong, who thinks Shu Gong is more boring than anything, an SOB just begging to get his lumps. Shu Nong looks out the window and hears a cat spring from the windowsill up to the roof. He sees the cat's dark-green eyes, flashing like a pair of tiny lamps. No one pays any attention to the cat, which is free to prance off anywhere in the world it likes. To Shu Nong, being feline seems more interesting than being human.

That is how Shu Nong viewed the world at fourteen: being feline is more interesting than being human.

If the moon is out that night, Shu Nong is likely to see his father climbing up the rainspout. Suddenly, he sees someone climbing expertly up the rainspout next to the window like a gigantic house lizard. Shu Nong experiences a moment of fear before sticking his head out the window and grabbing a leg.

"What do you think you're doing?" That is exactly how long it takes him to discover it is his father, Old Shu, who thumps his son on the head with the sandal in his hand. "Be a good boy, and shut up. I'm going up to fix the gutter."

"Is it leaking?"

"Like a sieve. But I'll take care of it."

Shu Nong says, "I'll go with you."

With a sigh of exasperation, Old Shu shins down to the windowsill, squats in his bare feet, and wraps his hands around Shu Nong's neck. "Get back to bed, and go to sleep," Old Shu says. "You saw nothing, unless you want me to throttle you. And don't think I won't do it, you understand?"

His father's hands around his neck feel like knives cutting into his flesh. He closes his eyes, and the hands fall loose. He sees his father grab hold of something, spring off the sill, and climb to the top floor.

After that, Shu Nong goes back and sits on his bed, but he isn't sleepy. He hears a thud upstairs in Qiu Yumei's room, then silence. What's going on? Shu Nong thinks of the cat. If the cat's on the roof, can it see what Father and Qiu Yumei are up to? Shu Nong thought a lot about things like that when he was fourteen. His thoughts, too, are like leaves floating aimlessly somewhere down south. Just before dawn, a rooster crows somewhere, and Shu Nong realizes he had fallen asleep—and had wet the bed. Mentally he wrings out his dripping-wet underpants, and the rank smell of urine nearly makes him gag. How could I have fallen asleep? How come I wet the bed again? His nighttime discovery floats up like a dream. Who made me go to sleep? Who made me wet the bed? A sense of desolation wraps itself around Shu Nong's heart. He slips off his wet pants and begins to sob. Shu Nong did a lot of sobbing at the age of fourteen, just like a little girl.

Shu Nong asked me a really weird question once, but then he was always asking weird questions. And if you didn't supply a satisfying answer, he'd give you a reasoned reply of his own.

"What's better, being human or being a cat?"

I said human, naturally.

"Wrong. Cats are free, and nobody pays them any attention. Cats can prowl the eaves of a house."

So I said, "Go be a cat, then."

"Do you think people can turn into cats?"

"No. Cats have cats, people have people. Don't tell me you don't even know that!"

"I know that. What I mean is, Can someone turn himself into a cat?"

"Try it, and see."

"Maybe I will. But I have lots to do before that. I'm going to make you all sit up and take notice." Shu Nong began chewing his grubby fingernails, making a light clipping noise: *chuk chuk.*

As for Hanli, she was one of Fragrant Cedar Street's best-known lovely young things. And she had a heart as fragile and tender as a spring snowflake. Hanli couldn't watch a chicken being killed, and she never ate one. The sight of a bloody, dying creature terrified her, and that trait became the keystone of her character. As youngsters, Shu Gong and Shu Nong often sprinkled chicken blood on the stairs to menace the sisters. It had no effect on Hanzhen but drained the blood from poor Hanli's face. Her terror evoked cruel fantasies in the minds of the Shu brothers. "So?" you say. Well, years later, mixed feelings would characterize Shu Gong's recollections of the girl Hanli, since he was always brutally punished by Old Shu for his cruel pranks: first Old Shu would pin him to the floor and gag him with a wet rag to keep him from screaming; then he would smack him across the face with his shoe until his arm tired. Old Shu would then drag himself off to bed and leave Shu Gong lying half-dead on the floor, his battered face looking like an exploded red windowpane. By then, the wet rag would be chewed into a tight little wad. "How had that come about?" you ask. Well, Shu Gong had considered Hanli his private plaything

from a very early age. She was like a katydid he held in his hand as
it screeched helplessly; he had her in his grip and wouldn't let go.
What I find strange is that the people in my hometown never
figured out the relationship between Shu Gong and Hanli, simply
writing it off as bad karma.

Let's say spring is giving way to summer, and Shu Gong is
washing his face at the tap when he hears someone walk down the
stairs behind him. He turns to see Hanli standing at the foot of the
stairs with a patterned skirt in a washbasin, her just-washed, shoul-
der-length hair a shiny black. Discovering Hanli's beauty for the
first time, he looks at his reflection in his own basin. The whiskers
on his upper lip are like a dark patch of weeds floating on the
water. But just as he realizes that he, too, has a certain charm, he
detects an indescribable stink and knows it is rising from his underpants, which he had put on that morning without washing them
first. He looks up at Hanli, who averts her eyes. Can she smell it,
too? A tangle of fantasies whirls around Shu Gong's head and tick-
les his sex like grassy filaments, invigorating it. He dumps the
water from his basin and puts the basin back under the tap, stalling
to give his brain time to sort out his feelings and desires. He hears
water spill over the rim of the basin and splash on the ground; the
basin is full again, but he still doesn't know what to do. Obviously,
he wants to do something to Hanli but doesn't know how to go
about it. What do I do? An idea forms. Draping the towel over his
shoulder, he walks over to the little storeroom beneath the stairs,
where he closes the door, takes off his underpants, and examines
the whitish stains in the crotch; then he puts his trousers back on.
Outside again, he carries his soiled underpants over to the tap and
crams them into Hanli's basin; water-soaked, they quickly sink to
the bottom. A shocked Hanli stops washing her face and hops
away.

"Wha——?" she shrieks, a curtain of hair covering her face.

"Don't have a fit. Just wash them for me," Shu Gong says as he
picks them out of the water.

"Why should I? I'm going to wash my skirt."

"Do as I say if you know what's good for you."

"You don't scare me, never did. Wash your own stuff."

"Really? I don't scare you?" A grin forms on Shu Gong's lips as his eyes bore into Hanli's face, in which an uneasy anger resides. He sees spurts of pink blood rise from the recesses of her body to just beneath the skin; he is always seeing Hanli's pink blood. That's why everyone says she is so pretty. With that thought on his mind, he picks up the washbasin and flings the water in Hanli's face. *Whoosh!* The strange thing is she doesn't scream. She stands there, soaked to the skin, and looks straight into Shu Gong's face. Pretty soon she wraps her arms around her shivering shoulders. Crystalline beads of water drip from her hair.

"Pick them up!" Shu Gong kicks the pair of blue underpants that have landed on the ground.

Hugging herself tightly, Hanli glances over at the stairs, but she doesn't move.

"No need to look. There's no one there. Even if there were, so what? I dare anybody to get me mad," Shu Gong says.

Hanli bends over and picks up Shu Gong's blue underpants, then tosses them into the basin.

"Wash them!" Shu Gong demands.

Hanli turns on the tap, closes her eyes, and scrubs them tentatively. Then she opens her eyes. "Soap. I need soap." Shu Gong hands Hanli a bar of soap. He grabs her wrist as she takes the soap from him and squeezes it hard. Not fondles, squeezes. On Fragrant Cedar Street, they say that was when the love between Shu Gong and Hanli was kindled. That may sound far-fetched, but to this day no other explanation has risen to challenge it. So let's keep the faith with Fragrant Cedar Street and move on.

The people's nostalgia for the river that flows through our southern city can last a hundred years. Our homes were built along the river until the banks were black with dense rows of them. It was a narrow riverbed, and the rocks on the sloping banks were covered with green moss and all sorts of creepers. As I recall, once the water got polluted, it never turned clear again: it was black and stank horribly. The river might as well have been the city's natural spillway, the way it carried rotten vegetable leaves, dead cats and rats, industrial oils and grease plus a steady supply of condoms.

Typical southern scenery. So why were there people who sang on the banks of the river? Why did people see tall-masted ships sailing at night? Fragrant Cedar Street didn't know; Fragrant Cedar Street, which ran along the banks of the river, had no idea.

Late that night, Shu Nong climbed onto the roof for the very first time. He prowled the dusty roof catlike in his bare feet, not making a sound. The world, having lost its voice, allowed Shu Nong to hear the wild beating of his heart. He walked to the edge and squatted down, holding a clothespole to keep from falling. He could see into Qiu Yumei's second-story room through the transom.

Simply stated, Old Shu and Qiu Yumei were in bed, making love.

In the weak light of the bedside lamp, Qiu Yumei's naked, voluptuous body gave off a blue glare; that was what puzzled Shu Nong. Why is she blue? Shu Nong watched his father ram his squat, powerful body against Qiu Yumei over and over, shattering then congealing the blue glare with lightning speed, until his eyes seemed bombarded with an eternal light. They're killing each other! What are they doing? Shu Nong saw his father's face twist into a grimace and watched Qiu Yumei squirm like a crazed snake. They really are killing each other! Darkness quickly swallowed up their faces and abdomens. The heavy, murky smell of river water seeped out from the room, and when it reached Shu Nong's nostrils, he was reminded of the filthy river flotsam. With the river flowing beneath their window, the one nearly merging with the other, the smells from the window polluted the river, and both created a barrier against Shu Nong's thought processes. He felt as if the world around him had changed, that he really and truly had become feline after falling under the spell of darkness and rank, puckery odors. He mewed and sought out something to eat.

That was the night Shu Nong began spying on his father and Qiu Yumei while they were carrying on.

Shu Nong the voyeur screeched like a tomcat.

Thinking of himself as a tomcat, Shu Nong screeched as he watched.

After each time, a little white object came flying out the second-story window and landed in the river. Shu Nong knew the things belonged to his father but couldn't tell what they were. So once he climbed down and headed for the river, where he saw the thing floating on the surface like a deflated balloon. He plucked it out of the river and onto the bank with a dead branch. It shone glittery white in the moonlight and lay in his hand like a little critter: soft and slippery. Shu Nong slipped it into his pocket and went home to bed. But soon after he lay down, a brilliant idea popped into his head. He took the sheath out, wiped it clean, and, holding his breath, stretched it over his little pecker; he was struck by a sensation of vitality that seized his consciousness. Shu Nong slept like a baby that night, and when he awoke the next morning, he was overjoyed to discover that for some reason, he hadn't wet the bed. Why was that?

The story goes that the sheaths Shu Nong fished out of the river solved his problem, but you needn't buy into that argument if it seems too far-fetched.

Shu Nong's night prowls atop number 18 went undetected for the longest time. Then one day, Old Shu found two yuan missing from his dresser drawer, so he searched his sons' pockets. In Shu Gong's pockets, he found one yuan and some change and a pack of cigarettes; in Shu Nong's pockets, he found three condoms. Needless to say, the unexpected discovery of condoms shocked and enraged Old Shu.

The first order of business for Old Shu, whose methods of punishment were unique on Fragrant Cedar Street, was to tie Shu Gong to his bed. Then he removed a cigarette from his son's pack, lit it, and puffed it vigorously. He asked the hogtied Shu Gong, "Want a puff?" Shu Gong shook his head. "Here, try it. Don't you want to be a smoker?" Before waiting for an answer, he shoved the

lit end of the cigarette into Shu Gong's mouth, and Shu Gong
screamed bloody murder. Old Shu clamped his hand over his son's
mouth. "Stop that crazy screaming. It won't hurt long. The cigarette will burn out in no time. You can have another one tomorrow
if you want."

Shu Nong's punishment was a touchier matter since Old Shu
wasn't sure how to handle the situation. When he called his
younger son into the little storeroom, he could barely keep from
laughing as he held the three condoms in his hand and asked, "Do
you know what these are?"

"No."

"Where did you get them?"

"The river. I fished them out."

"What did you have in mind? You're not making balloons out
of them, are you?"

Shu Nong didn't answer. Then Old Shu saw flashes of deep
green light in his son's eyes as he answered in a raspy voice:
"They're yours."

"What did you say?" Suddenly, Old Shu knew he had a problem. He wrapped his hands around Shu Nong's neck and shook his
puny skull for all he was worth. "How do you know they're mine?"

Shu Nong's face was turning purple, but rather than answer, he
just stared into the strangler's face, then let his gaze slide down past
the brawny chest and come to rest on his father's fly.

"What are you looking at?" Old Shu slapped Shu Nong, who
flinched although his gaze stuck stubbornly to his father's fly. He
was given another glimpse of the blue glare, which made him lightheaded. Old Shu grabbed his son's hair and banged his head against
the wall. "Who were you spying on? Who in the hell have you been
spying on?" Shu Nong's head banged into the wall once, twice, but
he felt no pain. He was watching blue specks dance before his eyes
like a swarm of wasps. He heard the screech of a cat on the roof; he
and the sound merged into a single entity.

"Cat," Shu Nong said weakly as he licked his torn gums.

Old Shu wasn't sure what his son was talking about. "Are you
saying the cat was spying?"

"Right, the cat was spying."

Some Fragrant Cedar Street neighbors passing beneath the window at number 18 stopped to gawk as Old Shu beat his son mercilessly. People living on Fragrant Cedar Street considered boys well raised if they were beaten often, so there was nothing unusual here. But the victim's behavior perplexed them. Instead of screaming and carrying on, Shu Nong appeared determined to bear up under the punishment, which was a big change from before.

"What did Shu Nong do?" one of the window gawkers asked.

"Wet the bed!" Old Shu replied from inside.

No one had any reason to suspect any different, since Shu Nong's bed-wetting was well-known up and down Fragrant Cedar Street. The neighbors were sensitive, alert people but not particularly adept at digging beneath the surface to get to the heart of a matter. When Shu Nong's destructive tendencies first began to manifest themselves, the people were too tied up in their belief that he was still fourteen and still wet the bed to spot the differences.

Shu Nong had stopped wetting the bed at the age of fourteen, but no one would believe it. Or better put, people found Shu Nong's bed-wetting interesting, but not the cessation of his bed-wetting. Take Shu Nong's mortal enemy, Hanzhen, for instance: she chanted the following when she jumped rope:

*One four seven, two five eight,*
*Shu Nong bed-wets at a nightly rate.*

Hanli, who rarely spoke to her mother, told a schoolmate, "My mother's a slut, and I despise her."

Folks assumed that Hanli was aware of her bloodline. Since half the women on Fragrant Cedar Street feuded with Qiu Yumei, any one of them would have happily let her in on the secret. But more to the point was Hanli's precociousness. She didn't need to be told what was what. You can't wrap a fire in paper, after all.

Hanli had not spoken to Old Shu for years. He bought her a scarf for her seventeenth birthday, but deaf to his entreaties, she cut him dead at the foot of the stairs. So he gave the scarf to Qiu Yumei, who tried to drape it around Hanli's shoulders. Hanli tore it out of

her hands and flung it to the ground, then spit on it. "Who needs
it? Who knows what you're up to?"

"Old Shu gave it to you only because he likes you. Don't be an
ingrate."

"Who asked him to like me? Who knows what you're up to?"

"What do you mean by 'what we're up to'?"

"You know what I'm talking about."

"No, I *don't*. You tell me."

"I'm ashamed to." Suddenly burying her face in her hands,
Hanli burst out crying. Then, with tears still streaming down her
face, she began combing her hair before the mirror. In the reflection, she saw her mother bend over to pick up the scarf, her face
frightfully pale. Hanli wished her mother would rush up and pull
her hair so they could have a real fight and get some of that
hatred out of their systems. But Qiu Yumei just stood there, wordlessly twisting the scarf around her fingers. Threads of pity
settled over Hanli, who said through her sobs, "I don't want it.
Give it to Hanzhen."

So Qiu Yumei took back the scarf, and the next day she wore it
outside. Eventually it was Hanzhen who went to school with Old
Shu's scarf draped around her shoulders. When asked, she said her
mother had ordered it from Shanghai and that her mother loved
her and not Hanli.

It was a different matter with Old Lin, whom Hanli treated
with fatherly respect. In fact, this alone was the source of at least
half the praise Hanli received on Fragrant Cedar Street. Whenever
Old Lin was in the middle of a neighborhood chess game, she
brought him food and tea, and back home she drew his bathwater.
She even trimmed his nails for him. Qiu Yumei told people Hanli
was trying to be an elder sister to Old Lin, treating him like a little
boy.

"And what about you?" they would ask. "How does that make
you feel?"

"It's fine with me," Qiu Yumei would say. "It makes my life
easier."

Let's say it's a blustery day and that the rain is pounding the sheet-metal roof of number 18, turning everything wet and forsaken at dusk. A frustrated Old Lin is searching for an umbrella beneath the stairs. He never knows where the family umbrella is kept. He opens Hanli's door. "Where's the umbrella?" Hanli looks at him but says nothing, so he tosses things around until he finds an umbrella with broken ribs and torn oil paper, which he can't open, no matter how hard he tries.

"Chess," Hanli says. "That's all you think about even when it's pouring rain. Don't come running to me if you catch your death of cold."

Old Lin flings the broken umbrella to the floor. "Don't tell me there isn't a working umbrella anywhere in the house!"

"There is," Hanli says, "but *she* took it when she went out. Would it kill you to stick around and pass up one chess match?"

Old Lin sighs. "Shit, what's there to do on a day like this *except* play chess?" He sits down and arranges the pieces just to keep busy, and Hanli surprises him by sitting down across the table.

"I'll play a game," Hanli says.

"Don't be silly, you don't know how to play."

"Sure I do. I learned by watching you."

"All right." Old Lin reflects for a moment. "I'll hand over one of my pieces. What do you want, cart, horse, or cannon?"

Hanli looks down at Old Lin's hands without answering. She's acting strange today.

"You can have two carts and a cannon. What do you say?"

"Up to you."

Old Lin removes two carts and a cannon and lets Hanli open. But she just moves her vanguard cannon and stops. Obviously, her mind isn't on chess.

"Papa, why don't you two sleep in the same room?"

"Just play, and no foolish questions."

"No. I want some answers."

"She doesn't like me, and I don't like her, so why should we sleep in the same room?"

"But I hear noises in her room at night."

"She walks in her sleep. She's never been a sound sleeper."

"No, I heard Old Shu from downstairs—"

"Keep playing, and stop with all that nonsense."

"Everyone says she and Old Shu—"

"You're getting on my nerves!" He picks up a chess piece and bangs the board with it. "What you people do is your business."

"What do you mean *our* business? It's your business, too. Do you know what people call you?"

"Shut up! Now you're really getting on my nerves!" He stands up, grabs the chessboard, and dumps everything on Hanli. "You bastards won't let me live in peace!"

Old Lin scoops up the broken umbrella and runs downstairs. Rain beating down on the sheet-metal roof has turned the dusk wet and forsaken. Hanli is on her knees, picking up the chess pieces, biting her lip to keep from crying out loud. She tries to figure out what's up with her father. What's up with this family? She can tell by the sound that the rain is picking up, and before long she fantasizes that it is about to innundate Fragrant Cedar Street. From where she sits on the floor, she feels as if the whole building were sinking. With darkness settling around her, she gets up to turn on the lights. Nothing happens, which scares her. Rushing over to the window to look downstairs, she sees Shu Gong poke his head out his window to pull in the line on which his blue underpants had been drying. Darkness claims Fragrant Cedar Street, all but a single bright spot on the crown of Shu Gong's head. Hanli runs downstairs, her flying feet making the stairway shake and creak. In the grip of a vaguely despairing thought, she hears her heart murmur, People should leave one another alone. I'll leave you alone, and you do the same for me.

Hanli bursts into the little room in the Shu flat and plops breathlessly into a wicker chair. Shu Gong eyes her suspiciously. "Who's after you?"

"Ghosts," Hanli says.

"The electricity is out, probably a downed wire."

"It's not the dark I'm afraid of."

"Then what is it?"

"I'm not sure."

"You don't have to be afraid of anything while I'm around." Unable to see Hanli's face in the darkness, Shu Gong grabs hold of the wicker chair and leans down to look more closely; but she turns away from him, the tip of her braid brushing his face.

"People should leave one another alone," Hanli says. "I'm not going to get involved in their affairs anymore, and they'd better not get involved in mine."

"Who's involved in whose affairs?" Shu Gong stops to ponder. "People should try to take care of themselves."

"I'm not talking to you," Hanli says.

"Then who are you talking to?" Shu Gong lifts a strand of her hair and tugs it.

"To myself." She slaps at his hand but misses, which he finds exciting.

"You're something, sure as hell." He yanks the hair out by its root. "It sure is long," he says, mesmerized by the strand of hair. "And really dark." A pulsating desire wraps itself around him; suddenly materializing, it emanates from Hanli, her natural scent making him limp all over. It is more than he can stand. He can hardly breathe. The time has come to inject life into the fantasy that visits him at night. Without warning, he throws his arms around Hanli, sticks out his tongue, and licks her lips. She screams and struggles to get out of the wicker chair, but the frantically licking Shu Gong covers her mouth with his hand. "Don't scream! Keep it up, and I'll kill you!"

Hanli recoils like a little bunny and lets him lick her face as much as he likes, calming herself by staring at the curtain of rain outside the window. "This isn't so bad," she says, sensing the time has come to see what it's like to be with a boy. She can show Qiu Yumei that she knows a thing or two about being shameless, too.

This isn't so bad. People should leave one another alone. Hanli smiles and gently pushes Shu Gong away. "We need a real date," she says in the darkness, emphasizing the word *date*.

"How do we do that?" Shu Gong asks, holding her hand and not letting go. He is breathing hard.

"Leave it to me, I'll teach you," she says. "Now let go."

"If you're playing games with me, I'll kill you." Shu Gong shoves her away. He is already very, very wet.

"I'm not." Hanli gets to her feet, puckers up, and gives Shu Gong a peck on the cheek. "I have to go upstairs. We'll do it. Just be patient."

In his search for some wire to make a toy gun, Shu Nong went into the storage room beneath the stairs. The latch was broken, so all it took was a good shove to open the door. Shu Nong found it strange that the room was deserted except for the cat sitting on an old slatted trunk, its eyes flashing. He wondered if the cat was up to no good, since cats are such inscrutable animals. When he walked over to pick it up, the cat sprang out of the way, leaving a pair of plum-blossom paw prints on the trunk. Shu Nong recalled this trunk as a place where his father stored all kinds of odds and ends. Maybe he'd find the wire he needed inside. He raised the lid and nearly jumped out of his skin. Two people were coiled up inside, and they were as frightened as he was.

Shu Gong and Hanli tried to make themselves invisible inside the trunk. He was naked, so was she. His face was scarlet, hers was ghostly white.

"What do you think you're doing?" Shu Nong nearly shouted.

"Playing hide-and-seek." Hanli covered her face with her hands.

"Liar," Shu Nong said scornfully. "I know what you're up to."

"Don't tell anybody, Shu Nong." Hanli grabbed his arm. "I'll give you anything you want."

"We'll see how I feel."

Shu Nong slammed the lid down and turned to leave. By then,

the cat was outside, so he walked toward it. Shu Gong jumped out of the trunk, grabbed him from behind, and dragged him back into the storage room. He easily knocked Shu Nong to the floor, then walked over and shut the door. "What are you doing here?"

"Looking for some wire. Nothing to do with you."

Shu Gong removed a piece of wire from the trunk and waved it in front of Shu Nong. "This it?" Shu Nong reached for it, but Shu Gong pushed his hand away and said, "I'll hold on to it for now. If you breathe a word of this, I'll seal your mouth with it, and you can spend the rest of your life as a mute."

Shu Gong was buck naked. Shu Nong noticed that his pecker was as stiff and big around as a carrot, with threads of purplish blood on the tip. As he stared at the bloodstains, his curiosity turned to fear. He looked over at the trunk. Hanli was sitting up, her face bloodless, her arms crossed over her breasts. Still, he detected the radiance of her body, the familiar bluish glare that characterized the bodies of Lin women. It stung his eyes. Shu Nong was feeling bad, real bad. He walked to the door again. By now, the cat was crouched on the first step. As soon as he was outside the room, Shu Nong threw up, the contents of his stomach spilling out in oceanic quantities. He had never thrown up like that before and had no idea why he was doing it now or why he couldn't stop. In the ensuing dizziness, he saw the cat hop up the stairs, one step at a time, until it disappeared from view.

One morning, Shu Nong instinctively knew that he had become Shu Gong's mortal enemy. At home, in the neighborhood, in school—wherever they were, Shu Gong gave him a glacial look out of the corner of his eye; Shu Nong had begun to cast a dark shadow over Shu Gong's secret happiness. Knowing that he was an obstacle in his brother's way, Shu Nong consciously avoided Shu Gong's stony gaze. It's not my fault, he reasoned. I'm a cat, and cats see everything. You can't blame a cat.

"Did you tell anybody?" Shu Gong grabbed Shu Nong's ear.

"No."

"How about Papa, did you tell him?"

"No."

"Watch out. Keep that mouth of yours shut." Shu Gong held up the piece of wire to show Shu Nong.

Shu Nong sat at the table, shoveling food into his mouth with his hand, a reprehensible habit with a long history. Old Shu could not get him to change, not even with his fists. No one knew he was just being catlike. That behavior symbolized Shu Nong's increasing inscrutability, but no one in the family realized it.

"If you tell anybody, I'll seal your mouth with this wire, understand? That's a promise, not a threat," Shu Gong said in measured tones before slicking down his hair with vegetable oil, putting on his white sneakers, and heading outside.

Shu Nong knew where he was going, and his thoughts turned to his father, who threatened him the same way when he was caught climbing the downspout. Who said I can't tell? If I feel like telling somebody, I will, and if I don't, I won't. They can't do a thing about it. They weren't fated to really shake people up, he reasoned; that was left to him. He followed people, seeing everything, and seeing it first. Is there a soul alive who can hide from the eyes of a cat?

They say Shu Nong followed lots of people, not just his brother and mortal enemy, Shu Gong.

As the sound of whistling faded away, Shu Nong calculated that his brother had passed the storage room and jumped to the street from the windowsill. Pinching his nose closed, he hugged the wall and followed Shu Gong to the limestone quarry, where Hanli waited. It was always the same: Shu Gong and Hanli hid between a wall and a waist-high stack of bricks, the space between stuffed with a battered bamboo basket, like a sentry.

Without a sound, Shu Nong flattened out on the ground and watched them through the gaps in the woven basket. Sometimes he saw their feet float and bob like paper boats. Shu Nong didn't think he could control the urge to screech like a cat, but somehow he managed. Afraid of being discovered, he lay on his belly and held his breath until his face turned purple.

\*   \*   \*

Fragrant cedars are long gone from Fragrant Cedar Street, replaced by acacias and parasol trees. Let's say the acacias are in bloom. When the first winds blow, we see a light-purple haze shimmer above the eaves of the dark building, illusory somehow; the air is heavy with the redolence of fauna. It's the outdoor season, so we all troop outside. Nineteen seventy-four, if memory serves, early autumn, late afternoon.

The boys gather in the courtyard of Soybean's yard, around a pile of stone dumbbells. Most boys on Fragrant Cedar Street can lift a hundred-pound dumbbell. We see Shu Nong push open the gate and stand on the threshold, wondering if he should go in or back out. He seems to be in a trance, standing there, picking his nose with the pinky of his left hand.

"Get the hell out of here, bed wetter." One of the boys runs up and shoves him.

"I just want to watch," he says as he leans against a gatepost. "Can't I even watch?"

"Come tell us what the young lovers Shu Gong and Hanli do."

"I don't know."

"Don't know or won't say? If you won't tell us, then get the hell out of here."

Shu Nong stays put, his free hand sliding up and down the post. After a moment, he says, "They hide in a slatted trunk."

"A slatted trunk?" the boys hoot. "Doing what?"

"Fucking," Shu Nong says maliciously. He bites his lip as he jerks open the gate and is gone like a puff of smoke.

Hanli realized it had been a long time since her last period, two months by her reckoning, and she didn't know why. She was nauseated and felt tired, limp, and sluggish all the time. Frequently downcast, she suspected it was a result of what she and Shu Gong were doing. But she couldn't be sure. When she tried to ask her mother, the words rose to the tip of her tongue and no farther. Deciding to ask a doctor instead, she slipped off to the clinic. When the doctor uttered that fateful word, his voice dripping with disgust, Hanli reacted as if struck by lightning; she was virtually paralyzed.

"Lin Hanli, you're pregnant. What school do you go to?" The doctor glared at Hanli, who snatched her sweater off the chair and dashed out of the clinic, covering her face with her sweater so people sitting in the corridor would not recognize her. She emerged into the blinding sunlight of a warm, breezy afternoon. The city and the streets closed in on her as always, but this time she was caught in the fetters of disaster and could hardly breathe. "You're pregnant!" Like a steel band cinched around her neck. How did this happen? What'll I do? Nervously, Hanli walked up to the post office and stopped to let her eyes wander up and down Fragrant Cedar Street. Few people were out and about on that peaceful afternoon; the cobblestones shimmered beneath the sun's rays. Hanli didn't dare walk down Fragrant Cedar Street since now it was an enormous pit waiting to claim her.

Hanli sat on the post office steps, her thoughts chaotic. She considered going to Shu Gong, who would be home asleep, but was afraid to enter Fragrant Cedar Street. Maybe she could wait till nightfall, when no one would see her. Where is all this sunlight coming from? How come the afternoon is so long? As hope faded, she felt like crying. But no tears came, for some strange reason. Maybe she needed to escape the eyes of Fragrant Cedar Street residents. Sometime after four o'clock, she spotted Hanzhen walking home with her schoolbag over her shoulder. She was eating candy. "Hey, what are you doing here?" Hanli grabbed her sister's bag and wouldn't let go. There was madness in her eyes as she looked into Hanzhen's round, ruddy face.

"Say something! What's wrong?" Hanzhen was nearly shouting.

"Not so loud." Like a girl snapping out of a daydream, Hanli clamped her hand over her sister's mouth. "Tell Shu Gong I need to see him."

"What for?"

"Just say I have to talk to him about something."

"No. You shouldn't have anything to do with boys like him."

"That's my business." Hanli pulled a handful of peanuts out of her pocket and stuffed them into Hanzhen's hand. "Hurry, and don't tell anybody."

Hanzhen finally agreed, and as Hanli watched her run toward the dark building at number 18, she breathed deeply to calm herself. This wasn't her problem alone—it was Shu Gong's, too. Would he know what to do? She'd wait for him there. The afternoon seemed endless. Later that day, Hanli and Shu Gong walked single file to their love nest, the limestone quarry, where Hanli sat down and hugged herself tightly as Shu Gong rested on his elbow. This was one of Fragrant Cedar Street's better-known love scenes a decade or so ago.

"What'll we do?" Hanli asked him.

"How should I know?" Shu Gong replied.

"Can we get rid of it?"

"How?"

"Don't you have any idea?"

"Who knows things like that? I can barely keep my eyes open. Let me get some sleep."

"No sleeping. You're the original sleeping dog."

"Who do you think you're talking to? I could beat the shit out of you."

"I'm talking to you. Why can't you figure a way out of this mess instead of always thinking about sleeping?"

"How should I know what the hell's wrong with you? Other guys play around with girls without getting into trouble."

"I don't know what happened either. What if we try to beat it out?"

"Beat it out? With what?"

"I don't care. Try one of those bricks."

"Where should I hit?"

"Here, and pretty hard."

"OK, here goes. It's going to hurt."

Hanli closed her eyes as Shu Gong swung the brick, really putting some arm into it and drawing shrieks of pain from Hanli. "Not so hard, you coldhearted bastard!"

"You're the one who said to hit hard. Do it yourself then."

Shu Gong jammed the brick up against Hanli's belly. He was mad, and it was her fault. He brushed the dirt off the seat of his pants as he turned to leave.

But Hanli wrapped her arms around his leg and wouldn't let go. She dug into his pant leg and held on for dear life. "You can't leave just like that." She looked up at him.

"Then what should we do?" Shu Gong asked.

"Kill ourselves," she blurted out after a thoughtful pause.

"That isn't funny."

"I mean it, we die together."

"You're crazy."

"Neither of us lives. We'll jump into the river."

"I can swim, so I won't die."

"No. We tie ourselves to a rock. That'll do it."

"Screw you. I'm not ready to die."

"I'll report you. That's a death sentence. You choose how you want to go."

"I'm not afraid, I'm just not ready to die."

"One way or the other, you're going to. Don't think I won't say you raped me."

Shu Gong sat down and scratched his mussed hair, giving Hanli a look of malignant hostility. On that afternoon, Hanli was cold and detached, like a woman rich in the ways of the world and familiar with the tricks necessary to get by. Shu Gong broke into a sweat on his back and felt nearly paralyzed. When he looked into the weakened sun's rays over the limestone quarry, he saw millions of dust particles spiraling lazily downward. Shu Gong snapped off a wolfberry twig and broke it into pieces, which he crammed down the sides of his high-topped sneakers. Then he rubbed the sneakers. "Whatever," he said. "If you want me to die, that's OK with me. So I die, so what?"

"So what?" Hanli sneered. "What does that mean? I didn't get into this mess alone."

"Don't be stupid. When are we supposed to go out and die?"

"Tomorrow. No, tonight."

Hanli took Shu Gong's hand. He shook her off. She threw her arms around his neck. He pushed her away. Shu Gong looked at the patch of skin revealed beneath the collar of Hanli's sweater, a piece of floating white ice. He pounced on her, pushing her to the ground and tearing the buttons off her coat, which he held in his hand to see clearly before throwing them behind the pile of bricks and pawing at Hanli's purple sweater. He heard the subtle sound of snapping threads.

Hanli was staring wide-eyed, her eyes taking on the subdued purple of her sweater, not a trace of fear in them. "Yes, it'll be dark soon." She appeared to smile when she said that, then obediently let Shu Gong have his way with her.

Shu Gong gasped as he ripped off her chemise: Hanli's small, firm breasts were covered with purple blotches, her nipples dark and enlarged. Shu Gong sensed that her body had undergone subtle changes. He had done what he had set out to do the past few months: he had fixed Hanli real good. "It doesn't matter to me," he said. "If you want me dead, then that's what you'll get."

Not far from the limestone quarry, a cat screeched mournfully, but they didn't notice.

The cat was Shu Nong.

After the curtain of night fell, Shu Nong followed Shu Gong and Hanli to Stone Pier, which is at the southern end of Fragrant Cedar Street but hasn't been used for years. It was Shu Nong's favorite spot from which to watch people swim. But this was not the swimming season, and he wondered what they were doing there. He climbed onto a broken-down derrick to observe them through the cracked windshield. From that vantage point, he could look down on the river that flowed through town, although when there was no wind, the water lay heavily, like molten bronze. A motley assortment of lamps were lit in homes along the banks; a new moon reflected in the surface of the water was a luminous oval of goose-down yellow. The two people sitting on the river's edge looked like disconnected marionettes. Not sure what they were doing, Shu Nong observed their movements. First they tied themselves together with a rope, then rolled a large rock up to the river very, very slowly, waddling like geese. Shu Nong assumed it was some sort of game. They stopped at the river's edge. A cat on the opposite bank screeched. Shu Nong heard Shu Gong announce to the river, "So we die, what's the big deal?" Then they wrapped their arms around each other and jumped in with a thud and a splash that sent silvery spray in all directions. The moon splintered.

Die? Finally, Shu Nong reacted. Shu Gong and Hanli are drowning themselves in the river! He jumped down off the derrick and made a mad dash back to number 18. His flat was quiet, deserted, so he ran upstairs and banged on Qiu Yumei's door. "In the river! Drowned themselves!" Shu Nong screamed at the dark-red door. He heard rustling noises inside.

Qiu Yumei opened the door a crack. "Who drowned themselves?" she asked.

"Hanli and Shu Gong!" Shu Nong stuck his head inside to look for his father. He spotted a shaky hand resting on a shoe under the bed. He knew the hand belonged to his father. With a squeal, he tore downstairs, shouting to the steps, to the accumulated junk, to the window:

IN THE RIVER!
DROWNED THEMSELVES!

To this day, if I close my eyes, I can see them fishing the bodies out of the dark river at the end of Fragrant Cedar Street as if it were yesterday. Every man who knew how to swim dived into the black, foul-smelling water. People thronged the neglected Stone Pier, where a single streetlamp lit faces that shimmered like the surface of the water. The Shu and Lin families from number 18 were central figures in the drama, and folks took particular notice of Old Shu, who dived to the bottom, came up for air, then dived again, over and over, while Old Lin stood watching on the bank, a chess piece in his hand. Some said it was a horse. Qiu Yumei leaned against an electric pole and sobbed into her hands, hiding her face.

Shu Gong was first out of the water. Old Shu flung his son over his shoulder and ran up and down Fragrant Cedar Street. Black, foul-smelling water spewed from the boy's mouth. Then they fished out Hanli, and Old Shu did the same with her. She looked like a lamb rocking back and forth on Old Shu's shoulder, but no water emerged from her mouth, not even when he had run all the way to the upstairs flat at number 18. She didn't even twitch. Old Shu laid Hanli's body on the floor and felt her pulse. "Nothing," he announced. "She's past saving."

Shu Nong elbowed his way up through the crowd to see what the drowned Hanli looked like, oblivious to the noisy babble all around him. Instinct told him that Hanli was dead. He looked down at her water-soaked body, still dripping as it lay on the floor, each drop the same blue color as her glossy skin. Hanli's staring pupils were more captivating than cat's eyes poking through the darkness. She was really, really blue, and Shu Nong was struck by the realization that all the females he peeked at were blue, even the dead ones. He assumed there was something blue about women and death. What was going on here?

Hanli's death became *the* topic of conversation on Fragrant Cedar Street's lanes and byways. People still loved her, even after she was dead, and they told anyone who would listen that like a tender flower growing in a dank cellar, she was fated to die young. This, you must realize, effectively captures the complex and veiled relationships among the people at number 18. The residents of Fragrant Cedar Street were incapable of glossing over the influence of Old Shu and Qiu Yumei on their children, so the suicide pact of Hanli and Shu Gong was overlaid by a film of tragic romanticism.

From then on, the black lacquer gate at number 18 remained shut to outsiders. Milk deliveries were placed in a small wooden box outside the gate, and if you peeked through a crack, all you saw was a dark building. It was just a feeling, but number 18 seemed off-limits in the wake of the Lin girl's premature death. By looking up, you could, if you were observant, see a change in Qiu Yumei's upstairs window: now it was sealed with sheet metal, which made it look from a distance like the door of a pigeon cage.

Sensitive folks tried to guess who had sealed the window, thereby forcing the trashy Qiu Yumei to spend her days in darkness. "Who did it?" they asked Hanzhen. She said she didn't know, adding, "Go away, and leave my family alone." So they asked Shu Nong, but he wouldn't answer, although his crafty eyes said, Oh, I saw, all right. Nothing gets past me. I see it all.

Let's say it's the night of Hanli's death, and Old Lin drags some used sheet metal and his tool pouch into Qiu Yumei's room, without knocking first. He bangs his hammer against the windowsill three times: *bang bang bang.*

"What do you think you're doing?"

"Sealing up the kennel door."

"Damn it, you'll block out the light."

"It has to be sealed up, and you know why."

"No. Have you gone mad?"

"Keep your voice down. I'm doing it for your own good."

"I'll suffocate in here. No one seals a southern window."

"I'm worried that Hanli's spirit will come looking for you. The river is right outside that window."

"Don't try to frighten me, it won't work. I did nothing to offend Hanli."

"I'm worried you might sleepwalk your way right out that window to your death."

Qiu Yumei climbed out of bed, then sat back down. She buried her head in the quilt and sobbed. "Go ahead, seal it," she said in a muffled voice, "if that's what you want." But Old Lin was too busy nailing up the sheet metal to hear her. He was so good with his hands that in no time the window was sealed airtight. Like I said, from a distance it looked like a pigeon cage in the dark.

How does it feel to return from the dead? To Shu Gong, the attempted suicide was a bad dream from which he awoke drenched. His family stood in the doorway, gawking at him. He felt terrible. "Bring me some dry clothes," he said to his mother. "I want to change." But Old Shu pushed Mother outside. "No changing. Since you didn't drown, you can just dry out on your own. Being wet shouldn't bother someone who can defy death. Go on, dry out, you turtle-egg bastard!"

Shu Gong lay there spent, thinking back to when they were sinking to the bottom of the river, to how Hanli's fingers groped frantically for him and how he pushed her away. He didn't want to die strapped to Hanli, whose finger reached out like a slender fish to peck him on the face before slipping away. Hanli was well and truly dead. He was still alive. Loathing and contempt lay in his father's eyes and in his as well, as they were reflected in the old-fashioned wall mirror; he also saw in them a cold enmity and guardedness. "Get out of here, all of you," Shu Gong demanded. "We have no use for one another, dead or alive." He jumped up and slammed the door shut to remove them from his sight. Slowly, he took off his wet clothes and opened his dresser.

*Creak.* The door opened, and Shu Nong slipped into the room. He leaned against the doorframe to watch Shu Gong change clothes. "I saw the two of you," he blurted out.

"Get the hell out of here." Shu Gong modestly held up his clothing to cover his nakedness.

"I saw."

"Saw what?"

"Everything."

"So you went and told everybody?" Shu Gong walked over to the door and bolted it, then grabbed Shu Nong by the hair with one hand and clapped the other one over his mouth to keep him from shouting. He slammed his brother up against the wall and heard it give and then snap back. Shu Nong's frail little body slumped to the ground as if it were made of sand. *Whoosh!* The breath escaped from Shu Gong's mouth all at once. This was the way to handle things now that something lost had been restored to him. This is how to do it: flatten that disgusting Shu Nong.

*       *       *

I saw Shu Nong out walking one cold early-winter day. He was dragging his schoolbag behind him; with his long, spiky hair, he looked like a porcupine. He was kicking dead leaves on his way home. Whenever there was some kind of commotion, he headed toward it, stood on the perimeter for a moment to see what was going on, then walked off. Once it became clear that there was nothing much to see, he was gone. Hardly anything captured his interest.

Shu Nong was being chased down the street, cradling an air rifle. His pursuer was the man who shot sparrows. "Grab him!" he shouted. "He stole my rifle!" The weapon was nearly as tall as Shu Nong, who finally got tangled up in it and fell in a heap in front of the stone bridge, where he lay rubbing the wooden stock for a moment while he caught his breath; then he tossed the rifle aside and crossed the bridge.

"Don't chase him," someone at the bridgehead teahouse said. "That boy's not all there."

If you knew Shu Nong, you'd realize how wide of the mark this comment was. Shu Nong was all there, all right, and if you have ever been to Fragrant Cedar Street, you know that this is the story of a very clever boy.

Shu Nong noticed a pair of new white sneakers, just like Shu Gong's, on his bed next to his pillow. He picked them up and examined them from every angle.

"Try them on." His father was standing behind them.

This was another major occurrence in Shu Nong's fourteenth year: he had his own white sneakers. "Are these for me?" Shu Nong turned around.

"They're yours. Like them?" Old Shu sat on Shu Nong's bed and inspected the sheet.

"I didn't wet it."

"That's good."

Shu Nong laced up his shoes almost hesitantly, as a result of lingering doubts. He kept glancing over at his father. Shu Nong never dreamed that his father would actually buy him a pair of shoes like this. Normally he wore Shu Gong's hand-me-downs.

"Can I wear them now?" Shu Nong asked.

"You can wear them anytime you like," Old Shu said.

"New Year's is still a long way off," Shu Nong said.

"Then hold off till New Year's," Old Shu replied.

"But that means I have to wait a long time," Shu Nong said.

"Then wear them now." A note of irritation crept into Old Shu's voice. "So wear them now." He began pacing the floor.

The shoes made Shu Nong spry and light on his feet. After bounding around the room, he turned to run outside, but his father stopped him with a shout: "Don't be in such a hurry to go outside. You have to do something for me first."

Shu Nong froze, his mouth snapping open fearfully. "I didn't wet the bed!" he screamed.

Old Shu said, "This isn't about bed-wetting. Come over here." Shu Nong grabbed the doorframe, lowered his head, and stayed put as he dimly sensed that the new shoes were a sort of bait. Old Shu raised his voice: "Come over here, you little bastard!" Shu Nong walked over to his father, who grabbed his hand and squeezed it. "I'll be sleeping in your room at night," Old Shu said.

"Why? Did you and Mother have a fight?"

"No. And what I mean is, sometimes. Like tonight."

"That's OK with me. In my bed?"

"No, I'll sleep on the floor."

"Why do that when there's a bed?"

"Never mind. I'll strap you to the bed with a blindfold over your eyes and cotton in your ears. We'll see how you do."

"Are we going to play hide-and-seek?"

"Right, hide-and-seek."

Shu Nong took a good look at his father, holding his tongue as he rubbed the tops of his new sneakers. Then he said, "I know what you're going to do. The upstairs window has been sealed."

"All you have to worry about is getting some sleep. And don't make a sound, understand?"

"I understand. You can't climb in with the window sealed."

"If your mother knocks at the door, just say you're in bed. And not another word more. The same goes for anyone else who knocks at the door. Understand?"

"I understand. But why not do it in the slatted trunk. Isn't it big enough for you two?"

"Don't tell a soul about any of this. You know what I'm capable of, don't you?"

"I know. You'll choke the life right out of me. That's what you said."

"That's right, I'll choke the life right out of you." Old Shu's bushy eyebrows twitched. "What were you mumbling just a minute ago?"

At this point, father and son had flat, expressionless looks on their faces. Old Shu crooked his little finger, so did Shu Nong; they silently hooked their fingers, sealing this odd pact.

Thus began the process that led to the most memorable nights of Shu Nong's youth. He recalled how the black cloth was put over his eyes, how he was tied to the bed hand and foot, and how his ears were stuffed with cotton. Father and Qiu Yumei made love beside him. He was in the same room with them. He saw nothing. He heard nothing. But he sensed their location and movements in the dark; he could tell who was on top and who was doing what to whom. A powerful blue radiance pierced the leaden darkness and touched his eyes, making sleep impossible and rendering movement out of the question. He gulped down large mouthfuls of the musky sweet air, then exhaled it in large puffs. He was getting uncomfortably hot, which he attributed to the dark-blue lights baking him as he lay strapped to his bed; the desolate howl of a rat lugging flames on its back emerged from his anguished soul. "I'm hot," he said, "I'm burning up." When Old Shu finally got around to untying the ropes, Shu Nong sounded as if he were talking in his sleep.

Old Shu felt his forehead; it was cold. "Are you sick, Shu Nong?"

Shu Nong replied, "No, I was asleep." Old Shu removed the blindfold. Shu Nong said, "I saw." Then Old Shu took the cotton out of his ears, and Shu Nong said, "I heard."

Old Shu grabbed his son's ear and barked, "Who did you see?"
Shu Nong replied, "She's very blue."
"Who's very blue?" Old Shu pinched the ear hard. "What kind
of damned nonsense are you spouting?"
Shu Nong was in such pain he thumped the bed with both feet.
"I mean the cat," he screamed, "the cat's eyes are very blue."
Old Shu released his grip and whispered in Shu Nong's ear,
"Remember, not a word to anyone."
Shu Nong curled up under his comforter and, with his head
covered, said, "If you hit me again, I'll tell. I'm not afraid to die. I'll
just turn into a cat. Then nobody will have anything to say about
what I do from now on."

Here is the kind of girl Hanzhen was: flighty, sneaky, and
headstrong. She loved to eat and was extremely vain. Plenty of girls
like that lived on Fragrant Cedar Street, and there isn't much you
can say about their lives outside of an occasional newsworthy episode that materialized out of the blue.
It might have been Hanzhen you saw out on the street, but it
was Hanli who was on the people's minds, a girl who had died too
young. When women took Hanzhen aside and asked, "Why did
your big sister want to kill herself?" she replied, "Loss of face."
Then when women asked, "Are you sad your sister died?" Hanzhen would pause before saying, "I inherited her clothes." If they
kept pestering her, she grew impatient and, arching her willowy
brows, said, "You're disgusting, the whole lot of you. All day long
you do nothing but keep your eyes peeled for juicy tidbits!" The
women compared her with her sister right to her face. "Hanzhen is
no Hanli," they would say, "the living is no match for the dead."
To the surprise of all, three months after Hanli's death, Hanzhen herself became the talk of Fragrant Cedar Street. Seen in retrospect, it had nothing to do with the real-life vicissitudes of
Fragrant Cedar Street. What the incident actually reflected was the
tragic significance of our story. Tragedy is an enormous closed box;
once it is opened, people inevitably get shut back inside. If not

Hanzhen, it would have been someone else. Can you understand what I'm getting at?

It starts with the sweetshop. One day as Hanzhen was passing the sweetshop on her way home from school, she noticed a jar of preserved fruit in the window. As she entered, Old Shi was hanging out a sign that said CLOSED FOR INVENTORY. Hanzhen checked the money in her pocket—she had just enough for a bag of dried plums. She thought she could make the purchase before Old Shi began the inventory. After closing the door, he asked, "What would you like, Hanzhen?"

She tapped the jar. "Dried plums," she said. "I want some dried plums." She was unaware that he had closed the door. She watched him walk around behind the counter, sit down, and start working his abacus. "I want a bag of dried plums," Hanzhen repeated.

"Wait a minute, I'm nearly finished."

As she waited for him to finish, she stared at the jar of dried plums, oblivious to the fact that the door was closed and that she was alone in the shop with Old Shi. Finally, he laid down his abacus. "Dried plums?" he said. "Come back here. I'll give you a special weighing, more than your money's worth." Hanzhen smiled bashfully and ran behind the counter, where she handed Old Shi the money in her hand. He looked at the crumpled bill, then wrapped his hand around hers. "I don't want your money," he said. "My treat."

"Why don't you want it?" Hanzhen asked wide-eyed.

"We'll work a swap," Old Shi said. "I'll give you the dried plums, and you give me something in return."

"Tell me what you want, and I'll go home and get it."

He scooped a big handful of dried plums out of a metal box. "Open your mouth, Hanzhen," he said. She did. With a giggle, he tossed in a dried plum. "Good?"

"Yum," she said.

Altogether, Old Shi flipped five dried plums into Hanzhen's mouth. "Now it's your turn," he said. "Let me see your belly button, that's all I want."

Unable to speak with all those dried plums in her mouth, Hanzhen just shook her head. The strange look on Old Shi's face was one she had never seen before, but the realization came too late, for Old Shi had wrapped his arms around her and was forcing her to the floor, where he crammed the rest of the dried plums into her mouth so she couldn't make a sound. The next thing she felt was Old Shi's sweaty hand pushing her undershirt up and rubbing her exposed navel. Then the hand pulled down her underpants and slipped between her legs. Hanzhen was shocked nearly out of her mind. She wanted to scream but couldn't, with all those dried plums in her mouth.

Old Shi said breathlessly, "Don't scream, don't make any noise. I'll give you ten bags of dried plums and three packages of toffee. Don't scream, don't you scream."

Hanzhen nodded and shook her head as if her life depended on it. She didn't know what he was doing to her; all she could see was Old Shi's gray head resting against her breasts. Then she felt a sharp pain down below and thought Old Shi was trying to kill her. She grabbed his gray hair with both hands and screamed, "Shame on you! Shame on you!" But there was no sound; it seemed like a fantastic, bizarre dream.

It was nearly dark when Hanzhen walked out of the sweetshop. She hugged the wall as she walked slowly, the schoolbag dangling from her hand, chock-full of preserved fruit that Old Shi had nearly forced her to take. "If you don't tell anybody," he had said, "you can have any treats you want." Hanzhen sucked on a dried plum as she walked. The place where Old Shi had done it felt as if he had left something sharp in there. Hanzhen looked down and was horrified to see a trickle of blood running down her pant leg and onto her shoes and the ground. *Whoop!* The dried plum came sailing out of her mouth as she gaped at the crimson blood. She sat down, hugged her bulging bag to her chest, and started to cry. Passersby ignored her. Sometime later, Old Shu walked by, pushing his bicycle home from work. He asked what was wrong. Hanzhen looked up and bawled, "Shame on Old Shi! Shame on Old Shi!"

The only resident of Fragrant Cedar Street ever thrown into prison was Old Shi from the sweetshop. They dragged him to the local school in chains to be publicly villified. We sat beneath the stage, gazing up at Old Shi's gray head and the look of dejection on his face. Hanzhen was sitting up front, where everyone could gawk at her, though she was oblivious to their looks. She stared blankly at Old Shi, trussed up and on display above her.

Her mortal enemy, Shu Nong, walked up and slyly felt her pocket. When he returned, he said, "She hasn't stopped eating those dried plums. She's still got some in her pocket!" He said Lin Hanzhen was trash, just like her whole family; none of the other neighborhood boys gave him an argument on that score since they had written her off as a worn-out shoe—damaged goods. Under their breath, they called her "a little worn-out shoe." Someone even made up a stinging nursery rhyme for Hanzhen, whose mother, Qiu Yumei, accused Shu Nong of authorship.

If you walked down Fragrant Cedar Street, the one thing you could not escape was the smell of the river that flowed beneath our windows. As I indicated early on, it was like a piece of rusty metal eroding the life of Fragrant Cedar Street. You could not overlook the river's influence, for the street's time was also the river's time.

The residents of Fragrant Cedar Street were tired of putting up with their river. It had taken on the color of its pollutants, and boats from the countryside no longer plied it. One day, an old-timer hooked a rotting sack with his bamboo pole and dragged it up onto the bank. Inside he found a dead infant curled up like a shrimp, a newborn baby boy with a wrinkled face that made him look like a sleeping old man.

The residents of Fragrant Cedar Street had arrived at a point where they didn't know how to deal with their river. It could drown them, but they couldn't do anything to it in return.

One day, Shu Nong had a brilliant idea: he spread a layer of flour over a spot beneath the bridge, then dropped in his fishing line. The minutes lingered until there was a violent tug on his line.

He jerked it out of the water. On the end was a worn-out leather shoe—dainty, T-shaped, made for a woman. An onlooker recognized it as one of the shoes Hanli was wearing when she jumped into the river. He threw it back in and murmured, "What cursed luck."

Why Shu Nong got into trouble isn't all that clear.

Let's say it's an ordinary winter morning and Shu Nong is searching for his schoolbag after breakfast. He can rarely find his schoolbag before departing for school. So when he spots it under Shu Gong's cot, he gets down on his hands and knees to get it. But a sleepy Shu Gong presses down on him. "Quit goofing off."

"Who's goofing off? I'm getting my schoolbag."

Shu Gong pins him to the floor and says, "Put a bowl of porridge on the stove for me before you go." A simple request.

"That's not my job," Shu Nong replies. "Do it yourself."

Shu Gong narrows his eyes. "You're really not going to do it?" he asks.

"No," Shu Nong says. "Get out of bed, and do it yourself."

Shu Gong snaps into a sitting position and throws off the covers. "OK, I'm up." He gets out of bed, grumbling, and takes the bowl of porridge over to the stove; then he gives Shu Nong a long look out of the corner of his eye. He jumps up and down to keep warm, bouncing straight into Shu Nong's little room. "You're a lucky bastard I don't feel like pounding you right now," he says as he pulls back the covers on Shu Nong's bed to feel the sheet. It is dry. With a grin, he undoes his pants and relieves himself on Shu Nong's sheet. When he is finished, he snaps his fingers. "Father will come in pretty soon and see you've wet your bed again. I'll let him pound you for me."

Shu Nong stands there stunned, hugging his schoolbag to his chest, his face turning red; instinctively, he runs over to the water vat, scoops out a ladleful of water, and dumps it on Shu Gong's bed. Shu Gong doesn't move a finger. He dresses and says, "Go ahead, sprinkle away. No one will believe I wet my bed, and you'll still be the one to get pounded."

Shu Nong leaves for school after soaking his brother's bed. By lunchtime, he has forgotten the morning's incident—until he sees that Mother has hung out the sheets to dry. Old Shu glares darkly at him.

"I didn't wet the bed, Shu Gong did it."

Old Shu roars, "Liar! You're not only a bed wetter, you're a liar!"

Shu Nong defends himself: "Shu Gong pissed on my bed."

Old Shu jumps up angrily. "Stop lying! Shu Gong was never a bed wetter. Why would he want to piss on your bed?"

"Ask him yourself," Shu Nong says as he sits down at the table and picks up his rice bowl.

Old Shu rushes up and grabs the bowl out of his hand, then picks him up and flings him out the door. "Fuck you, you little bastard!" he bellows. "Nothing to eat or drink for you. Then we'll see if you still wet the bed. And if you still feel like lying!"

Shu Nong sits on the ground in front of the door, looking up at his father and tracing words in the dirt with his finger—*fuck* is one of them. Old Shu slams the door shut, and Shu Nong thumps it a time or two as he climbs to his feet and brushes off the seat of his pants. The cat chooses this moment to spring out through the window. It mews at Shu Nong. It seems to be chewing on a piece of cooked fish.

"Meeow," Shu Nong mews like the cat, then follows it down the street, heading east, all the way to the auto-repair shop, where he loses track of the cat. Shu Nong enters the repair shop, where some greasy mechanics are working on cars, their heads hidden under the hoods. Shu Nong squats nearby and watches them work. "What are you doing here?" one of them asks. "Get out right now."

Shu Nong says, "I'm only watching, what's wrong with that?"

A can of gasoline sits on the floor in front of some beat-up cars. Shu Nong is squatting next to it. He sniffs the air to breathe in the gasoline smell. "I know that's gasoline," he says, "and that a single match will light it off."

"You're right," the mechanic says, "so don't play with it. If it goes up, that's the end of you."

Shu Nong hangs around watching them for a long time, and when they realize he is gone, they also discover the missing gas can. They don't associate the one with the other.

Shu Nong walks home with the gas can. People see him, but the problem is no one knows what he plans to do with the stuff. He walks up to the dark building at number 18 and, after hiding the can behind the door, tiptoes inside, where he notes that both his father and Shu Gong are asleep. He softly closes his father's door and jams a toothbrush into the eye of the latch hook. Then he approaches his brother's bed. Shu Gong, whose head is under the covers, is snoring away. Shu Nong curses the covers under his breath: "Watch me even the score, you bastard." He fetches the gas can. The cat has returned home, he discovers, and is perched atop the can, staring with its lustrous-green cat's eyes. Shu Nong makes a face at the cat and shoves it off the can, which he carries over to Shu Gong's bed. He pours gasoline on the floor under the bed, smelling its aromatic scent as it spreads silently throughout the room and hearing the dry floorboards soak it up. He walks, and he pours, and he watches the clear liquid seep under the door into Father's room. That should do it, he tells himself. Confident that the gasoline will ignite, he puts the can down and takes a look around; everything is napping, the old, wormy furniture included—all except for the cat, which is watching him with its shiny green eyes. Cat, Shu Nong muses, watch me even the score now. He takes a box of matches from Shu Gong's pocket. His hand shakes; he attributes that to mild fear. So he grits his teeth, lights a match, and drops it to the floor, releasing a brief red flame. The fire takes hold under Shu Gong's bed and begins to spread. He hears the cat screech in agony and watches it streak ahead of the flames.

Shu Nong rushes desperately upstairs, without knowing why. The Lins' door is closed. Qiu Yumei and Hanzhen poke their heads out the kitchen door. "What's gotten into him?" Qiu Yumei asks.

"He's going crazy," Hanzhen says.

Shu Nong ignores them in his race to the rooftop. The first chaotic sounds rise to greet him as he crawls to the roof's edge. He believes he can hear Shu Gong scream as if his soul had left his body and Father trying with all his might to yank open the toothbrush-jammed door. He can even hear bumping sounds as Hanzhen tumbles down the stairs. By then, Qiu Yumei has thrown open a window and is shouting at the top of her lungs: "Fire fire fire fire fire fire . . ."

Shu Nong sees no sign of fire and wonders why. From his vantage point on the roof, he notices a red glow in one of the roof vents, then sees the cat emerge amid a ball of flames. The cat screeches as it burns, giving off a strange charred smell. Its eyes turn from green to purple; it seems poised to pounce on Shu Nong, who contemplates going over to pick it up. But he has second thoughts because of the flames licking its body. How could the cat have caught fire? How could it have followed me onto the roof? Shu Nong watches the cat slink forward a few steps, then crouch down and stop moving. The flames on its body die out, leaving a ball of cinders behind. Shu Nong realizes that his cat is dead—incinerated. He reaches out to feel the corpse—it is hot to the touch. He rubs the cat's eyes. They are still alive—deep purple and shiny bright.

People from all over Fragrant Cedar Street converge on number 18. To Shu Nong, the mob on the run looks like a pack of skittish rats bearing down on his home with loud screeches. He assumes that the building is about to be engulfed in flames, so what possesses them to enter it? He pokes his head over the edge to see what is going on down there. Black smoke pours out of the windows but no flames that he can see. How come? His thoughts are interrupted by a shout from below. "Shu Nong, it's Shu Nong, he's on the roof!" It's Shu Gong down below, brandishing his fists at Shu Nong. He's in his shorts—no sign of flames. Shu Nong wonders why Shu Gong hasn't been burned. Maybe he was pretending to be asleep. Shu Nong sees someone bring up a long ladder and lean it against the building. It's Old Shu. Shu Nong is getting lightheaded. Things aren't working out as planned. Everything is going wrong. He tries to push the ladder away but can't budge it. Old Shu, his face blackened with soot, is climbing toward him. Shu Nong clings to the top of the ladder. "Don't come up here!" he screams. "Don't come up here!" Old Shu keeps coming, silently, menacingly. Again Shu Nong tries to push the ladder away, but still he can't budge it. He watches his father's smoke-blackened face draw nearer and feels something cold drip from his heart. "Don't come up here!" Shu Nong screams hysterically. "I'll jump if you take another step!" A curtain of silence falls upon the crowd below. Everyone is looking up at Shu Nong. Old Shu stops his advance and joins the others in gazing at Shu Nong for about three seconds before continuing up the ladder. When his cramped fingers touch the roof, he sees Shu Nong leap high into the air like a cat and sail over his head.

With their own eyes, the residents of Fragrant Cedar Street see Shu Nong plunge into the river. Amid shrieks of horror, Shu Nong's voice is the shrillest and loudest of all. It sounds like a cat or, in the final analysis, just like Shu Nong's own voice.

It was an autumn day in 1974 on Fragrant Cedar Street. I think it was some southern holiday but can't recall which one. At dusk, two young northerners were walking from one end of the street to the other. They had stopped off on their way from Shanghai to Nanjing. As they headed down Fragrant Cedar Street, they saw a white ambulance tearing down the narrow street and a crowd of people running toward a dark building. They joined the surging crowd. The building and the area around it were packed with men, women, and children, all seemingly talking at the same time, not a word of which the two northerners could understand. But they detected the subtle odor of gasoline coming from inside the building. "Children playing with fire!" a woman said in Mandarin.

Afterward, the northerners were on the bridge, looking down at the river, its green-tinged black water flowing silently beneath them. When debris from upriver floated under the bridge, it bumped against the stone pilings. They spotted a little white sheath floating past and smiled at each other. One kept silent, but the other said, "Well, fuck me." They were still watching the river when they spotted a charred little animal float by, lying heavily in the water as darkness settled in, making it disappear from time to time. One of the northerners pointed to it and said, "What was that?"

"It looked like a cat," the other one said.

TRANSLATED BY HOWARD GOLDBLATT

# A String of Choices

## Wang Meng

It all began with that toothache of mine. In the beginning, it was just a little nagging pain. At the time, I still believed in medicine as a science, in science leading the way on the path to freedom and happiness, that knowledge is power, and all the rest.

Believing is acting. Never doubting science, I had bestirred myself and sallied forth the night before to stand in line at the you-know-where. Umbrella over my head, galoshes on my feet, and raincoat wrapped around my shoulders, I stood in the line. I don't remember whether it was a starry night or a drizzling night or if it was pouring bucketfuls. The stronger shock to the nerves always drowns out the weaker. (You'll know what I mean if you keep on reading.) That particular dental clinic was famed far and wide for constructing removable root canals under your cavities. It had been written up in the papers for "exemplary performance," and since then the long lines outside its gates had grown even longer. A mountain-climber friend whom I had always admired offered me his tent and suggested that I install myself outside the registry office, right under its little window slot. He also made me a present of compressed biscuits fortified with vitamins and iron.

A formidable lady doctor, despite the fact that she did not seem to weigh over one hundred pounds, took custody of me and jabbed a needleful of Novocain into my upper jaw without wasting time on preliminaries. She vanished before I had time to make out if her eyes were double lidded. Following on her heels, a creature whom I deduced to be an intern shoved a coldly glistening pair of pliers into my mouth. From the viewpoint of patients, I would propound the view that interns are the fountainhead of all our woes. On this assumption, I deduced with dead certainty that that particular ultra-efficient muscle-rippling athlete was none other than a blasted intern. "Do you feel anything?" he asked.

I nodded. Would it be toothache if I didn't? Wasn't it on account of this particular feeling that I had undertaken to quarter myself in front of the registry office? Would anyone be spiritual enough to do it just for the sake of the experience? All living creatures are in possession of the senses, so who among the living would own to being so bereft? And anyway, when a formidable medical personage puts such an awesome question to you, what can you do but nod? One of the golden precepts of life is that nodding your head is always better than shaking it. To be more precise, taking into account all aspects of the problem, I might add that if the question hanging in the balance is whether or not to chop off a head, then shake your head by all means, and let the other head stay on. But as a general principle, I'd say that nodding is always better than shaking.

And thus he proceeded to pull out my tooth. He pulled at my chin, he pulled at my neck, he pulled at my head, he crashed through my cavities. And why not? It is not for nothing that dentistry here is formally categorized as surgery. It refuses to be designated as tooth extraction but must puff itself up as surgery. Under such a heading, it is transformed into something profound, refined, erudite. The pliers of surgery pulled my soul out of its internal sockets into the external light of day. I broke into a cold sweat, I saw sparks, I fainted.

What a sissy!

As I was gasping for breath, I thought to myself that I should bring in a piece of self-criticism within three days at the latest. Being a sissy was no laughing matter. It was a serious lapse. The proletariat are all offspring of the legendary Guan Yu, otherwise known as Yun Chang, who had his flesh cut open and his bones scraped of a poisonous infection while he played chess.

It was only on the bus on my way back that I felt the area where the pliers had attacked suddenly turn to wood. Praise be to anesthetics, fruit of science. The workers and businessmen who have brought you into the world have not stinted on the ingredients of the recipe, after all. After the dissemination of extreme pain, I then experienced the transcendence of numbness. God help my jaw!

Now you understand why I, a professor living in the twentieth century, squarely facing the problems of modernization, would cringe at the thought of tooth extraction. You now see why I look on the various branches of dentistry as the torture chambers of the Japanese military police, why I look on all dental clinics as versions of purgatory. Teeth, for the last dozen years, have been my supreme concern. To protect my teeth, to protect my wife, to protect my honor—the three-protect principle reaches tragic dimensions, tugging at my heartstrings. In compliance with this principle, I brush my teeth five times a day, once in the morning, once in the evening, and once after each of my three daily meals. I have tried countless brands of toothpaste. My monthly expenditure on toothpaste far exceeds my spending on cigarettes and wine put together. I have become a collector of toothbrushes: long handles, short handles, long bristles, short bristles, stiff bristles, soft bristles, a bristling little tuft. I never touch cold or underdone food; I gave up sweet-and-sour; I avoid hot soup and sticky porridge and everything hard on the teeth. I not only quit cracking melon seeds, I even keep away from roasted peanuts!

But, disaster of all disasters—one day, the toothache struck again! Oh the avenging heavens!

Now you can easily understand why with this new toothache, I moped about, dragging out my days. Should I go to the hospital? I just couldn't muster the courage. I was faced with a paradox. Why go to a hospital? Because of the ache. What, then, if you go to a hospital? It will ache a hundredfold, a thousandfold. But after the ache, there will be some relief. The power of medicine lies in the fact that it will concentrate your lifetime of suffering into twenty-five seconds of agony. Which is better? A mind-racking question. It all depends on the value system you live by. With the world as it is—beauty and ugliness mixed in a medley, old and new side by side, ideas scintillating, concepts chasing one another, east confronting west, north in dialogue with south, schools and trends as numerous as trees in a forest, a sea of flapping banners shutting out our view of the sky—when the multitude of views exceeds the sum total of all the teeth of the world population by who knows how many times—in such a world, at such a time, I felt the real dilemma of *choice*.

History raises a question only when the solution itself has ripened. Just as I was suffering unspeakable agonies from a toothache and the perplexity of indecision, the president of a certain toothology association moved into our apartment building. We shook hands on the landing, and the wings of freedom fluttered on his back as if he were the archangel himself. He gave me his card: THE INTERNATIONAL TOOTHOLOGY SOCIETY CHINA CENTER. SHI XUEYA, PRESIDENT. ADDRESS: RUNNING IN PLACE. TELEPHONE: 0000000.

Oh heaven-sent succor! Toothache, thy days are numbered! Armed with two packs of the famous ginseng and deer-antler kidney-enhancement mixture, I called upon President Shi. President Shi refused the gift offering with evident delight and then accepted most reluctantly. Then he proceeded to enlighten me. The aching tooth, he said, is divided into five categories, each category subdivided into five species. Five fives, that makes twenty-five. They are all but interplay of the elements: gold, wood, water, and fire. Or variations of inflammation, decay, heat, or cold. Or imbalance of calcium, magnesium, phosphorus, and potassium. Encompassing medicine and surgery, braces and orthopedics, dentistry as a field of medicine is divided into three schools, which in turn are subdivided into nine branches. West of Mount Tai, it forks out into two main schools, European and American. Busily pulling, drilling, and filling in deadly competition, stopping up with cement, substituting with glass beads, pouring in mercury, tinkering from inside and capping from outside, they are all out to enhance the beauty of youth. Ancient Chinese medical practice, he went on, traces the complaint to its source and then removes the manifestations. All forms of toothache, according to Chinese medicine, begin with heat syndrome: liver inflammation, stomach inflammation, heart inflammation, kidney inflammation, lung inflammation, and spleen inflammation. Inflammation rises from irritation. Water quells fire, but evil fires are resistant. The quelling of inflammation is an art, and one must seek a doctor. North, south, east, west—there are four famous practitioners. There are also folk prescriptions, which have their special folk flavor. Curing toothaches by the art of *qi gong* is to work through control of the vital energy and other paranormal functions. When teeth are pulled out by *qi gong,* new ones will sprout that can withstand heat or cold. . . .

President Shi's eloquence flowed on; he was conversant with all the famous examples of toothache as well as all pertinent theories and schools of thought, from ancient to modern, native and foreign. From the fifth left upper molar of Napoléon to the auction of the dentures of Hitler's mistress, Eva; from the front teeth of the newly excavated female mummy of the Eastern Han dynasty to the qualities of the Buddha's tooth and its efficacy on various occasions—he was conversant with them all. Then he went on to the great controversy between the conservative and the radical schools in treating toothache, which has been raging for centuries. Just as he was at the height of his eloquence, I screamed, "It's killing me!" and fainted dead away.

President Shi was most apologetic. He was also modest. He declared that he was only the president of the Toothology Society and was not a practicing doctor at a dental clinic. He explained that the society was an academic organization and then proceeded to inform me that all dentists at the county level were supervised by the Handicrafts Management Office of the county government and that their licenses were issued by Agricultural Market Control officers. He kindly pointed out to me that my toothache was too down-to-earth, too mundane for his own interests. He offered me the use of his collection, including *The Toothache Encyclopedia, The Complete Guide to Toothache, Suggestions for Tooth Protection,* and other reference books. As the ancient saying goes, The master points the way; the key to the cure is in your own hands. How could I have doubted it? I was reluctant to wear out my welcome. So, restraining myself according to the ancient rites, I picked up two volumes and left.

Reading those books plunged me into the depths of confusion. I realized with pain that teeth are mortal but knowledge boundless. In the act of pulling, the teeth are there, but after the act teeth are nonexistent. Lost in boundless despair in a toothless, boundless world, I woke up and found myself a *modern* man.

My wife's elder brother, who had just returned from research and study abroad, scolded me roundly for my ignorance and condemned President Shi for wallowing in useless words. He pointed out that fleeing the hospital with an aching tooth held hostage in my jaws was like Ah Q hiding from his own baldness.* He said that if Ah Q had taken steps earlier to treat his baldness, like taking vitamins and applying hair lotions, he might now be flaunting a mop of hair down to his waist. My brother-in-law warned that a toothache, if unattended, may develop from a single infected tooth to periodontal disease, to pulpitis, to osteomyelitis, to bone tuberculosis, and from there with one quick leap to cancer of the spinal marrow. Then if you're lucky, it's amputation. If not, you're a dead man. Examples were legion. In A.D. 1635, 5,488 people died of tooth disease in Europe alone. He pointed out with great perspicacity that there was no such branch of science as toothology, that none of the developed countries recognize it as such. He would recommend that a group of oral surgeons form a team to investigate the feasibility of toothology as a branch of dental science. I mildly objected to his way of setting up the non-native rhinoceros, metaphorically speaking, as a measure of all things. But I thanked him for his advice. The truth grates on the ears, as the saying goes. He had

*Reference to a comic character in Lu Xun's short story "The True Story of Ah Q."

pointed out the stern effects of my dilatoriness in dealing with my tooth. As I did not want to lose a limb, much less my life, on account of one bad tooth, I decided to act.

I geared myself up for another pulling. That there might be anything else in that particular dental clinic apart from pulling teeth was beyond my wildest imagination. The chairman of the department where I teach told me that extraction is the fastest, the most pleasant, the most sanitary, and the most thorough way of dealing with a bad tooth and that drilling, filing, or filling is a much more painful process, with no end in sight. My colleagues at the department admonished me to make sure that I got hold of a male doctor for the operation, because tooth extraction is heavy labor. According to them, the grain allotment of dentists should be on a par with that of dockworkers. I took in everything gratefully, keeping to myself the fact that it was precisely a male doctor who had nearly killed me with his pulling. Friends and colleagues poured out their own experiences, lessons to be drawn, warnings for the future, tricks for an easy way out, rules to stick by, and so on, all relating to the art of dealing with the aching tooth. As the sayings go, The scholar offers words, the rascal offers gifts, and Birds of a feather flock together. Thus it may be deduced that both I and my community fell into the category of scholars. Alas for my scholarly tooth.

I stood in line for three days running, waiting my turn, but my turn never came. It was said that all the registry slips had slipped out by the back door. The masses at the front gate, tormented by bad teeth, were seething with anger. I wanted to make a scene then and there, but thinking of my status as a professor, I desisted. I would be in the middle of a scandal and still stuck with a bad tooth. I went home and told my wife everything. My wife said, "We have our own back door!" Back door, back door, enter ye who has the key.

I set out with two bottles of Maotai wine (don't blame me if they were fake; I can't tell the difference) to call on my wife's cousin many times removed, a certain Mr. Liu who was department head at one of the offices at the Ministry of Health. Mr. Liu told me first that he was supervisor for hospitals of Chinese medicine, that he had nothing to do with Western medicine, even less with dentistry, and second that he disapproved of Western medicine on principle. The entire scope of Western medicine, he pronounced, was to take the human body apart for vivisection, a reflection of the outlook of the early days of the Industrial Revolution. If your tooth aches, they'll attack your tooth; if your foot aches, they'll tackle your foot. All they can do, he continued, is to alleviate the manifestations. They're miles away from the root and source of the complaint. They resort to scalpels, forceps, hypodermics, saws, and clamps, treating people like machinery with so many parts. As to teeth, he added, all they know is to pull and fill, fill and pull, and they won't stop until they've rid you of your last tooth. With Chinese medicine, however, it's another story, and here Mr. Liu waxed eloquent. Chinese medicine treats the human body as an entity, a system, a construct of assimilation and dissemination, a system where the yin and the yang contend and supplement each other and the five internal organs move in unison. Even a puny little tooth has its roots in the heart, the lungs, and the kidneys, he assured me. And thus fuzzy mathematics, modern logic, total intuition, and sensory experience represent the postindustrial fifth wave. Mr. Liu informed me that famous physicians of the West had personally told Chinese medical students studying abroad that the future of medicine is embedded in China and will flourish in China, that it was preposterous for them to go west to study, that in fact it was scholars from the West who should make the pilgrimage to China to pluck the fruits of wisdom. He added that Picasso had owned up to Chang Ta-ch'ien that art is found only in China. Likewise, it is China, and China only, that is home to the genuine tooth. To sum up, Mr. Liu volunteered to help me get into the Hospital of Chinese Medicine for treatment.

I was so overjoyed that for the moment I even forgot my toothache. I have only myself to blame for my previous ordeal of that barbarous tooth extraction. Why did I have eyes only for Western medicine? I could kick myself. Mr. Liu went on to write a letter to link me up with a connection of his. I thanked him over and over again.

That first time I had trouble with my tooth, I had still believed in Western medicine as a science that would be the savior of my tooth. So infantile! Since then, times have changed, the years have chased one another down the aisle of history. As for myself, having passed through countless ups and downs, I have finally learned that science without philosophy or science plus philosophy but without the arm of backdoor connections will get me nowhere, cannot even save my tooth.

Department Chief Liu's letter, in his own calligraphy, read:

Dear Director Zhao:

How have you been? I have been terribly busy and thus remiss in paying my respects. Please excuse.

Regarding the affair entrusted to me, I have made arrangements. Please do not worry.

All these whispers about you-know-what, I think there must be some basis. Therefore please accept my early congratulations.

By the way, a friend—Professor Wang—has a toothache.

Thank you in advance for your attention to this little matter.

So this was the road to the salvation of my tooth!

There was a milling crowd at the Hospital of Chinese Medicine, not unlike Shanghai's Temple Fair. There were even lines at the men's and women's rest rooms. People would exit still belting themselves up, such was the crush. I looked around in silent astonishment. Before liberation, Chinese medicine had been in such decline, but the scene in front of me now was bursting with activity. And to think that I alone had a letter for Director Zhao. This gave me a sense of superiority as I watched the crowd of patients rushing madly to and fro.

I said to a nurse, "I want Director Zhao. Show me the way to Director Zhao!"

She walked away, completely expressionless. Did she have an ear infection? I asked several other nurselike figures standing around in white jackets. No response either. Nobody seemed to have heard me.

"I have a letter from Department Chief Liu!" I shouted. But all to no effect.

I thought I had come to the wrong place and went out to check the sign at the gate. No mistake, it was the Hospital of Chinese Medicine. By the time I reentered the hospital grounds, I had lost my confidence and rushed about like the other patients. "I want Director Zhao. I have a personal letter from Department Chief Liu!" I insisted. But my demands gradually subsided into spineless whimpers.

While the hospital staff completely ignored me, the other patients turned on me with fury: "Go line up!" I looked around but could not find anyone in particular who had his eye on me. Just as I thought I was safe, again I heard the furious tones of patients shouting in one voice: "Go line up!"

In a sort of daze, I made my way to the registry office. Through the little window slot, I said to the nurse sitting on a raised seat, "I want Director Zhao!"

The window slot was tiny and situated very low. I had to bend and put my head down and then lift up my eyes to make out the (presumably) dazzling beauty of the nurse in charge. All I could make out was the fuzzy contours of someone high and mighty, looking down on the patients as so much trash. I shouted, "I want Director Zhao!" and waved my letter, which by now had become limp in my hands.

"Room seven," the unmoving, unmoved, and immovable figure behind the window slot mumbled. Was it *one,* or *seven,* or *eleven?* My neck had become stiff, as I was trying to bend my shoulders and lift my head at the same time.

I didn't have a second chance, for the people behind shoved me aside. I rushed to the consulting rooms, fighting my way through the crowd. I was continually pushed by other patients. This infuriated me, and I myself began pushing right and left, only to be swung to and fro by the human tide. I made my way into room 1. A woman was sitting behind the desk. A woman? That could not be Director Zhao, I said to myself. I fought my way out through the mass of people craning their necks at the door. A young man was sitting behind the desk. No, that could not be Director Zhao either. Again I pushed and was pushed on my way out. Like a bubble on a boiling sea, I rolled into room 11. An elderly person with venerable white locks—"Director Zhao!" I shouted gleefully and was immediately shoved aside. I found myself in room 8. The doctor in room 8 was in a loud altercation with a patient, who pointed a finger at the doctor's nose and said in disgust, "I've never seen the likes of you!" The doctor pointed his finger at the patient's nose and reciprocated: "I've never seen the likes of you either!" I was sure this was not Director Zhao. Director Zhao would never quarrel with patients, nor patients with Director Zhao. But I had learned something in a flash of inspiration. It seemed that *have never seen* is a term of extreme opprobrium. What has never been seen is decidedly bad. But I had never seen Director Zhao, so why should I look so hard for him?

By now I had floated willy-nilly into room 9, and found myself face to face with a young fellow with long hair. Unlike the other crowded consulting rooms, this one was quite deserted. Obviously, he was not trusted by patients. I sat down and said hesitatingly, "I'm looking for Director Zhao . . ."

"I am Director Zhao," he said in firm tones.

I had no reason to dispute this, though I felt in my bones that something was wrong. Toothache, however, overcame my scruples. Leaving aside the verification of his identity, I began to tell him the history of my woes.

In friendly tones, the young fellow asked me to open my mouth. He began poking at my teeth with a steel prod. When he knocked on my bad tooth, I howled in pain.

The alleged Director Zhao nodded in sympathy and wrote out a prescription with many flourishes of the pen. I tried to make out his calligraphy on my way to the pharmacy. Suddenly, I deciphered: "Pain reliever 2 × 3 × 7."

Which means that all I was getting for my pains was pain-reliever pills to be taken three times a day, two at a time, for one week! Then I looked at the signature; it was even more undecipherable. It looked like Liu or Zhou or Xu; but whatever it was, decidedly it was not Zhao.

I had been cheated!

My pent-up feelings of anger exploded, and I made a scene then and there. Four individuals, male and female, young and old, all of whom claimed to be Director Zhao, tried to handle the situation. They said that Chinese medicine is quite all right, especially for chronic complaints, but for toothaches it is no panacea. Sad but true. Of course, this is only one view, for internal reference only, not for dissemination to the general public. All in all, Chinese medicine is superb, acknowledged by Western practitioners. But pain relievers are quite potent in relieving pain, they conceded and suggested I take some and go to a dental clinic. We are touched by your faith in Chinese medicine, they assured me. In theory, they continued, one cannot say that Chinese medicine is helpless when it comes to toothache. The root of toothache is an attack of sinister heat. For this, you may take the powder of crushed rhino horn, deer antler, and mountain-goat's horn mixed with mint and other medicines with cooling properties. But please remember first that these medicines require at least a month to take effect. Considering the pain you're in, can you afford to wait even a week? Second, all these medicines act as laxatives. If taken in small quantities, they don't work; if in great quantities, you will suffer from diarrhea. Considering the state you're in with your toothache, can your constitution tolerate an attack of diarrhea? Third, the most important ingredient among the cooling medicines is the powder of crushed rhino horn. The Ministry of Health has issued a document—x year, x month, x day—stipulating that rhino-horn powder be taken off the national medical-care program and paid for privately. It's a damned nuisance, as this medicine is very expensive. Of course, that was the point of the new regulation.

"Do you mean to tell me that I went through all this trouble, and even had to look up Department Chief Liu, just for a measly pack of pain relievers?" I shouted in anger.

"All right, all right, all right, we'll try acupuncture. . . ."

They inserted a needle into the *hegu* acu-point between my thumb and index finger and another into my earlobe, and I had no choice but to leave with a pack of pain relievers in my pocket.

Actually, acupuncture and pain relievers did help. My symptoms were relieved, and so was I. What does it matter, Chinese medicine or Western medicine, so long as it works? Likewise, it doesn't matter, expensive medicine or cheap medicine, so long as it cures. On the problem of a toothache, there is no need for the differing schools of medicine to exclude one another.

Five days later, before I had finished my pills, the pain returned. This time, it was not only the tooth; one whole side of my head was throbbing. I could neither sleep nor eat nor even sit, much less work. I lay in bed groaning and moaning all night. Through the stillness of the night, our whole apartment building rang with the echoes of my lamentations. Much to my chagrin, I had disturbed the sleep of our neighbor on the floor above, President Shi Xueya of the Toothology Society.

President Shi came down to give me his personal attention. Dressed in a Western suit and leather dress shoes, with pin and tie and a matching handkerchief tucked into his breast pocket and exuding the faint aroma of Parisian cologne, President Shi had become a new man in a matter of days. I was impressed. He shook his head when he saw the state I was in.

"How could you let a petty little tooth reduce you to such a state? Our Toothology Society is an academic institution, now participating in an exchange program with the Royal Society of Holland. A complaint such as yours is beyond, as well as beneath, our concern. But your groans disturb my rest. This is a case of physical babblings interfering with metaphysical contemplations. Out of humanistic concern, I will alienate myself from my true identity and stoop to cure your toothache."

Then and there, as if in an epiphany, I realized that

*Chinese medicine confounds by abstractions,*
*Western medicine is lost in technicalities;*
*Tradition leads back into the mists of obscurity,*
*While transplants from abroad are vulgar.*
*Pills merely kill the pain,*
*And thus medicine is degraded;*
*Acupuncture needling under the skin,*
*Is scratching the boot for the itch on your foot.*
*Western medicine tackles the tooth,*
*By steel and iron implements,*
*Whizzing and whirring,*
*As in a machine shop;*
*The worker pulls out your tooth,*
*Like any machinery part.*
*But onward from today,*
*To the people I turn.*
*The people have magic prescriptions,*
*And miraculous cures.*
*The people are all-powerful,*
*They move mountains and rechart rivers,*
*They change the course of the sun and the moon,*
*And turn the universe upside down.*
*So what's in a tooth!*

President Shi got together a few old women, who prepared to scrape my back with copper thimbles steeped in vinegar. (Attention, readers, neither tin nor aluminum nor any other metal would do; it must be copper.) I exposed my back to their fingers. Up and down, up and down—the copper thimbles went the length of my back; from the neck to the tailbone, they left three blood-red trails. My whole body exuded the fragrance of vinegar, stronger than that of the sweet-and-sour fish at the Seafood Delight Restaurant, where the price had gone up three times running.

President Shi then went and procured a muscle-rippling *qi gong* master to instill vital energy, the *qi,* in me. First, the master placed his left foot lightly on the floor and slightly bent his right knee. Then he stretched his left hand toward me and withdrew his right hand as he proceeded to rally his vital energy, the *qi*. It is common knowledge that this kind of *qi gong* performance can split rocks; even iron swords have been made to bend under the influence. How, then, can a tooth withstand its spell? It occurred to me that its potency would crush my jaw or even my head into smithereens. The thought made me shake in fear, and surprisingly my toothache disappeared. President Shi pointed to me shaking in bed and said to my dear wife, "See how *qi gong* works. See how the evil negative *qi* inside him is quivering under the potency of the positive *qi*!"

The words were barely out of his mouth when the *qi gong* master rolled his eyes fiercely and, calling up the *qi* from his own *dan tian* acu-point under the belly button, cried in a loud voice, "Open!"

I was soaked in sweat, but my toothache was gone. I ate a bowl of egg custard and slept peacefully.

From then on, my toothache stopped bothering me. I was very touched by the experience and went about singing the praises of folk medicine. Looking sideways, it was better than Western medicine. Looking backward, it was better than traditional Chinese medicine. Reporters for an evening paper interviewed me and wrote up my story, "Magic Cure in the Hands of the People," which was later included in the pages of the popular *After Eight Hours* magazine and *Reader's Digest*. Ironically, my toothache has boosted my reputation. An elderly expatriate Chinese living in Los Angeles read my story and wrote to me, saying that he was suffering from a toothache and thanks to my story has decided to return to the motherland in hopes that I will put him in touch with the magic folk cure. My experience with toothache has actually contributed to attracting China's sons back to the bosom of the motherland! The Ministry for the United Front was interested and also came to make a note of the case.

Pretty soon President Shi moved away from our apartment building. It was said that he had moved into quarters commensurate with his elevated position and his contribution to the Toothology Society. Two months later, news got out that Shi Xueya was arrested and his society dissolved. It was said that he was a fraud and that many people had been his dupes. This news had me completely rattled. I couldn't help reflecting back upon my relationship with ex-president Shi. Had I been currying favor with the president for the sake of my tooth? Had I fabricated the records in his favor? Was my gift offering of ginseng and deer-antler kidney-enhancement mixture a form of bribery? Had I, consciously or otherwise, contributed to inflating his false reputation? Now he was arrested, and that of course was proof that he was guilty. If he was a con man, then what am I, given our close association? What had been my motive in associating myself with him? Apart from the urgency of my toothache, was there something else lurking beneath my consciousness? What about the exhilaration at seeing my name in the evening paper? Look inward! Was it not vanity and self-seeking? The more I thought about it, the more my tooth hurt. Oh, the pain was killing me!

This last attack was not limited to teeth; my whole body was affected. My head was spinning, I had nausea, I ran a high fever, and I trembled from head to toe. All my colleagues came to commiserate. They deplored my dilatoriness resulting from a fear of tooth extraction and advised me not to trust to luck anymore and to seek out an oral surgeon without delay. The chairman of my department was full of admonishments. The first rule in life, he said, is to be honest. If your tooth aches, let it ache in an honest, down-to-earth way. Take it to a hospital honestly and get it pulled out honestly. All that dillydally-shilly-shallying was due to your fear of pain. Fear drives out honesty, and without honesty you'll get nowhere. Now without some pressure, he said, how can you expect to cure your toothache? The matter was insignificant but the philosophy behind it profound.

I was completely bowled over. I made haste to concur that the honest attitude is the scientific attitude and that without science there could be no oral hygiene. I conceded that this was the princi-

ple of two negatives negating each other but that however you ne-
gate, you can't do without science! The problem with me, I con-
fided to my chairman, was not that I rejected science but that
science had persisted in eluding me—in a word, I couldn't get registered in the clinic. With only one dental clinic in a city of over a
million, those of us without back doors must begin lining up the
night before to get a registration slip. But now that my wife and I
were advanced in years, I said, we did not have the inspired energy
to start lining up the night before, as I had done on my previous
visit many years ago. Without that kind of inspired energy, one
could not pull off a great performance; without the required kind
of great performance, the registration slip could not be had; and
without the registration slip, any kind of scientific treatment was
beyond our grasp. On the other hand, I continued, those with back
doors could sit at home comfortably without having to line up at all.
All they needed to do was greet their elder maternal uncle or second paternal uncle or third paternal aunt at the hospital gate,
and they could sail in and get the best treatment at the least ex-
pense. . . . But why am I saying this?

Actually, I was not familiar with the registration policies of the
dental clinic and had no more grudge against the clinic than anybody else. But being blamed for rejecting science, I got worked up
in spite of myself and recited a litany of grievances, ending with a
tragic flourish. It always boosts your self-esteem to blame others.

The chairman of my department then said that a new mayor
had just been installed, a certain Mr. Zhu, who made much of intellectuals and had helped many scholars with particular grievances.
He advised me to write a letter to this man. His word of support,
my chairman argued, would materialize in action, and then getting
into the hospital would be child's play. An example of "spirit con-
verting itself into material results," he added.

I hesitated. But my colleagues were keen. They offered to write
the letter for me, seeing that I was incapacitated by illness. The
words flowed easily from their pen, and in no time at all the letter
was read out to me. It described the pain of my toothache with pas-

sion and eloquence and exposed the pernicious backdoor practices with indignation. As I could not raise any objections to the contents, I was asked to sign. Just as I was deliberating as to whether sending such a letter was advisable, my wife took out my seal and stamped it on the letter. So there it was, my own red seal staring back at me from the sheet of paper. My colleagues snatched up the letter and promised to put it into the yellow-capped fast-service mailbox with stamp and everything. Such comradeship! I felt funny around the tear glands.

The letter was sent, but I was still uneasy. Should I have disturbed the mayor over such a petty affair as my toothache? It seemed an inglorious, unconscionable thing to do. Just think, the city's population numbers one million, and every one of them has thirty-six teeth, making altogether thirty-six million teeth. Supposing all thirty-six million teeth were to go and bother the mayor—how could the man do his work? Perhaps this was a vestige of the Cultural Revolution, a resurgence of the rebel spirit. I felt ashamed.

The day after my letter was mailed, I received a missive from ex-president Shi Xueya. He told me he was safe and sound and that what had transpired was all a misunderstanding. I was welcome to look him up if I had trouble with my teeth. He also informed me that he was about to chair the governing board of the Society for the Treatment of Scabies and that they had received academic support in the form of fifteen thousand deutsche marks. He asked me whether I had trouble with hair loss or scalp itch and said that help would be available. I was so alarmed I kept putting up my hands to check my scalp several times a day.

The very next day, in confirmation of ex-president Shi's words, news of the founding of the Society for the Treatment of Scabies appeared on TV, showing a lot of local celebrities in attendance. Mr. Shi Xueya was the most active on the scene, beaming with recovered glory. It was said he was a real pioneering spirit.

The following day, I received an official letter from the dental clinic. The gist of it ran thus:

Your letter to Mayor Zhu has been relayed to us. Your criticism of backdoor practices in registration is correct in principle and basically grounded in facts. Considering that you fall within the category of intellectuals over fifty years of age who have made contributions to society and, having been approved by the mayor's office, it is now determined that you are eligible for Special Services and assigned to the care of Dr. Zi Wutong, physician-in-charge. Please be at the Hospital before eight o'clock on the 28th and proceed straight to Special Services, room 54. You need not register on arrival. You will be charged after the consultation. Hoping for our further co-operation, you are welcome to offer more criticism of our work. Our clinic is the Best Choice for toothache sufferers.

I was exhilarated. Such a good mayor, loving the people as his own children, as the saying goes. And such a good clinic! Such modesty! Such efficiency! Immediate results! Better than Tokyo! And such a good doctor assigned to me, even his name sounded reassuring: Zi—"high qualifications"—and Wutong—"no pain"! Such heaven-sent good tidings. I had neither killed nor had I coveted my neighbor's wife, and now all the virtues I'd stored up in a life well spent were being rewarded.

But I was also frightened. Now that I was really going to the dental clinic to deal with my tooth, I began to have doubts. Could I avoid having it pulled? Inspecting it in the mirror, I saw that it had nearly all rotted away. Things having come to this point, how could I still cling to the forlorn hope that the remains might still be preserved? Or even think of putting off the pulling? Or hope for pulling without pain? Dental clinic or heavenly haven, Dr. No Pain or Dr. Screaming Pain, how could you avoid injections of Novocain? How could you avoid pliers and pincers? Or blood? Or a big black hole? I had spent the energy of nine bulls and two tigers, as the saying goes, and for what if not to avoid the pain of tooth pulling? And then I had spent another round of energy of the same dimensions, and for what but to undergo the pain of the ultimate pulling? Now the case was closed. There could be no more procrastination. The best choice was already made. How could a tooth have led me to such absurdities?

I reckoned the time hour by hour until finally it was the night of the twenty-seventh. Then I reckoned the time minute by minute and didn't sleep a wink all night. My thoughts roamed over the sufferings that teeth bring into the life of man. Born without teeth, sprouting front teeth at eight months, a full mouth of baby teeth at two years of age, and then another set of teeth in early childhood—all his life, man's sufferings are linked to teeth. Keeping them is a trial, but losing them is worse. Sprouting them is a pain, but eliminating them is torture. Even after death, when one's remains are stuffed into the ash container, the poor injured and insulted teeth are often disturbed in their last rest. Why do humans have such sharp and durable teeth?

Time dragged on until morning arrived at long last. My wife fed me fried eggs. We looked at each other dejectedly. The wife said, "Fear not! Be firm and firmer still!"

The repetition of *firmness* nearly drew tears to my eyes. I said to my wife in the tragic tones of a last parting, "I am on my way. Take care of yourself!"

How sublime! I had finally overcome the psychological obstacles, conquered the fear of pulling, the fear of pain. With head held high and swinging steps, I marched into the dental clinic; I swept past the gatekeeper with the dignity of a man about to meet his maker, stepped into Special Services, room 54, and stood before the nurse—I was a new man.

"Have you come for your teeth?" The smiling nurse flashed her teeth at me. I tried to smile back, with my hand on my aching, swollen jaw.

I explained my business and showed her the official letter. The nurse spread out her hands: "How unlucky. Dr. Zi Wutong had a stroke last night and is now in the emergency ward. The other doctors are not informed about your case. You know, of course, that our consultations are all planned beforehand. Please go home. You may leave the letter here; I'll make some inquiries, and let you know later . . ."

Was this possible? Treating me like dirt! But . . .

I made my way out of the hospital; I fought my way onto the bus, and after riding three stops, it suddenly occurred to me that my tooth was spared that particular day, that I need not go through that excruciating pain. It was not my fault; I had done all I could, but it was just not in the stars that I should have my tooth pulled on that day. What could I do? The tooth was willing, but the pulling was put off. What can it be but the will of heaven?

I was so overjoyed my bad tooth had even stopped hurting. Marvelous it was that although my tooth was not pulled out, I was just as gratified as if it were—actually, even more so. From the Taoist viewpoint of Laozi and Zhuangzi, pulling was not pulling, not pulling was pulling. From the Buddhist viewpoint, the tooth was the sorrow, the great sorrow was suffering, suffering was boundless; but turn back your steps, and salvation was at hand. From the Freudian viewpoint, pulling out the tooth was release. From the Keynesian viewpoint, pulling out the tooth was a process of value accumulation. From the Sartrean viewpoint, the aching tooth was the externalization of the essence. From the viewpoint of systems, pulling the tooth was system engineering. From the Nietzschean viewpoint, a toothache was the proof of degradation and misfortune, was the pain of you not feeling my pain, the proof of the isolation of misunderstood greatness, proof that the culture of teeth was more unbearable than the aching tooth . . .

My tooth has not been pulled out yet, but it has acquired more profundity than if it had been.

TRANSLATED BY ZHU HONG

# Sham Marriage

## Li Rui

He thought it felt like a sham right from the start. When the pro-
duction-team leader, who was standing as guarantor, grinned and
led the woman and a three- or four-year-old girl into the courtyard,
he was pretty sure the one thing guaranteed was that the team
leader had already boiled her noodles. But he steeled his heart and
took in the woman and child anyway. His wife had been dead for
twenty years, his two daughters married off, and after enduring a
bachelor's life for twenty years, his lonely rod was all dried out with
thirst. While the man and woman pressed their fingerprints onto
the guarantee, the team leader broke off a straw from the kang mat,
picked bits of green onion and egg out from between his teeth, and
stuffed them back into his mouth, which reeked of alcohol.

"Good, yet another made-to-order family! A lonely rod like
you, so poor you can't even marry. And you, with your man dead,
you come begging at harvesttime, and as soon as you open your
mouth, the food is there. One poor devil bumps into another: a perfect match. Everywhere you go in this world, it's the same: men
sleeping with women, women having kids, and all of them sticking
it out together. And don't you worry about that official commune
wedding certificate yet. When you're all settled down, you just ask
somebody to write home for a letter of proof to make up for it."

As they were walking out the gate, the leader pressed up
against his ear and added, "You can't go wrong. She's from Hejia-

liang, Yulin County, Shaanxi. I got Liu the schoolteacher to check the map, and it's right where you'd expect it to be. She's not going to go running off the map. So tonight you just have yourself a good time taking care of that thirst of yours, but don't get too rough or anything. There'll be plenty more nights from now on. Heh heh, some goods she's got, nice and plump; I guarantee you, you can't go wrong . . ."

Suddenly, a flame rose up inside him. "You fucker, what's guaranteed is that you boiled her noodles!" But even as this rage flared up, it had already passed. Say what you will, he brought you a wife you didn't have to pay a thing for. And besides, even if it wasn't the team leader who boiled them this time, you sure won't be the first—or were you still dreaming about marrying some un-plucked lily? At this point in his thoughts, he had to laugh at that indescribable flame of rage: he was just like the old toad that lusts after a swan's flesh.

As soon as he had returned to his room, he pointed out the rice, flour, oil, and salt to the woman. He showed her how to get a fire going. He shouldered a couple of pails and filled up the cistern. Then, putting down the shoulder pole, he took up his ax and headed for the woodpile. For twenty years, he had put up with fetching enough water and cutting sufficient firewood just to make do, and after marrying off his daughters, he had lost interest in the flavor of even oil and salt. But today was different: his body was suddenly flooded with a rush of energy. He had really guzzled it down with the team leader, and now as the liquor burned fiercely in his chest, he felt slightly tipsy. The ax he wielded in the yard nearly rocked the mountains and shook the earth; with each thud, pure-white wood chips burst from beneath the razor-sharp blade. The ground around him was blotted with flowery white patches, like falling snow. As he was chopping, the woman came out to col-lect the firewood, and when she bent over beside him, he suddenly caught a glimpse of heavy swelling breasts jiggling provocatively. It was as if she had hidden a plump goose under her dingy clothes. He clamped his lips together and laughed inwardly: Nice fat tits like those—I'll bet you could balance a couple of temple guardians on top of them!

Actually, he had seen the woman the day before, after hearing that someone had come to the village begging for food and that she was staying overnight at the team leader's house. When he went over to take a look, he was unaware that she was looking for a husband. But seeing her now was a lot different from looking at her then. Yesterday it was a matter of looking at somebody else's woman; today he was seeing his own. With these thoughts in mind, his eyes locked onto her, betraying a possessive, wanton gleam: he eyed her up and down, from in front and from behind, her head, her legs. . . . The woman clearly felt the scorch of his gaze. Enduring it in silence, she kept at the work in her hands without pause. Now and again she raised her eyes slightly to meet his but quickly let her eyelids drop in submission. His male intuition could sense the composure of her silent yielding, her calm of having bowed to fate. And yet he felt she shouldn't be so calm. The force of this calm collided with the surging heat in his chest: this coolness of hers was too unfeminine. Still, he couldn't imagine what kind of woman she would have to be to fulfill his masculine desires. Three people who had never laid eyes on one another in their lives had abruptly been made up into a family—even an opera has to have a prelude. But this was no opera. This woman before him had long since found out what goes on between men and women, and not just eight or ten times, either—she even had a child of three or four. A penniless, lonely old rod like you, what were you thinking, anyway? The liquor was still burning in his chest, and now yet another force was churning with it. He grasped the ax firmly in his hands, relying on his masculine strength to hold down that force stirring inside him. He couldn't let the struts supporting him collapse, and he certainly couldn't lose his male strut in front of this beggar woman. As he watched the woman's outline disappear behind the door, those full breasts appeared again before his eyes; that strange thought of his, that they could balance a couple of temple guardians on top, made him laugh. You dumb fuck, so you're still picky about whether you get a fat one or a lean one. Anything that satisfies hunger is a good meal!

After the midday meal, the lamp was lit; three strange shadows swayed up and down upon the kang mat and against the wall. Before the afternoon was half over, the woman had already wiped the room sparkling clean. A few embers still burned in the stove, where the woman stood leaning against the wall; set against the dusky lamplight, her face flickered in the glow. Steeped in a warmth and tenderness that seemed a little strange to a body and heart that the years had ground down coarse and crude, he was inexpressibly moved in the dusky lamp shadows and flickering glow of the fire. Yet even this emotion felt strange.

Everything he should ask and everything he should say he had already asked and said. Even the few words he had managed after searching and scraping the bottom of his belly had been said, too. About all that was left had to do with, well, with that coming moment, with *that*. All those struts he'd brought out, knowingly or not, to prop himself up had lightly and easily drifted away, like late-autumn leaves, leaving the tree standing naked.

The woman was waiting. Her face, flickering in the firelight, maintained its look of calmly bowing to fate.

The child was oblivious to what was going on between the man and the woman. She was fiddling with his deer-hoof pipe, turning it over and over in her hands while now and then a childish sentence or two of some local dialect slipped out between her lips.

A surge of impatience and resentment rose in his heart. The look of calm on the woman's face made him uneasy, and with a sweep of his hand he snatched the grimy bandanna off of his head and ordered her: "Here, wash this!"

The woman came over with a smile and reached out for it; he clutched her shoulder and with one yank twisted her toward him.

"Mama, a gun!" the girl shouted in her broad accent, pointing to a long rifle propped against the wall.

The woman didn't struggle; she simply lowered her eyes. "Let's wait till she's asleep."

"No. The side room's empty." He flared up and, without knowing why, thought back to how the team leader had boiled her noodles the night before. *I have to eat his leftover noodles, and she tells me to wait?*

The woman didn't utter another word; silently, she pulled over a pillow for the child, took her into her arms, and laid her down, then pulled out a gummy piece of candy that had been stuck in her pocket for who knows how long and pushed it into the child's mouth.

Without lighting a lamp, he dragged the woman onto the kang as if she were his prey. And there, in that lacquer-black darkness, the floodwaters that had been choked off and swelling his chest for twenty years came gushing out in a savage frenzy. Two lives were fused into one body in that primal darkness, where it was impossible to distinguish between you and me, between man and woman, between what was somebody else's and what was your own.

A rat scrounging for food lost its footing, slipped through the roof, and dropped down, screeching shrilly; in its frantic flight, it bumped into a scalding yet supple mound of flesh; it couldn't make out what this thing could be, and the scrabbling of its tiny, piercing claws on the kang mat left behind only its frightened, scattered soul.

On the first day, that is how it went.

On the second day, that is how it went.

On the third day, that is still how it went.

He could tell he was in the grip of madness, but he didn't have the strength to stop this gush of insanity surging from the very core of his body. And he had only to think of that night before the woman belonged to him, how another man had already boiled her noodles, for that gush of madness to swell ten times over until it was many times larger than his own flesh-and-blood body, as if a hairy monster, panting heavily, stood there confronting him.

But over time, this gush of madness spent itself, drop by drop, on the woman's warm and soft, broad and giving bosom. Once that rabid nature had calmed down, his masculine self-respect and confidence were reborn in his body. One day after he had finished breakfast, he waited until the woman had cleaned and tidied everything up and then pulled out ten yuan from his chest pocket.

"Here."

The woman stared blankly without taking it.

"Too little? Here's ten more."

The woman still stared blankly.

"Don't try to fool me. You've already got a home, you've got a man, he's not dead, you've got other kids, they're all back home waiting for you."

"No, no . . ." The woman shook her head, alarmed.

"Go fool your own devil!" His anger was rising. "You'll live here for three months, five months, maybe a year or more, but when you see your chance, you'll be gone, and here I'll be, all alone again. Right? What do you think I'm after? Feeding you two all for nothing? So go! Go, if that's what you want. I am a man, you hear, and no one's going to make a monkey out of me!"

Tears trickled from the woman's eyes.

For some reason, he actually got some satisfaction out of those tears. He'd been feeling like a fool for days, knowing he hadn't broken this calm woman. As for himself, he'd kept getting flustered, waiting for nightfall, and as soon as it got dark, he'd get skittish about doing it. But now everything was all right. He'd poked through the blank-paper window that seemed to veil her, and she was clearly under his control.

The woman sobbed and cried, "Elder Brother—"

"Oh, so now you call me Elder Brother." Deep down he laughed grimly. So you can't keep it up after all, can you? If you've got what it takes to pull off something like this, then you've got to have what it takes to keep it up right to the end. But he didn't say these words aloud; he just squatted on the kang and smirked, feeling that everything was firmly in his grasp.

"Elder Brother, we've had a terrible harvest at home this year. We had no choice. I know I haven't done right by you. If you don't want to let us stay here, then we'll go. And your quilt, I pulled out the padding and washed it yesterday, but I haven't had time to sew it back up yet. After I finish that, I'll go."

Suddenly, a gush of tears stung his eyes, and he fought mightily to keep it back. His quilt hadn't been washed since that day three years ago, on the eve of his second daughter's wedding. For the past few days, this woman had been working in and around the house as if there were no tomorrow; in town, everybody said he'd stumbled upon a god of wealth right in the middle of the road. To tell the truth, he'd also tossed around the idea of keeping the woman and her child tied down here. He'd even thought about going back with her to Hejialiang to get that letter of proof. She was a good woman, but then a sham was still a sham. What angered him was that she had faked it so realistically that she had stirred his heart.

Yet in the end, her eyes, puffy and soft with tears, softened his masculine heart.

"If you want to stay, stay. If you want to go, go. I can't tell you what to do."

The woman fell to her knees in front of him. "Elder Brother, the girl's father and I will never forget you."

His temper flared up again; he was in a rage. "You go back, and tell your man that maybe my bullets can't reach him, but if they could, the first person I'd shoot would be him. The bastard!"

"Elder Brother, he's just a poor wretch, too. I'll do up the quilt for you. We'll leave tomorrow."

The little girl didn't understand what was going on between the adults; all she cared about was holding her mama tight, crying and yowling.

He had thought that they might make a scene, but now that it was actually happening, he felt totally at a loss—what kind of show did he think he was putting on anyway? But as he recalled the two fingerprints stamped on the guarantee and thought of how this woman who should have been his wife had really been somebody else's wife all along, surge after surge of the wildfire in his heart rose to his head. Husband and wife—the whole show had ended as quickly as it had begun.

That night after dinner, it was time once again to light the lamp, but the two of them stiffly and wordlessly held their ground. The child had already flopped over to a corner of the kang to sleep.

The woman was waiting for him.

He smoked; his heart rankled. He couldn't let this night pass, he couldn't knowingly let go of this final opportunity. After this evening, who knows how many years he'd have to go parched with thirst all over again? Lighting his deer-hoof pipe, he satisfied his craving for a smoke. He smoked bowl after bowl, and bowl by bowl he knocked out the ashes against the edge of the kang. A hopeless hope was shattered; a sham that had been a sham from the start was over. But the heart of this lonely rod, who had endured somehow for twenty years, was suffering endless torment from the whole affair. And the greater his torment, the more agitated and rancorous he became. He did not know how he was going to release that agitation and rancor; meanwhile, the woman who would be leaving tomorrow was waiting for him. Abruptly, he snatched up his splendid pipe and smashed it against the stove, whirled around, and ordered: "Sleep!"

The woman undid her buttons, and her dingy clothes revealed those two full breasts. Suddenly, a thought burned in his head. He demanded, "Did that fucker of a team leader touch you?"

The woman bowed her head bashfully and covered her exposed chest back up.

"Say it! Did he touch you or not?"

The woman hesitated a moment, then nodded reluctantly.

"That fucker. Make me eat his leftover noodles, will he? I'll fuck his ancestors!"

The wild wave in the man's chest plunged and split his head open. He lunged for the woman, brutal, rabid, giving vent to the bitterness of half a lifetime, which had turned even more bitter because of all of this. It was as if the net of this life and this world, which could never be thrown off, now lashed him even more tightly, and all because of this woman. With his savage spasms and gasps, the torment and suffocating bitterness he could never find words for and the body and soul he could neither tear nor break apart—all pulverized into fragments, into a foul slime of flesh and blood as it spurted into the woman.

She put up with it in silence; her warm and soft, broad and giving bosom, under the lashing of the driving waves, was as warm, soft, and giving as always.

A flame of lamplight the size of a bean burned dimly on the oil lamp, struggling to sustain a faltering smear of light in the unyielding darkness.

It was after the driving wave had finally calmed that the man's thickly calloused palm brushed across the warmth of tears on the woman's face.

**TRANSLATED BY WILLIAM SCHAEFER AND FENGHUA WANG**

# The Day I Got to Xi'an

## Duo Duo

From a good distance away, I spotted the medical academy's sign, but then another sign leaped into view next to it—the business school's. I was about to stop one of the students to ask directions when I heard—no, saw her coming toward me with a "Hey!" Relieved now, I eased out of the big manic strides I had been taking. I walked along beside her. Suddenly, I felt as though someone had been added in between the two people here and that this other someone was me. Whatever this feeling was, it trapped inside me everything I had intended to say to her.

All I said as we walked through the medical academy was her name, Xiao Tong, in a flat, dry voice. Was I afraid of never being able to call her name again?

Inside the dormitory, clothes were hung up all over the place to dry. I had to push through at least three or four layers of laundry before I could make out the door to the inside room. Once inside, we stood there, facing each other, then sat down. A bed, a desk, two chairs (one for me, one for her), a radio–cassette deck, four bare walls, and a table, which would have been bare as well if it hadn't been for the dust. Just then I noticed I'd forgotten to bring cigarettes. I hardly asked anything about her. None of the usual "How's it going?"—a commonplace I'm sick of. What does that mean, *how*? How *could* it be going? But she wasn't exactly making me feel at home either, I noticed. I rested my arms on the table, rapped out a little beat with my knuckles, crossed my legs, recrossed my legs, and knew this visit was not going to be a pleasant one. In a year and a half (she'd been transferred to the medical academy a year and a half ago), she'd had maybe four visitors. She'd got fat, ugly, and she was telling her favorite stories about herself. My heart sank when she said she hardly drank any water except at the three meals in the cafeteria (Sundays she often didn't go at all). Now I had no choice but to ask her to please bring me a glass of water. I was waiting for that water.

So that was about it. Then from somewhere or other, out popped that little gem of a phrase, *nervous breakdown*. She perked right up, hearing that. She hadn't slept a wink last night ("You've just *got* to get sleep after sweating heavily"). Except for lectures (she was a teacher) twelve periods a week, she slept through everything, all through those two years she didn't have classes, and on Sundays, too.

"Oh really? . . . Is that right?" When did I start humoring her like this, I wondered. It probably got this way because she had no interest at all in anything I could have said to her but was perfectly content with the way her own life was going these days. Compared with someone like me, who is always criticizing himself, who tries hard to straighten himself out, she came across as being as neat and composed as could be. I had the feeling, though, that she treated everyone as if he or she were her doctor. That would explain why everything we talked about had to do with pathology and why I suddenly found myself playing psychiatrist, racking my brains to come up with the most pedestrian advice: "No, that won't do. . . . No matter what, you can't go on like that. . . . You've got to do something, anything, just do it. . . . Do it along with other people . . ."

This was leading nowhere. For two hours, it was as though she were someone perpetually waiting at a bus stop, and I was the bus. No cigarettes, no water—just me trying to help an overweight, imperturbable woman try to figure out how to get her life together. I mean, I was trying to think it through for her: one way is to see that people are different, that they behave differently. She didn't make that derisory little sniff when I got on the subject of behavior, or at least I don't think I heard one, but even so the second I said the word *behave,* my confidence drained away. She was totally wrapped up in herself—her reactions had slowed, making her useless to herself and to anyone else. "So . . . you should love . . ."

I told her how I had rescued myself—that is, how I had admitted to myself that I had a problem: lonely to the edge of madness, disgusted, hiding from everyone. I told her how I missed my cat so much after it ran away that I spent a month looking for it; how every night coming into the stairwell, I would stare ravenously at my mail slot, though I couldn't remember having written to anyone, not even a simple card; and how after work, I let myself pedal my bicycle on and on, oblivious to where I was headed; and then how I finally understood something. "You should . . ."

You should help others, abandon the idea of self-worth—or rather, making your own life more worthwhile is what it's all about. One day around noon at a greengrocer's stall, I saw a boy dragging his younger sister along the ground. I broke through the crowd of indifferent onlookers, shoved the little brat away, helped the girl to her feet, and ordered the boy to take her home. I told Xiao Tong about the throb of joy I felt at doing this good turn, how from then on, I kept on doing good turns, and how I felt happier than ever before. Then I couldn't take it any longer: "Can I—may I have a glass of water?"

She was a long time registering my request. First, she said she'd run out of tea; then she said there wasn't any water ready boiled and the fire in the stove had gone out. She talked on and on, sitting there in her chair. Finally, she said, "Love?"

For the seventy-second time, I thought to myself, I've got to go. But somehow I couldn't make myself get up. The sun, three hours of whose light I'd squandered while sitting in there, had sunk down past her kitchen. In that room in the fading light, I noticed her foot had gotten fatter, too, cocked up on her knee and squeezed into a sneaker. Still, there was no way I could bring myself to say, I've got to go. In the silence, I could almost see her after I'd gone, still sitting there.

I finally did get the drink of water. I was the one who lit the stove. When the water was just about to boil, I broke the silence: "How about a stroll over to Wild Goose Pagoda?" She said it was all the same to her whether she went or not. Then another half hour of silence before I suggested again that we go to the pagoda. In the meantime, she had turned on some music, let it play for about a minute, and turned it off again. At last, I found the strength to stand up and say, "I've got to be going." Her eyes (they looked fatter, too) seemed to say that she wouldn't oppose the wishes of anyone in the world. In other words, I was free to come and go as I pleased.

We went out, and she escorted me across the campus. Some students were playing volleyball. I said I had to use the rest room. She gave me directions on how to get there. It seemed so complex: I had to turn several corners and go all the way inside some building. When I came back, she had changed her mind. (I thought that it was fine for her to have made up her mind in the first place; if she changed it back again, all the better.) I told her what I had just been thinking, and she told me that we could take a shortcut to Wild Goose Pagoda, that there were a lot of vendors selling Xi'an-style snacks near the pagoda, and that we could have for dinner some things I couldn't find in Beijing. That interested me. I didn't remind her, though, what a terrific gourmand she used to be.

I practically had to force her to decide whether or not she was going to climb the tower, and then I had to tell her three times, "If you don't want to climb it, you can wait for me at the bottom." As far as I recall, this was all we said along the way. Walking together, riding the bus, stepping off the bus, and continuing to walk on, we were locked into an acute awkwardness. She said she may as well climb the pagoda, so I went to buy a couple of tickets. Going up (seven stories in all), I wasn't sure if I should give her a hand or if we should each make our own way. I figured I'd let my elbow bump hers on the way up—that way, she could decide what to do. I

kept thinking that's what I was going to do, but I may not actually
have done it. Through the four windows of the pagoda's top story,
we gazed out at the city and suburbs of Xi'an, spreading out as far
as the eye could see. . . . If it had been just me going up the pagoda,
that last phrase wouldn't have stuck in my mind.

We left Wild Goose Pagoda and walked along at a moderate
pace. "Shall we get something to eat?" She seemed to have forgotten about the eating part. Neither of us was hungry at all, but we
each had a deep-fried dried persimmon. All I could think about
was rushing to the bus station and getting away from her as soon as
possible. Then of all things, she started going on about how there
used to be so many snack vendors around this place, but now there's
hardly anything except for stuff like bean noodles. As for me, I was
still thinking of the twenty cents I'd spent on those two dried per-
simmons. She said she knew of a good restaurant near Dachai Market but didn't say if she thought we should go or not. I said, "Let's
head over there." We headed over.

Dachai was bustling and brightly lit. She led me into a food
shop selling pastries. I asked her, "What's the point of coming in
here?" So we went right out again and started on a search for that
unfindable restaurant. Already it was seven-thirty, and most of the
restaurants had shut down. Red faces of drinkers careened out of
restaurant doors. We kept on, walking from street to street with no
idea what we were after. All I could think of was hurrying to a bus
stop so I could get away from her. But the city buses were so
crammed full of people that we didn't feel like getting on any of
them.

The stores all sold cassette players, leather jackets, shampoo—
stuff like that. We walked into yet another restaurant, a dumpling
place, where everybody was eating standing up. We walked right
out again, but as we did, she kept looking over her shoulder, back
inside. Then there was another place, which had run out of everything but pig organs. She said she just couldn't remember where
that one good restaurant was. We slipped into a wonton place
and had a bowl apiece; I paid, of course. Then I asked her if she

was taking the number 3 bus or the number 1. I figured if she took the 3, I'd take the 1. She said either would do. I said I wanted to go to the long-distance bus station to order a ticket and asked her if she wanted to come along. Why I had to suggest that to her, I don't know. We went all the way through the night market again, through all the boiling and frying and clouds of steam, through all the people milling around and bumping into me. I had no idea, none, what the connection was between her and me or why we absolutely had to walk along here, getting shoved and elbowed, or if I really had to buy a long-distance bus ticket. When she saw me actually holding a bus ticket for early the next morning, she pointed to a shop next door selling southern-style foods and then pointed inside the place at some kind of soft, fluffy cake. I ignored her. Then we stood in a corner of this city where I didn't know a soul, waiting for the local bus to come. It came.

I managed to grab an empty seat for her. "Bye," I said when I got to my stop (which came before hers). She turned her face toward the window. I got off the bus but wasn't relieved at all. Nine-thirty in the Xi'an suburbs, walking through mud, suddenly I was hungry. As luck would have it, there ahead of me stood a place selling meat pastries and, incredibly, it was still open for business. I had a couple of the pastries (good ones, too) and washed them down with a bowl of hot sticky-dumpling soup. When I walked outside, I thought I saw the bus carrying Xiao Tong still coming toward me down the road, and I wondered whether I really *had* seen her.

"Next stop Xi'an—end of the line. One of our nation's renowned ancient cities, Xi'an has served as capital for more than ten dynasties over the long history of the Chinese people. . . ."

Xi'an.

The woman conductor had just yanked the woolen blanket out from underneath my pillow. I hopped down from the upper berth. Xi'an. No need for the woman on the PA system in that tiny one-and-a-half-square-meter booth (every time I went to the toilet, I saw her sitting there, right next door to the toilet) to make the announcement; from the train's deceleration, I already knew Xi'an was coming up. Just like all the other times I had shouldered my satchel and prepared to step into the press of disembarking passengers, I thought perhaps I ought to make some sort of parting remarks to the acquaintances I'd made on the trip. But I didn't. I did, however, make a rough calculation of my expenses since I'd started out just the day before: two box lunches, one beer, a cold plate of beef, and the noodles for breakfast. Altogether . . .

The comrades sent to greet me had the sign for the conference held high, so I spotted it from a good distance away. I relaxed when I saw it. The first words spoken by the first comrade to shake my hand gave me a start: "Say, didn't you run into trouble on the way?"

What trouble? What was this all about? It seemed someone had passed the word that my train had been delayed by a flash flood in the mountains, which is normally no big deal. This comrade, though, for some reason couldn't believe that I had managed to arrive in one piece. He gave me a good firm handshake but left me stuck with a grim thought: *somehow* I'd made it through safe and trouble free!

The conference was to open the following day, and we were going to drive out there bright and early in the morning. The plan, meanwhile, was to take the afternoon to do some sightseeing. I got a clear idea of the arrangements and checked my watch: still just a bit past ten in the morning. A van hauled us from the train station to the hostel, where we were to spend the night before heading off to Luxian and the conference. I went over to the check-in desk to make a phone call.

I gave her a call. Xiao Tong.

As soon as I began thinking of Xiao Tong, that summer three years ago drifted back into view. I was separated from my wife, feeling low and foul, as if she and I were involved in some sort of warfare. (I had no heart for fighting it out. We could have been happy together—if only, that is, I hadn't become what I am now.) It was in a gray fifties-era building that I had first met Xiao Tong. I was there with some journalist friends at a get-together called the Journalists' Trust, as we were all in the same line of work. But since each of us was either already divorced or in the process, it might have been better named the Singles' Club. I think it might have been I who came up with that Singles' Club tagline while proposing a toast. As for a good journalistic subheading to go with it, no one ever came up with anything. The opening speech was called "The Independent Woman." The speaker was Xiao Tong. She had recently got a divorce from a husband dead set against splitting up. Originally an athlete, she was powerfully built, proud, and bursting with an unreasoning drive to go out and take on her new life. (I have to admit that for me, it wasn't like that at the time.) She had prepared the lunch: fried sausages, ham, pickles, even cheese, and a ginger nutcake she herself had baked. And then that magnificent chicken. Even the way she carried it out to the table: unforgettable. She knew how to live and live well. The talk she gave, delivered in a strongly speculative vein, left a lasting impression, too. I remember only one phrase from it, when she said, "If a woman can love only one man, then she's not affirming the emotion of love but the man; only if a woman loves continually does she give affirmation to love in and of itself."

At the end of the get-together, our friends left Xiao Tong and me behind on our own; each one of them shook our hands as if wishing the two of us well in some unstated sort of way. I can't remember what she and I talked about then, except that she seemed to want me to stay for dinner (the get-together had been a lunch party), and I felt that wasn't really necessary. We met several times after that. She told me how she wrote compositions in English and how she spoke French in her sleep. She was the one who recommended that I read some of the world's most abstruse books. (I think I still have two that I bought after consulting the list she wrote out for me.) Later on, mutual friends were always filling me in on the latest about Xiao Tong: Xiao Tong's in love again, or Xiao Tong's gone through another breakup. The explanations of why she went to Xi'an conflicted. I tended to believe the one I could accept most readily: that she switched job assignments with a teacher who wanted to get back to her husband and child in Beijing. Then, of course, there were other factors in the background: after another frenetic breakup, Xiao Tong, in a huff, had stopped talking with her family.

This was where it stood when I arrived in Xi'an and gave her a call.

She would be happy to have me over for a visit but made it clear that she had nothing to offer me as her guest.

So after lunch at the hostel, I started out. The medical academy would be easy to find, I was given to understand, but even so I kept trying to talk myself out of going there right away: should I rush to get a quick look at the sights of Xi'an first, or should I spend the entire afternoon seeing Xiao Tong? Then again, we could take in the sights together. I decided on the latter.

Walking alongside a muddy road, at last I spotted the sign at the gate to the medical academy, and then I saw Xiao Tong.

A half month later, I'd finished the conference report and gone to see the terra-cotta soldiers, Empress Wu Zetian's Tomb, and the Tomb of the Yellow Emperor. Getting ready to leave on my return flight to Beijing, I wondered if perhaps I ought to make another trip to Wild Goose Pagoda or perhaps see Xiao Tong again. I decided on the former. No—I went to Xiao Tong's place first and then to Wild Goose Pagoda, because at her dormitory I saw a big padlock on the door. I knocked at the next-door neighbor's, but no one even knew who she was. When I said I'd been here a half month ago to see her, the neighbors suggested I go to the dean's office to check the personnel files. Check the files, or trust my memory? I decided on the latter.

When I got back to Beijing, would I tell my friends about Xiao Tong, or keep it to myself? I decided on the former. So I told a friend about what happened with Xiao Tong. He smiled. Xiao Tong had been back in Beijing for over three months, he said; he saw her almost every day. He could take me to her right away, too, since she was still around. Really? Terrific. It looked as if I'd really done a good turn—I'd deceived my own memory, or maybe my memory had deceived me. In any case, I didn't care to talk about it anymore. I started in telling my friend about my experience on the trip back from Xi'an, how I had had to stand up on the train for twelve hours straight. He interrupted—which number train had I taken? "Number one twenty-six, of course." He smiled again, almost laughed this time: "Then you've come from Nanjing." He was right. I must have taken the plane back to Beijing!

But that sensation of standing on the train still lingered in my legs.

As soon as the train pulled up to the platform, I used my usual trick of flashing a journalist's ID and an interview-approval letter until I located the head conductor. To get a sleeper, you have to move in fast—you can't wait until after you've claimed a hard seat in third class. Unless you've made reservations four days ahead of time or waited five hours in line, this is the only chance there is to get some sleep on the trip. The head conductor very civilly led me to the dining-car corridor, pointed to a ten-centimeter-wide ledge along the wall, and said, "Sorry, but that's the best I can do—the sleepers are full. How about the third-class seats? ..." I looked over and realized that I had no choice but to sit on the little ledge. The adjacent hard-seat car was impassable—this train was more of a city bus, what with people pressed up against one another so tightly that even turning around was impossible. The head conductor took me toward the door leading into the next car and, after making me promise three times not to let anyone into the dining car from the hard-seat section, let me have the spot. I promised and sat down. It felt like sitting on the rim of a toilet. I'd boarded the train at ten in the evening. It was due in Beijing at seven-thirty the following morning. For nine and a half hours, I would have to sit here, stuck in the position of someone taking a crap.

Half an hour after the train started moving, I went to see the head conductor again. He let me know that he'd already explained how things stood, that sleepers were out of the question that night, although something might be available tomorrow morning (which would be two hours before reaching Beijing). I said, "Then how about giving me a hard seat?" He said that would be more difficult than getting a sleeper. ("We can't pull someone out of his seat to make room for you. Take a look around, and if you see one, take it.") The third time I went to talk to the head conductor, he guided me out of the dining car, took his keys, and "clack," locked the dining-car door. I was left for good with the people standing in the hard-seat car.

It dawned on me that I was being held close by a mass of warm, sweaty bodies. All the connecting doors were open, allowing me to see straight to the back of the train, about a quarter of a mile away, people standing all the way to the end. We stood like horses, staring at one another, breathing into one another's faces. Next to us was a boiler room, so that with the dining-car door locked tight, the car I was in warmed up like one gigantic boiler. The windows were sealed shut, and there wasn't much air to begin with. At every stop, a few more people squeezed on, swelling the ranks of the standing passengers. No one was getting off the train. I had to grip the floor with my feet to keep myself upright, as there was only enough floor space for about half of either foot. I wondered how long I'd be able to keep this up.

A little over two hours into the ride, someone came up with the idea of getting off at the next station and waiting to get on the following train, which would probably be less crowded. Someone else said that was right, seeing as our train had left at ten at night and there wouldn't be anyone else getting on the trains after midnight. Sounded reasonable. But when a group of us climbed down onto the platform at the next stop and asked around, a short, fat platform attendant flatly advised that we get back on our own train. He couldn't guarantee we'd be better off on the later trains. In fact, he insisted that the next train through, the one we hoped to catch, would be even more crowded than this one. The only slight hope was a train coming out five hours later. "On the whole," he said with a wave of his hand, "you may as well stick with what you've got."

When we climbed onto the train again, the conductor asked why we were back. We told him what had happened. He immediately dismissed the platform attendant's remarks as a pack of lies. By then, the train had been moving for ten minutes. Nothing left to do but check and recheck the time on my watch: six and a half hours to go, six and a quarter hours to go, six hours and fourteen minutes to go, six hours and thirteen minutes to go. . . . It reminded me of a long-distance bus trip I'd taken two years before in Henan . . .

I was sitting right behind the bus driver. Anytime a pig or chicken crossed the road or when we came up on a bicycle rider, he would blow the horn. The horns on those buses are as loud and harsh as they come. Every blast lasted about ten seconds, and then the sound rang in my ears for at least another fifteen seconds. Each time he hit it, I thought my heart was going to heave up out of my mouth. By a rough calculation, I figured that the two-hundred-mile trip would take around seven hours. With the driver blowing the horn about once every two minutes, that meant 210 horn blasts, each ten seconds long, plus the fifteen seconds of ringing in my ears. . . . But why go on? I thought. Ten minutes into the bus trip and my nerves were shattered. What would be left of me after half an hour? I realized I didn't care anymore—my ears had already hardened like iron . . .

In much the same way, I passed the nine and a half hours of that night numb to all feeling. The train didn't stop until seven in the morning. Just a half hour to go, but I felt sure I'd be able to stand for another nine and a half. Someone stuck his head out the window and reported that the train was temporarily held up.

"Clack." After being locked all night, the dining-car door opened. A conductor gave us an update: the train wouldn't be signaled into the station before ten-thirty. This meant that even though Beijing was only twenty-five minutes away, the train had to stay put for three more hours. No one's eyes registered any disappointment or anxiety, and no one said a word. The interior of the car was silence itself; everyone had to wait and endure. The connecting doors were locked—no one was allowed off the train even though all anyone had to do was walk to the nearest bus stop and catch a bus into the city . . .

It's a feeling I have, that even now I'm still on that train. My feet seem to be planted on the floor of that railway car, regardless of whether the train is stopped or moving, regardless of whether it's going anywhere at all. I have no way of telling this to my friends in Beijing—that I don't know when that arrival will ever come about . . .

By that I mean I may have never been to Xi'an at all.

TRANSLATED BY JOHN A. CRESPI

# Sunshine Between the Lips

## Chen Ran

### Another Rule

I am a young woman whose job is very mechanical, as mechanical as the hands of timepieces, always making circular motions with the same radius and in the same direction; as mechanical as a fatigued truck traveling invariably down a fixed route. Usually when I am reading the study materials delivered by my work unit, especially articles about the new trends in struggles, I can never remember whether Iraq annexed Kuwait or the other way around or if the Scud stopped the Patriot or vice versa, even if I read the same news item ten times. But I am able to commit to memory all the typos in the articles. For instance, in the lower-right corner at the end of a line, I will easily spot an apostrophe that should be a comma, and so forth. That's what comes of being a proofreader.

This simple work keeps my chaotic mind from making many mistakes, I am glad to say, since I am a daydreamer who finds it hard to play by the rules. Let's say, for example, that the faint-hearted son of a cold-blooded murderer accidentally kills someone. When the death sentence falls upon the frightened son, the father, who has always been able to escape the net of justice, mysteriously takes his son's place at the execution ground. This act must be regarded as a mockery of the law, but I will be moved by the loving sacrifice of a brutish father who kills without compunction, until my face is bathed in tears; I will even hold him in some regard.

When I see an accomplished surgeon refuse to treat a class enemy's wife who is in great pain and in need of help, I am disgusted. My problematic views and a tendency toward aberrant thinking are enough to deprive me of the chance to become a doctor or lawyer.

They say that to be a writer, you must follow even more rules. I know only too well that my deviant thinking and convoluted logic keep me at odds with those rules. Fortunately, I am aware of these flaws and have never expected or hoped to become much of anything.

Yet there may be another possibility. You might happen to share my way of thinking, which means you could interpret my unorthodoxy as a rule in its own right. Anything is possible.

## Fear of Hypodermics

Dentists always fire Miss Dai Er's imagination. The fantasy begins when she approaches the dentist's office and hears the whir of the drill. As she enters, the sound courses through every nerve in her body. At the same time, in the space taken in by her gaze, countless teeth dance and fly around her like snowflakes. Whirling and spinning, they send forth the delicate fragrance of falling pear blossoms.

At this moment, Miss Dai Er is fantasizing as she sits in dental chair 103, assigned to Dr. Kong Sen, in Hospital 103. Dai Er, twenty-two, possesses a nearly pathological tenderness, charm, and melancholy. A painfully impacted wisdom tooth has brought her here. She looks around carefully: there is a spittoon and a cup on the left armrest; above it are a gadget on an adjustable arm and a small electric fan; directly overhead is a large lamp, like a golden sunflower whose petals move around the patient's mouth; alongside the right armrest is a swivel chair with wheels, on which the young dentist is currently sitting.

He is a reticent young man, tall but stocky and sedate, with focused yet limpid eyes. (Miss Dai Er will never forget his eyes. In the future, she will spot him amid a sea of people by his eyes alone.) His nose and mouth are obscured by a snow-white gauze mask, and it is this hidden part that bestows upon him a space open to imagination and a mysterious, fathomless aura.

Once you lean back in the chair and the lamp lights up the area around your lips, you clench your fists nervously and lay them in your lap. The young dentist presses up close to your face from the right. You open your mouth wide and let him work on your teeth with probes, forceps, and scalpel. His large, strong fingers move ceaselessly in the cramped space of your mouth. Because of the narrowness of the oral cavity, there is tremendous cohesive force as he pulls your tooth. He exerts all his strength, and you exert all yours. If you are a young woman like Miss Dai Er and have a vivid imagination, it will be easy to associate this with another activity.

Dr. Kong Sen leans over to a patient in the chair beside Dai Er to give the gray-haired woman a shot of Novocain in her upper jaw. Then he turns back to Miss Dai Er.

He asks, "Any physical problems?" His voice is low and deep, as if sealed in an underground tunnel.

"No," she says.

"Heart trouble?"

"No."

"High blood pressure?"

"No."

"OK, let's begin."

His comments are terse and precise. She gains a dialectical fascination from such an either-or dialogue.

He turns to get the Novocain. To Dai Er, the ailments he has mentioned pertain to old folks, not to her. But knowing that the questions are routine, she smiles her gratitude to him.

He has fetched the syringe filled with Novocain, the needle pointing upward. He lightly pushes the injector, and tiny droplets spurt from the tip of the needle. The spray fans out in an exaggerated arc; white mist, curling upward, drifts out of the room and into the corridor, then slowly descends the staircase. It glides over twenty-eight stairs, passing through more than a decade, and on toward the internal medicine ward. There Miss Dai Er was barely seven and a half years old.

Dai Er, front teeth missing and two terrified eyes staring out at a white world, was a weak, sickly child. She had just come out of a fever-induced coma caused by meningitis.

"Do you recognize Mommy?" A young woman about the same age as the present Miss Dai Er sat beside her seven-and-a-half-year-old daughter, expecting a response as if awaiting a fateful verdict.

"Do you recognize Mommy? Where is Mommy?" the young woman repeated.

Dai Er struggled to open her eyes, which seemed dried out and enlarged by the debilitating illness; she searched the confines of the room. The walls were white; a hovering sound was white; a smile at the upturned corners of the mouth behind the sound was white. Over there stood a large man holding a hypodermic syringe in his right hand; the needle was pointing upward, like a bleak wilderness, awaiting the passage of humans. Long and hollow, it would enter her buttock. He may have been smiling at his young patient, but his expression was changed into cold indifference by the gauze mask.

"Can you recognize Mommy? You see, Mommy is smiling at you!"

Dai Er remained motionless as her eyes followed the movements of the needle. Concentrating all the strength in her little body in her eyes, she was trying to ward off the approaching instrument.

"Mommy is right here, don't you recognize me?" The young woman was losing her composure.

The needle kept coming, with its cold glint and tiny shriek.

"Mommy, I don't want a shot." Dai Er sat up suddenly and draped her arms around her mother's neck. "Mommy, I don't want a shot," Dai Er cried loudly.

The young woman burst out crying, her sobs punctuated by laughter: "My baby's alive again. She's not a mindless vegetable, she's alive again . . ."

The white uniform and the needle had moved up next to little Dai Er.

"Put her down, and leave us alone, please. It's time for her injection," the mouth above the white uniform said. The huge hypodermic in his hand was cold and hard, like a pistol.

To Dai Er's chagrin, the young woman put her down, shedding tears of happiness, and left the room.

She knew that her mother, too, was afraid of the man. Her leaving was testimony to this. She could not protect Dai Er. Now Dai Er was alone. She stopped crying, for she knew she had to face the cold needle by herself.

"Lie on your stomach, and pull down your pants."

It was useless to resist. Even Mommy obeyed him. She rolled over obediently and pulled down her pants.

For two whole months, the seven-and-a-half-year-old Dai Er experienced the world through the unvarying command of "Lie on your stomach, and pull down your pants." She learned that no one else could take that resonating needle for her. Everyone had his own needle to face.

The long needle entered her buttock and stabbed at her heart. She grew up with that needle.

The dental office resounds with the provocative screeches of teeth being drilled and scraped. They grate on Miss Dai Er's nerves and make her shudder.

The stocky, young dentist approaches her, holding a hypodermic syringe.

"No!" Miss Dai Er's scream disturbs the rigid operating protocols of the dental office.


## A Fortuitous Encounter

That I actually met him was certainly the will of heaven. It happened five years ago. One day at dusk when the feeble face of evening had already faded, night's curtain fell in a rush, allowing no explanation. At that time, my persistent nostalgia invariably led me from a stage pieced together by historical fragments to a theater displaying the passage of time. On that day, I walked alone into a grand theater decorated with a mix of luxurious splendor and religious decline. It was at the entrance where I ran into him; to be precise, at first I was captivated by the eyes of a handsome, bright young man, and then I recognized him by his voice.

"Is it really you?"

I collected myself and looked at him, able to identify the focused yet limpid eyes. The space beneath the eyes, however, appeared only in my imagination; except that in my imagination, the chin had been broad, with sharp edges and corners, whereas the one before me was steep yet smooth. The Grecian nose was just as I had imagined, belonging to the right person.

"Yes, it's me. I know you . . . part of you, anyway." To be acquainted with a handsome man in this way—how could I help but smile?

He was smiling, too. He stroked his chin with his right hand, and the large palm slid along with a lively whistle. Neither of us mentioned the event we had experienced together.

"Are you . . . alone?" He asked.

"Yes."

"If you don't mind, I happen to have two tickets."

"I've got one." I showed him the ticket in my hand.

"But mine are in the front row."

"Um . . . aren't you going to wait for her any longer?"

"Who?"

"Um . . ." I turned and looked around.

He took my arm gently before I turned back around. "I'm waiting for a girl just like you."

I smiled and shook my head but followed him nevertheless.

The heavy curtains opened, the lights dimmed, and all was quiet. I've always thought that the biggest difference between an office and a theater is that an office is a stage and that even if you don't like to perform, you must play a role regardless of how unimportant it is. There is no escape. Even though your office is tranquil as still water and only one or two people—actors—are around you, you are still unable to indulge in your inner world: your facial expression will betray you. The office is a stage, an outer life, an unclosed space. In a cinema or a theater, however, once the lights are turned off and the darkness spreads around you, you are swallowed up by a vast emptiness. Although in the darkness, countless heads are hidden and the air is filled with whispers like a tired night wind quietly perched in a vast forest, you gain a peaceful space where your heart is able to wander freely. You watch a miniature world and telescoped time on the stage; your pearllike tears flow, you giggle, you can't help yourself, you let yourself go.

That day's play was about love, and the actors performed with wild intoxication. A man poured out his heart to a woman as beautifully as if he were lying, and a woman lied to another woman as beautifully as if she were telling the truth. I was totally immersed in the story and the passion on stage. When the curtains closed and the lights came on, I was dragged back to the theater from somewhere within my heart by the noise of movement around me, and once again I saw his focused yet limpid eyes.

I said thanks.

He also said thanks.

We walked out together. We made our slow way through the excited crowd, his arm shielding my back to protect me from being jostled. From time to time, his arm was pushed up against my back or waist by the crowd, and to me it felt like a gentle, comforting caress. When we reached the exit, he helped me with my coat. This act, subtle and natural, made my coat warmer and more velvety.

To get from the theater to the bus stop, we needed to pass down a narrow lane with buildings on both sides. I had already thought about the hidden dangers in the cramped space on the way to the theater, but since it had not yet been entirely dark, the imagined danger had been no more than a fleeting concern. Now the darkness was thick as ink as we left the theater, and the moon, like an eroded boulder, showed only a tiny sliver. Completely caught up in the dangers of the long, narrow, dark passage, I asked him to stand at this end of the lane and wait until I ran to the other end and said good-bye to him.

He laughed. "Why so complicated? I'll go with you."

"No."

"I don't mind. Really."

"There's no need. I . . . really no need . . ."

"But why?"

"I'm just afraid . . . suddenly somebody might . . ."

"Oh! Including me?"

"Um . . ."

"You really are a little girl. You need me, but you're also afraid of me. OK, you go first, then shout, and I'll come over and see you home."

I accepted happily.

I ran the whole way without taking a single breath, as if it were a hundred-meter dash. His eyes and silhouette remained behind me, exactly where I'd left them. As soon as I reached the other end, I shouted, "I made it."

And from the other end, his footsteps sounded.

When we were together again, he earnestly guaranteed my safety. I felt I could trust him. This trust originated from a shared memory, which I cannot reveal here.

As we walked, reluctantly we recalled that event. I told him how impressed I had been by his eyes and by his voice—the low, gentle voice of a cello filtering out from behind closed doors and windows. Unexpectedly, every detail of the event, including my manner and behavior, remained fresh in his memory.

"I knew then that you'd never return," he said.

Walking slowly along the deserted night street, we talked about things far and near, including the romantic play we had just seen. I said I didn't agree with one of the leading man's lines. The "rib theory" is ridiculous, I said. However intimate the original Adam and Eve or their future replacements might have been, they each had their own heads, their own thoughts, and their own spirits. Women were independent.

He agreed.

"Maybe that's why I have no religious beliefs," I said. Five years ago, I talked about love as earnestly as I did about death.

We parted a short distance from my house.

He stroked my hair gently and said, "You talk like an adult."
He emphasized the word *like,* implying that I was really only a little
girl.

"There's no contradiction." I ignored his implication.

"Contradictions are beautiful. You're a contradictory girl."

His silver-gray raincoat softly flapped against my body, and I
felt a sort of moist tenderness. He leaned toward me slightly, but
that's as far as it went.

The moon was full, and the pale yellow streetlamps shimmered
at the tips of our shadows. Feeling his breath caressing my cheek, I
lowered my head, not knowing what to do.

I freed myself from the embrace of his flapping raincoat and
said, "Don't."

"Don't be nervous. I just want to hear your story."

I looked into his face; I felt safe and relaxed.

## The Reappearing Shadow

Miss Dai Er is sitting in the dental chair of Dr. Kong Sen, her head
tilted slightly backward, her left leg stretched out straight, her right
knee bent inward and tucked under her left calf. Her hands lie
stiffly on her flat abdomen. A slight tremble causes her shapely
breasts to jiggle like a pair of startled little heads. The young dentist
is gazing absorbedly at the nervous body of the young woman, who
seems solitary and helpless under the strong light of the lamp.

Watching the approaching Dr. Kong Sen, who is holding a full
hypodermic, Miss Dai Er is in a great panic. She opens her mouth
wide, and the brutal syringe, which is about to stab her upper jaw,
makes her pale and sends her out of control.

"No! No!" she screams.

The young dentist puts down the syringe and says indifferently,
seemingly devoid of sympathy, "If you don't feel comfortable, we
don't have to do it now."

Dai Er's face is cold; the corners of her mouth and the tip of her
nose twitch uncontrollably, making it impossible for her to open

her eyes. Her mind is a blank; her body, enfolded in leaden clouds, is spinning upward and upward . . .

One dense, heavy cloud followed another, as though the sky were covered by the dark-gray wings of a multitude of birds. The air was damp. The huge birds, hovering in the universe like fine steeds, swooned earthward. Their feathers were shot down one by one by peals of thunder and thudding raindrops, and the dark-grayness fell at a leisurely pace to stick on the window. On that rainy day in that damp and gloomy room, what the seven-and-a-half-year-old little Dai Er saw was as tangled as matted hair. In the dim light, little Dai Er was shocked to see a huge hypodermic, growing in the body of a man, pointing right at her face. The scene has remained in a secret place of her memory; on all rainy days, a dark mass of birds always swoons . . .

There is a commotion in the dentist's office. Beyond the window, it sounds like rain, and a dark-green mildewy smell rises into the sky. She feels her chair being tipped backward by someone, forcing her head down.

"It's all right. Nothing serious. Just a case of nerves." She hears the young Dr. Kong Sen's voice.

Following the brief commotion, she senses that the blurred white shadows around her have dispersed and that the office has resumed its normal order.

Miss Dai Er feels the pressure of the young dentist's fingers on her cheek, and her twitching facial muscles gradually relax. It is raining outside, the watery threads flowing softly down the windowpanes, as if stroking her cheek. With a white towel, the young dentist is wiping away the cold sweat on her face. Vaguely, she sees a patch of white like a junk sailing into view from the far edge of the sky. The junk now hangs at the window, peering inside and questioning the dim light. She breathes hard, feeling her lungs being tinted a dirty yellow, bit by bit, by the fouled air in the room. She gazes at the white junk as a thousand thoughts swirl through her mind. Making an effort with her arms and both eyes, she strains to grasp the fleeting white.

Miss Dai Er opens her eyes and takes a deep breath, recovering gradually.

"Feeling better?" asks the dentist.

Dai Er sits up with difficulty, "I . . . I'm finc."

The young dentist smiles. (Dai Er can only imagine his smile since all his expressions are hidden by the gauze mask.) "Did you faint because of the needle?" he asks.

"No. Not exactly. The hypodermic . . . makes me think of something else."

"This is not a good day for you. Why don't you come back in a couple of days, when you feel better?"

Ashamed and remorseful, Miss Dai Er steps down from the dentist's chair on rubbery legs. She knows she will never come back here. She looks at the young dentist, who has touched her cheek and whose limpid eyes have already been carved in her mind; the feeling of profound loss is so dominant that she doesn't even say good-bye to this young dentist who has fired her imagination and made her want to stay longer with him. She leaves amid the gloom of disappointment.

## Love in Winter

Winter is a serene old man walking calmly out of an ardent summer, out of the bigoted, romantic, and dangerous air of the tropics, then gradually quieting down. I like summer, but my love sprouts in a winter setting. Of course, this may be seen as the nature I have bestowed upon this love.

Before I ran into him again, my winter had been long and desolate; the icy north wind whizzing past my window was like a shadowless, invisible man panting as he runs. A bald-pated, commodious sky greeted my window. I sat facing the window in my warm room with a book of some sort in my hands and the sunshine more trustworthy than any of my imagined lovers. Creeping languidly all over my body, the sunshine alone stayed to embrace me during the chilled months and years, soothingly melting the pent-up sorrow and despair in my heart and restoring a sense of composure.

During this winter, my trust in him gradually increased until it was second only to my trust in the sunshine.

After he burst into my life, I felt as if I were living in a world of unreality. My body was but a stationary launching pad for thoughts. Most of the time, I was unable to keep my gushing thoughts from wandering all over the place like a cloud, like a mist. I frequently pinched my cheeks in the hope that the real sense of touching would somehow make me more real.

We started dating regularly. I believed I liked and trusted this man. He steadfastly avoided mentioning the incident at our first meeting, when my loss of control had impressed us both so deeply.

We went out every night. During those years, my sole amusement had been walking. So we walked along Jianguomen Avenue for hours, taking in the sights, a refreshing breeze kissing our faces and colored lights glittering all around. This man, born in the year of the male horse (he always added the male gender to the animal representing his birth year), had the tall, powerful physique of a stallion. I hung on to his left arm as we walked leisurely. Actually, only he was walking, propelling both of us forward. Like the earth itself, he bore my all.

Finally one day, he asked me, "Why didn't you come back after you left that day?" I knew he meant our first meeting. "If I hadn't bumped into you at the theater, I'm afraid you might have disappeared forever. I hate to even think about it—I might have lost a whole world."

I was suddenly quite moved.

There in the middle of the brightly lit street, we kissed. My heart emptied, my limbs turned weak. For a timid young girl tasting a man for the first time, this act was indeed soul shattering. I found myself longing desperately for his body; the strange fear hidden within me gradually dispersed.

He drew me into the shadow of some roadside trees. And there in the leafy mosaic of moonlight, we kissed and fondled each other for a long time. Making an effort to contain his excitement, he unbuttoned a young woman's blouse for the first time in his life, as nervous as a boy who has just learned how to unbutton his clothes being told by his teacher to take his shirt off. Also for the first time, he roamed a woman's body with his eyes. We held each other tightly; a young man and a young woman new to the clouds and rains of sex were sent into ecstasy. I felt drained, nothing but a hollow container. The top of my head felt cold and numb, my body became a vast wasteland; a sort of void, the likes of which I had never experienced before, spread unhindered, as if the surrounding area were full of stony peaks and swimming fish.

I do not intend to describe our love here because I simply don't know whether or not it can be called love. Today, five years later, I'm still unable to judge accurately my feelings at that time, since I have never known all the implications of love.

I remember how, when I was burning to take his body into mine, I stopped suddenly, clung to his waist without moving, and sobbed softly, tears glistening in my eyes. I said, "I don't want to see it, don't want to—"

"What's the matter?"

"I just don't want to see it."

"What's wrong? Why?"

I could answer only with low sobs and tears like pearls.

He stopped and caressed my face. The repression concealed in my body for years was like a fish bone lodged in my throat. At last, I plucked up the courage to remove whatever it was from the bottom of my heart and hand it timidly to this man. In a low voice, I implored him to share my burden, for only he could shoulder my fears.

I gave myself over to the protection of his arms and his profession. I had never felt so relaxed because I had never lost control in anyone's arms before. One by one, my sobs transported me to a joyful realm I'd never known existed. But I had never felt so burdened

either: I had to face the blurred past of my childhood again in order
to share it with him.

## A Clinical Conversation

Finally, Miss Dai Er called the young dentist one rainy afternoon.
She said she had to see him.

The rain had stopped by the time they strolled through the hospital district, with its verdant trees and rain-soaked leaves. The sun
was out, and the sky appeared a fresh, tender pink that dripped
down onto the steamy lawn. Old people talked to themselves as
they sat idly on park benches, nodding off from time to time. The
young Dr. Kong Sen smelled of disinfectant, which made Miss Dai
Er feel like a patient.

"So, you've come . . ." he said. "Are your gums inflamed
again?"

At first, Miss Dai Er held her tongue, but then she started talking about something totally unrelated. She talked on and on, delighted to be able to unburden herself of her past.

Miss Dai Er said that in her childhood she had a friend, an architect, a gaunt, weary, middle-aged man who was her only friend.
He lived next door to her. At that time, children's toys consisted of
sand, cobblestones, and water. Things like building blocks and simple rubber, nonelectric toys were luxuries. Day in and day out, little
Dai Er was immersed in the joy of playing in the sand. She dug
countless small holes around herself and put a blown-up paper ball
into each of the holes (she called the balls mines), then crisscrossed
two or three twigs over the holes, covered them with paper, and
buried the whole thing with sand. When that was done, Dai Er
stood there surveying the area like a general devising strategies in a
command tent, while arrayed around her were hidden accomplish-
ments. Closing her eyes, she spun around several times, then
walked out of the minefield in the grip of excitement. This was a
game she had learned and adapted from the movie *Mine Warfare,*
and she was absorbed in it for a long time.

The grown-up Miss Dai Er recalled her childhood game, whether at the office or out among the crowds, and only now realized how her present life resembled that game.

Little Dai Er spent a great deal of time with her architect friend, a reticent man who grew lively only when he played symbolic games (the term *symbolic* was a modifier the grown-up Dai Er bestowed upon the word *game*). He taught little Dai Er some games she'd never dreamed of; for example, he taught her how to build high towers by mixing crushed stones with mud. He built them high enough for the child Dai Er to think them truly lofty. They were always in danger of collapsing with a loud crash: a strong wind could blow them down. And as they stood there, lofty and tottering, the architect would lead Dai Er in squeals of delight.

They also played faucet. At the southwest corner of the yard was a long trough with three faucets. The architect often turned them all on at the same time, releasing three powerful streams of water, which nearly drove him wild. He would howl excitedly; the sounds reverberating through the deserted yard sounded especially horrible, both thrilling and frightening little Dai Er.

He was an excellent architect, whose certificates of merit covered a wall in his home. But his wife was never proud of that. In Dai Er's memory, these neighbors, her only neighbors, quarreled constantly. When little Dai Er asked her parents why that was, they became evasive, avoiding the important and dwelling on the trivial; or they equivocated, saying that Uncle was busy with his work in architecture and didn't have time to take care of the family and so Auntie was unhappy with him. Children wouldn't understand and shouldn't ask so many questions. Dai Er was never satisfied with this answer. She constantly sought an opportunity to ask her architect friend—until one rainy day, when the event that Dai Er would remember all her life happened. After telling her mother tearfully that the architect had exposed himself in front of her, they were not friends anymore.

Now that she is grown up, little by little Miss Dai Er has come to understand the connection between his frenzied need to work and play and the loss of his manhood—a compensation for failure.

Finally one day, a white ambulance, its siren blaring, took the architect away from the yard where little Dai Er played her games. They said he was taken to the asylum in the northern part of the city. They also said that after pacing up and down a gloomy, remote, and shaded pathway for a long time, he did to a young female passerby what he had done to little Dai Er on that rainy day.

When Dai Er was in elementary school, she experienced a fire. At first, people were driven out of their homes by a strong, scorching odor and the acrid, choking smell of smoke; then they saw the architect's windows being lapped by countless bright-red dog tongues. Bit by bit, those hissing dog tongues merged into a wall of hot flames. On that afternoon, after being suspended from his duties, the architect had locked himself in his room, where he set a fire amid the suffocating smell of gasoline that brought an end to his vexations, regrets, and powerless desires. The billowing smoke and crackling flames enveloped the quiet yard, the twisting alley, and Miss Dai Er's serpentine childhood, which was lost in the hidden recesses of that alley.

The young dentist laid a hand heavily on Miss Dai Er's shoulder, as though to keep her from being carried away by the billowing smoke in her memory. That was the arm for which Miss Dai Er had long been yearning. She had been waiting for just such an arm to rescue her from her memories. For the first time in her life, she became a patient, giving herself up weakly to the arm that had rooted out so many decayed teeth. The arm itself was the warmest and safest bedside practitioner, the most accurate psychoanalyst.

## The Beginning of Birth or Death

One breezy, sunny morning a few months after I moved in with him, we cut through the busy district of town, then crossed a vacant lot and a yard piled high with rusty metal, rotting wood, and crumbling bricks. I had always felt a strange affection and melancholy toward all those relics; the desolation never failed to spark feelings of nostalgia: maybe that junkyard held my childhood and early youth. We stood silently for a while, then walked toward a small hut—for years, it had been regarded as the cradle of love as well as the source of the graveyard; people said it was a stage that accommodated both comedies and tragedies. I was incapable of naming this place, just as today I am incapable of naming my love of that time.

A warmhearted young man received us, one who habitually punctuated his speech with *fuck* (used in place of commas, this word evinced neither joy nor anger). From this small hut, we obtained a red certificate that read

> Registration No. 13
> Dai Er (Female), 23
> Kong Sen (Male), 26
> Wed of their own free will.
> Investigation confirms that their marriage conforms to the marriage laws of the State.

We each kept a copy, knowing that the paper was thick as sheet metal and thin as a cicada's wing.

## A Ceremony for Hovering

On an afternoon after her marriage, Miss Dai Er finally shows up again at dental chair 103 in Hospital 103. She looks especially beautiful, her face radiant with softness and charm. The panicky eyes exist no more; now her gaze has a dazzling fascination, like a shining constellation.

Sitting peacefully and confidently in the chair, she says to the young dentist beside her, like a mistress commanding her attendant: "Let's begin."

In his right hand, the young dentist holds a full syringe, the needle pointing straight up as if it were a loaded pistol ready to fire. He waves it in front of Miss Dai Er and asks, "Are you sure?"

Dai Er smiles. "I'm sure."

She opens her mouth wide, calmly accepting the highly symbolic hypodermic as it stabs her soft palate. Following a momentary sting, her mouth is suffused with a warm, sweet numbness. Sunshine enters her mouth, penetrates her jaw, permeates her tongue; it dances trippingly and sings gracefully in her mouth. A pink smile spills out over her lips.

The young Dr. Kong Sen bends over her, and even though the white gauze mask hides his lips, Dai Er can still feel the hot breath greeting her. The dentist holds forceps or scalpel in his right hand, and with his left arm he presses against her chest for support. This weight stirs her imagination wonderfully. The young dentist deftly extracts two impacted wisdom teeth from Miss Dai Er's mouth, one from each side. When they work together like that, Miss Dai Er feels no pain. She cooperates obediently and meekly. They seem to be hovering together, distantly light as a feather, the sky covered with their rainbow arcs. This intimate cooperation and harmony resurrects the memory of sharing her husband's bed on their wedding night.

When the young Dr. Kong Sen noisily drops the two bloody wisdom teeth onto the milky tray, the secret anguish deeply buried in Miss Dai Er's remote past is finally uprooted.

TRANSLATED BY SHELLEY WING CHAN

# Grass on the Rooftop

## LI XIAO

This story was ignited by being cooked up over a fire. Perhaps you think this is an exaggeration bordering on sensationalism: after all, how can a fire cook up a story? Now if we were talking about cooking a bowl of soup noodles or something. . . . But in our little village of thirty or forty households, where a story about somebody's chicken dying is front-page news, a fire is really a major event. So you can imagine the stir that was created by the unusual fire that hit the house of the pensioner Old Mr. Chen. The old-timers of the village, who say that everything in this world has a cause and an effect, concluded that the fire was a result of the ancestors' spirits having somehow been offended, maybe because the house wasn't situated just right or because of some evil deed carried out by an earlier generation or because of an act of defiance initiated by the younger generation. But the fact is that even if Mr. Chen, a childless old man, had committed any terrible offenses, he'd certainly have owned up to them by now, and he'd never provoked anyone. So how could a huge fire strike him? That's why we've all maintained there was something fishy in the way this incident occurred.

Of course, not everyone agrees with this interpretation. Our friend Xie doesn't. He insists he saw flames coming out of a crack in Old Chen's chimney a long time ago, and not just once, either. It was as if the lower part of the chimney had a piece of crimson cloth fastened to it that flapped in the wind. The team leader was a little miffed over this and asked him why he hadn't spoken up about it at the time, but Xie (whom we called the Crabman) countered, "How was I supposed to know it could burn through to the roof? If you look up at my chimney, you'll notice a few fingers of fire leaking from it, too."

The truth of the matter is if there were a blacklist of firetraps, there's little doubt that the house occupied by those young high school graduates from Shanghai would have been on it. If you don't believe me, you can go stand at the entrance to the village and look up at the roof of each household. There'll be no need to ask who's poor, who's well-off, and who's really able to manage his resources—your eyes won't deceive you. The roofs of the poor people are smoothed out and covered with rice straw and wheat stalks; those of the well-off families are covered with a reddish grass brought all the way from Dahong Mountain; and those who are even a little richer have smooth, gray tiles attached to the eaves. The rooftops of those who can really manage their resources are fashioned from wheat stalks and shiny green tiles. But regardless of whether the people are rich or poor, the straw for the eaves has been clipped off, all nice and tidy, and the top is as smooth as a mirror. Not only is it attractive, but the rainwater drains well and isn't always backing up. Now take another look at the house of the students from Shanghai—who knows how many dynasties it has endured? The wheat stalks have been washed white by the rains, the eaves are so soaked they've started to turn black, and the tip of the roof is so full of bumps and hollows it looks like a small pasture where sheep graze. The wind has blown some grass seed up to the rooftop, so a patch of new grass is growing there. Then there's that chimney, all crooked and slanting, as if it were about to topple to the ground; even if it doesn't fall, you never know when it might spray sparks onto the ground.

There's another factor that must be taken into account. It was a scorcher on the day of the fire, so hot that sweat gushed off the workers. Out in the countryside, there aren't any thermometers, so I can't tell you the exact temperature, but I heard someone say that if you stood facing the sun for half a second, you'd be gasping for air, and the sweat would wash out of your pores and evaporate in the air without leaving a speck of salt on your body. The physics textbook we used in middle school said there are two factors needed for combustion to occur: oxygen and high temperature. Since both these factors were at optimal conditions, a fire was inevitable. What's odd is that our book mentioned nothing about cause and effect. But as we said before, this was a middle school textbook, something for kids to read; seldom do such books touch upon matters involving adults or elderly people.

Since it was so hot, they went to work extra late that afternoon. Some of the guys who lived under that grassy roof were just returning from dreamland. The one called Four Eyes by his friends was tossing about on his bed. He turned and faced south, trying to determine by the patch of sunlight on the door across from him what time it was. His friend, who was nicknamed the Professor, was holding a book to his heart, chanting poetry with his eyes closed. The Crabman was reading a letter. Abe Lincoln (so named because of his idealistic belief in truth and justice) had already got up. Of course at the time, none of them imagined there was a fire; all they were thinking about was how to get through the rest of the day. The team leader, who was in his own backyard and separated from these fellows by two mud walls, stretched and gave an earth-shattering yawn, signifying that he was ready to pick up his hoe and sling it over his shoulder. He stuck his whistle into his mouth, but instead of blowing it to send the men back to work, he savored that last remaining second of leisure.

When the sound of his whistle did finally pierce the silence, the Crabman and the Professor were both talking, but what they were saying didn't necessarily have any direct bearing on the fire. The Professor was reading a poem that went something like this:

> An entire life spent delighting in spreading out my books;
> As I approach old age, this earlier madness remains.
> At midday, I read in the southern sunlight;
> As the sun sets, I scurry to catch the light at the east window.

What the Crabman was saying went something like this: "Nowadays what's really great is for a guy who's stuck here like us to have a girlfriend in Shanghai, whether she's got a job or not!"

Both Four Eyes and Abe Lincoln sneered contemptuously. All three of them responded to the Crabman's little speech by looking at one another in blank dismay, as if they couldn't make heads or tails of what he meant. When the team leader walked past the door carrying his hoe, the four of them reluctantly straggled out of the room. If there's any truth to what the old-time villagers say about how hot it was that day, the students should already have been able to taste the scorched, charred flavor of the sun's rays.

They started hoeing corn. When they'd finished about half of that field, the team leader ordered half of the men to hoe the sorghum up on the ridge. Four Eyes and the Crabman held on to their hoes and didn't budge, so the Professor and Abe Lincoln went. Actually, the two of them didn't have to go; Four Eyes and the Crabman certainly could have gone, but Fate stepped in at this point, dictating that those two go up the hill and the other two stay behind. And that is how the task of being the main character of our story fell to the Crabman. As Abe Lincoln and the Professor walked farther and farther away from the house that was destined to burn down (of course, they were oblivious of this), they discussed the Crabman's puzzling comment.

"What do you think the Crabman meant? I believe I've heard him say it before," said the Professor.

"I don't know," said Abe Lincoln, "but have you noticed that the Crabman only goes on like that after he's got a letter from Shanghai?"

If conditions had allowed them to continue probing into this matter, no doubt they'd have soon figured it out. After all, we know that once the waves settle, the truth surfaces. And had that been the case, our story would have ended here. The two of them were racking their brains when suddenly they heard shouts from below the ridge. As they looked toward the village, they could see a hazy, nearly transparent speck of red flickering intermittently atop Old Chen's house. At that second, those with the quickest reactions sped down the hill. Abe Lincoln and the Professor ran after them.

Anyone who had the good fortune to see the huge fire at the Cultural Square in Shanghai or the disastrous department store blaze in Beijing or the even more impressive fire in Changsha will doubtless be deeply disappointed by our story. Old Chen's single-room house was off in a corner by itself, in the western part of the village. Even had it been possible for the mud walls to catch fire, I rather doubt that the building could have gone up in a really big blaze. But of course, the small scale of the fire should not detract from the courage of those brave and daring villagers who quelled the flames, not in the least. Any fire is life threatening, whether it's a major conflagration or a lesser blaze.

So when the Crabman charged into Old Chen's house, he unquestionably put his life on the line for at least a few seconds. What happened then was stated accurately in the article that ran in the *Eastern Anhui News:*

> It was a raging inferno, the thick, suffocating smoke from which threatened the life of Mr. Chen, a poor farmer. In this life-and-death crisis, the Crabman recalled the heroic efforts of Huang Jiguang and Qiu Shaoyun during the Korean War, and he remembered those modern revolutionary figures Ouyang Hai and Lei Feng, who sacrificed their lives for the good of the country. It was as if the flames directed him to act—he scrambled in front of his fellow villagers and, like a powerful, intrepid eagle, rushed toward the raging fire . . .

Here there's a slight problem: who actually was the first to jump in at the scene of the fire? By the time the Professor and Abe Lincoln raced over, that particular act of our little drama was already concluded. It's true that Four Eyes stood outside the house, immobilized, like a piece of wood nailed to the wall, but it's difficult to say why he did so. The villagers were divided over the issue of who entered the house first: some said it was the Crabman, some said it was the team leader. However, that's relatively unimportant.

In any case, it was the Crabman and the team leader who helped Old Chen out of the house, one on either side—that much was obvious to everyone.

After he helped Old Chen out, the Crabman charged back into the sea of flames and succeeded in rescuing an old quilt. At the same time, the villagers managed to take out of the house anything of the slightest value. (Frankly speaking, there was nothing of any real value. If there had been, how could Old Chen have qualified for a government pension for all these years?) According to the newspaper, as soon as the Crabman's foot was out the door, a burning beam crashed and knocked a millstone-sized hole in the floor. Of course, the hole was no larger than the size of a teacup, and the beam hadn't caught his leg, as the report implied. The rescue work was completed by the time the people on the ridge came racing down. They watched the fire burn for about six or seven minutes before they heard the crash of the burning beam as it fell to the floor. But no one questioned this point. After all, when writing a story, how can you keep from spicing things up a bit? Everyone understands that. Don't forget that even though most of the villagers aren't literate, they still possess a fair amount of common sense.

The fire was extinguished. Everyone breathed a sigh of relief, except for the pensioner himself, who was sitting on the ground and bellowing cries of anguish. Things could have been worse: at least no one died. And anyway, what's one house? At most, it came to a mere two thousand catties of straw, and since the beam wasn't made of solid pine or fir, it could certainly be replaced easily enough by any odd-shaped piece of lumber.

Because of all this, the team leader was feeling quite good. He was pleased that they'd now be able to take the rest of the day off, and it appeared that for all intents and purposes, the incident was over and done with.

After he returned home, our hero, the Crabman, changed into his swimming trunks and went for a dip in the large pond beyond the village. Four Eyes, the Professor, and Abe Lincoln were busy getting dinner ready. They had just made the dough, rolled it out into wheat cakes, and were now waiting for the wok to heat up. As they stood near the hot stove, a quarrel erupted because Abe Lincoln kept pestering Four Eyes about why he hadn't helped put out the fire.

Four Eyes, defending himself, said, "There were already plenty of people inside the house. If I'd gone in, it would only have added to the confusion."

"That's no reason," said Abe Lincoln.

"I *couldn't* go. 'I think therefore I am; if I take action, I shall perish,' " Four Eyes said.

"That's the Prince of Denmark speaking—not Four Eyes," the Professor said.

Four Eyes flew into a rage. "So then what am I? It sounds like you won't be satisfied until my body is consumed by a sea of flames! I know what you want me to say. OK, I'll admit I was scared. Now are you satisfied? The truth is I wasn't scared at all, and I was quite clearheaded about everything. But for some reason at that moment, I just couldn't get my feet to move."

That was one minor episode. There was another. The team leader was squatting near the doorstep, smoking a pipe. After he'd had enough nicotine to satisfy his craving, he knocked out the ashes, then vented his moral outrage over the way the Crabman had shamelessly paraded by in a pair of low-cut swimming trunks. The team leader was speaking in behalf of the untainted youth of the village. As the Crabman splashed about in the pond, the teenagers were so shocked that they covered their faces and cried out. "We don't go in for that sort of thing in our little village," the team leader remarked. "Just look how skimpy his trunks are. Why, you can see his pubic hair!"

Just then the team leader's wife broke in, shouting at her husband at the top of her lungs that there wasn't any water in the vat, and he rushed off to get some. This left unresolved the question of whether the teenagers had cried out from shock or whether they were just joking around. Were they so scandalized that they'd run off, or were they still hanging around at the edge of the pond?

When they covered their faces and closed their eyes, had they, in fact, peeked through their fingers? Although these suspicions filled everyone's head, the answers remain unknown. This, however, is irrelevant. The reason we include these minor episodes is merely to prove that at this point in our story, no one in the village considered the Crabman much of a hero. Nor did anyone forgive his lack of modesty because of his earlier show of bravery. But did the team leader really have the right to berate him this way? After all, the two of them had dashed into the sea of flames at practically the same moment. In any case, by the time evening fell, neither the Crabman nor anyone else in the village, apart from the team leader (who was still concerned about the couple of thousand catties of straw he would have to give Old Chen to rebuild his house), was thinking about the fire that afternoon.

The whole matter would have been forgotten if it hadn't been for the team leader's son, Little Shuanzhu, who was a student at the commune middle school. Since he couldn't come up with anything better to write about, the event found its way into one of his compositions. And if it hadn't been for his teacher, who had always wanted to be a writer herself and who corrected and practically rewrote the story by turning it into a radio script; and if it hadn't been for the fact that the commune broadcasting station stepped in and sent the script to the district; and if it hadn't been for the fact that when the script arrived at the district broadcasting station, a reporter from the *Eastern Anhui News* happened to be there (God only knows why: did he have some official business, or was he visiting friends or relatives, or was he just so tired from walking that he'd stopped there to take a break?)—in any event, he was there and he happened to see the script; if it hadn't been for all these coincidences, the entire incident of the fire would certainly have been closed. Now you know, were it not for all the "if it hadn't been for's" that one encounters, one's achievements and potential ability (in politics, military service, cultural and artistic endeavors, etc.) would no doubt sink into oblivion. Some people have, in fact, disappeared into oblivion precisely because they lacked the "if it hadn't been for's" in certain situations. When you think about it, don't you just want to sigh in despair?

At this point, "coincidences" fade into the background as we touch upon the reporter from the *Eastern Anhui News* who happened upon the script. At once, his keen, X ray–like investigative abilities surfaced as he realized the potential value of this bit of news. He put aside the work that had brought him to the broadcasting station in the first place (God only knows what it was), hopped onto the last bus of the day, and spent the night cramped up in the dark, dingy, commune hostel. The next day, he found the soundman at the commune broadcasting station, through whom he was able to contact the middle school teacher, who in turn put him in touch with Little Shuanzhu. On the third day, he personally went to visit the small brigade.

I don't need to tell you that from the very first day Shuanzhu brought home the news that the fire would make the papers, the entire village was in an uproar. "Reporters—""coming—" "to investigate." Investigate what? The villagers whispered among themselves and engaged in endless debates—after all, nothing like this had ever happened before. The eldest resident in the village, the venerable Mr. Liu, could date events as far back as 1905. But no one knew much about anything that had happened before then. In any case, no one with comparable experience of those early days had come to this little village. Even during the time of the Great Leap Forward, when more than fifty people in the village had starved to death, no one came to investigate. So the older people said assuredly, "This, and I'm speaking of the peculiar circumstances surrounding that fire, is going to cause a real stir, just you wait and see."

Sitting on his heels by the students' doorstep, the team leader puffed on his pipe. Then he said, in a voice that showed how deeply troubled and exasperated he was, "You guys have got to come up with an idea to get me out of this mess!"

You haven't heard what Shuanzhu told the team leader, his father, so naturally you can't understand why the team leader was so upset. The reporter had told Shuanzhu that since this was the very first time a Shanghai high school graduate had risked his life to rescue someone from a local fire, he wanted to write a story about the Crabman. He wanted to interview the Crabman and Old Chen, and he also wanted to meet with all the high school graduates, the team leader, the secretary of the Party branch, and the representative of the peasants' association. You might be saying to yourself, So they have a meeting, what's the big deal? But you must realize that in this village, the team leader was, in fact, the secretary of the Party branch, and the secretary of the Party branch was, in fact, the representative of the peasants' association. In short, all these positions were held by the same person, and this person happened to be Shuanzhu's father. The team leader was not concerned about whether the reporter held a high official rank, nor was he worried that the reporter was in a position to have him removed as Party-branch secretary or representative of the peasants' association. What concerned him, apart from having to hold meetings for a few days (for which he wouldn't earn a penny), was how in the world his one pitiful mouth would be able to spit out enough words for three different people.

For all intents and purposes, there simply was no solution to the dilemma faced by the team leader. But then again, you have to understand the temperament of these Shanghai students—they never give up in the face of adversity. "I've got it," Four Eyes said, *"I'll* be the representative of the peasants' association. I look old for my age."

As good as his word, he did indeed carry out the scheme. The team leader brought a white Chinese-style jacket from home and gave it to Four Eyes to wear. Four Eyes also changed his shoes for a pair of small cloth "peasant" slippers. He took off his glasses, and Abe Lincoln rubbed a few ashes on the bridge of his nose to cover up the red indentations. The Professor said he looked just right: when Four Eyes blinked, it looked like he had trachoma. The Crabman was still worried that the effect wasn't complete, so he found a towel (one of those brand-name towels from Shanghai) and tried to wrap it like a turban around Four Eyes' head. Four Eyes absolutely refused to wear it. "You're not going to make me look like a hick," he said.

The next day, the reporter came to the village, and the team leader made such a fuss you'd think somebody was getting married. Bare-bottomed toddlers shouted and squealed with excitement as they escorted him to the students' house. On the other hand, the adults, without exception, slammed their doors shut and stayed inside. The Crabman, the Professor, and Abe Lincoln sat on the bed, leaving the three stools for the reporter, the team leader, and the representative of the peasants' association. Several bold youngsters pressed close to the reporter and stared at his notebook and even rubbed the material of his clothing with their fingers. No matter how experienced and knowledgeable a reporter might be, he'd still find it difficult not to fidget in circumstances such as these. The team leader and the representative consulted briefly and decided to kick the people out and shut the door. Actually, by the time they closed the door, the villagers were already pretty fed up. "So this is a reporter," someone outside the room was heard to say. "How come he looks just as poor and hard up as a schoolteacher? Is there something we're missing? Do you think he can sing local opera?"

Whether or not the reporter could sing local opera remains unclear, but he certainly could talk! Almost all the talking that day was done by him and the representative of the peasants' association (you of course remember that this was Four Eyes); the former monopolized the first half of the discussion, and the latter dominated the second half. Every now and then, the team leader and the high school graduates somehow managed to get in a word or two. There's no need to relate the reporter's opening remarks here since everyone can more or less imagine what he said. We also don't intend to go into what Four Eyes said, for that can all be found in the editorials that came out in the revolutionary newspapers and magazines that year. What we *do* want to reveal is a few words that were spoken right before the meeting adjourned. After all, as experience has shown, there comes a moment in steeping tea when it tastes just right.

"Well, that's enough for today. I think I have the overall picture," the reporter said as he closed his notebook. "But I can't help feeling the material is a little too ordinary. How should I put it? It doesn't quite have enough punch. It needs something special to catch the reader's eye."

"Something special?" asked Four Eyes. "I've been stuck in this village for some thir-thir-thirty years, and I've seen hundreds of fires put out, but I can't say I've ever seen anything *special* about them."

"What I meant was the second time he rushed in to the sea of flames," the reporter said, pointing to the Crabman, "all he came out with was an old quilt. I mean, don't you think that's rather anti-climactic? Don't you think it would make a flashier story if he had come out with, say, a few scrolls of Chairman Mao's writings or a sacred portrait of the chairman?"

"But an old quilt was all I brought out," the Crabman insisted. "And anyway, Old Chen's house didn't have a picture of Chairman Mao."

It's at this moment that we discover the difference between being a reporter and being a high school graduate. We can also see how someone who consciously makes use of his brain approaches problems.

"Comrade, you can stop with the 'I' and 'my,'" the reporter said with a smile. "We are not the least bit interested in using you, as an individual, for propaganda. What's an individual, anyway? We owe all our achievements to the Party and to the people. The reason for reporting a story about you is to provide a good model, so that other high school graduates can learn from your example. The potential power of such a model is boundless! Do you follow me? Now do we want people to imitate your dragging out some old quilt, or would we rather have them emulate your undying dedication to the chairman? Why don't you think about it for a while? You can write a short statement and give it to me tomorrow, OK?"

That night, if you had rushed over to the room where the students from Shanghai lived, you'd probably have thought they were holding an open discussion meeting. Four Eyes was sitting in front of the oil lamp, pen and paper in hand; the Crabman was standing behind him with an expectant look on his face; Abe Lincoln and the Professor were already in bed. Even though the seating arrangement was casual, they expressed their opinions with utmost seriousness.

"So do we vote for or against the reporter's proposal?" asked Four Eyes.

"Against! That man is an out-and-out liar," Abe Lincoln said firmly.

"Yes, we should vote against it. Otherwise, people will say that all I can do is show off," the Crabman said somewhat hesitantly.

"However," interrupted the Professor, "as the saying goes, When it comes to important people, not every statement can be believed, and not every act comes to fruition."

"So should we just write what happened?" Four Eyes asked.

"Of course the facts demand it," Abe Lincoln said, remaining resolute.

"But in that case, maybe he won't use the story," the Crabman said, still somewhat uncertain.

" 'Look not upon something that is not proper; act not upon something that is not correct,' " quoted the Professor. "Who cares whether or not he uses the story?"

"I've got a plan that might satisfy everyone," Four Eyes said as he picked up his pad of paper. "Listen to this: 'After I helped Old Chen the pensioner out of his house, I remembered his portrait of Chairman Mao. Of course it would have been impossible to leave that bright and glorious portrait in the fire. So, burning with righteous fervor, I charged back into the sea of flames. The thick smoke stung my eyes so badly that tears blurred my vision; the tongues of fire leaped toward me, but driven by ardent loyalty, I summoned up the courage to forge ahead. When I felt the wall, I looked up and—it was as if a weight pressing up against my heart suddenly fell to the ground—there was no portrait on the wall! I grabbed a quilt from the bed and rushed out of the room.' " Four Eyes was triumphantly smug as he looked around at his three friends. "What do you think?" he asked. "A case of going in like a lion and out like a lamb. You must admit it's a lot more lively."

"But can I really say that?" The Crabman was still somewhat hesitant.

"What's wrong with it? I ask you, if at that moment there really had been a sacred portrait of the chairman in the fire, would you have carried it out with you?"

"Probably, I would have."

"So why are you being such a stick-in-the-mud? Be a little more positive. When it comes right down to it, would you have taken it or not?"

"Most likely, I would have."

"Well, then, I rest my case."

Consequently, this was the statement they gave to the reporter. And so once more, we have proof that these students from Shanghai were not in the habit of being overcome by difficulties.

After the reporter returned to his district, many days passed without incident. And since the villagers spent their days fiercely hoeing the fields of corn and sorghum, they apparently forgot the matter. But the Crabman hadn't forgotten. After all, for him, it had been a personal experience, so his feelings about the subject were quite different from the gossip passed back and forth by mere observers. He sent letter after letter to Shanghai in which he boasted of his achievement to friends and relatives. The Professor could see him consulting the statement Four Eyes had written for him as he wrote these letters.

One day, Four Eyes and the others caught the Crabman completely off guard. He had just finished writing a letter and was standing near the kitchen stove, sealing the envelope with some sticky rice. As you know, some people feel elated after they have accomplished some task at hand. Take, for example, the way the team leader acted each time he got a haircut: he'd get a blissful look on his face, close his eyes, and hum a few bars of his favorite opera. The Crabman said, "Well, for guys like us, whoever has a girl-friend in Shanghai—"

"Whether she's got a job or not," Four Eyes interjected.

Abe Lincoln took up where Four Eyes left off, "A guy like that—"

Now the Professor chimed in, looking quite pleased with himself: ". . . is truly great!"

The Crabman, who still had the word *Shanghai* on his lips, registered a shocked look.

On their way to work, Abe Lincoln asked Four Eyes about the underlying meaning in the Crabman's comment.

"It's black and white," Four Eyes explained. "When he says, 'For guys like us, whoever has a girlfriend in Shanghai,' he means he has a girlfriend in Shanghai. 'Whether she's got a job or not' means his girlfriend doesn't have a job. She just hangs around the house, living off her family. In short, it means he thinks he's one great guy. I can read him like a book!"

Four Eyes might have analyzed the man's thoughts a little more thoroughly (maybe he was thinking of doing just that), but at that precise moment someone was running down the path, shouting. It was Shuanzhu, running like a scared rabbit. With one hand, he was holding his book bag tightly against his chest; with the other, he was waving a wad of—no, wait a minute, it was newspapers. If you'd seen the way he looked, you'd have thought he was a paper-boy shouting out the latest hot-news item.

There's no need to tell you, since you've all guessed by now, what was written up in that newspaper. Four Eyes picked up a copy, opened it, and there on the front page was a banner printed in red: LOYAL HEART SEEN IN BLAZING FLAMES OF ROARING FIRE: SHANGHAI HIGH SCHOOL GRADUATE RISKS LIFE TO SAVE POOR PEASANT. Why, you didn't even have to read the article. Just looking at the color of the print was enough to make you think of red flames!

The contents of the article were more or less the same as the first draft that Four Eyes had come up with. To be more precise, the first part was exactly the same; just the ending was a little different. Phrases like "burning with righteous fervor," "charged back into the sea of flames," "the thick smoke stung my eyes," "tears blurred my vision," and "ardent loyalty" had all been left in. They had just been changed from the first person to the third person. But there was an added twist after the part that recorded his courageous advance. The article read: "He felt the wall, very carefully lifted the portrait down, and stuffed it under his jacket, pressing it close to his fervently burning heart. Next he turned around, yelled out, 'Long live Chairman Mao,' then rushed out of the building." Sometimes there is no such thing as compromise. Either the "east wind will prevail over the west," as Chairman Mao said, or the west wind will prevail over the east. How could Four Eyes fail to understand this fundamental concept? If you could take a minute to look at our characters now, you'd see that the Professor was scratching his head, Abe Lincoln was muttering something, Four Eyes was wide-eyed and tongue-tied, while our hero, the Crabman, had just plunked his butt down on the muddy ground as if somebody had kicked him in the shins.

Actually, the Crabman was afraid that the villagers would revile him for being such an egomaniac, and for the time being he didn't even dare raise his head. But regardless of what had happened, nobody was going to say anything disagreeable (didn't we already tell you the villagers said they'd seen just about everything?). After dinner, the team leader brought the newspaper over and sat on his heels by the doorstep. Once again, the Crabman was overcome by a sense of guilt and slipped away to hide behind the mosquito netting. Actually, he'd jumped to the wrong conclusion; the team leader had come there to ask one of the students to mark in red the passages in the article that referred to him. You see, since he couldn't read, he didn't know which parts featured him. As Abe Lincoln picked up a pen, he discovered that there really were quite a number of passages to be marked. Of course, the Crabman's exploits were inseparable from the topic of reeducating the poor and lower-middle peasants; so at each mention of poor and lower-middle peasants, how could the article not refer to the Party secretary, the team leader, and the representative of the peasants' association? Four Eyes asked the team leader why he hadn't told Shuanzhu simply to underline the relevant passages for him. The team leader threw down his pipe and swore, "That damned kid! I haven't seen a trace of him since dinner." Actually, we shouldn't blame Little Shuanzhu. Just think, from the time he finished hoeing the field until after dinner, he had already read the entire article to his father twenty times.

Henceforth, there were *two* famous people in our village. One was the team leader—he tucked that newspaper with all the red marking into his pant pocket, right next to his beloved pipe and his house keys, and took it with him wherever he went. Whenever he ran into a cadre from the production brigade at the commune or someone he was close to—a friend or a relative or even just the neighborhood street vendor—he would take out the article and show him the passages that were marked. And what would he do? He'd silently sit off to one side with a big grin on his face and smugly puff on his pipe.

Of course, the other famous person was the Crabman. The elementary school run by the people at the production brigade invited him to give their next presentation. The middle school at the commune also invited him to give a talk. The commune called a huge gathering of all the young high school graduates in the commune for the express purpose of having him speak. Just look at him as he takes the podium—he appears composed and at ease, and his words flow so eloquently, not a trace of guilt to be seen. Before long, there was a large meeting of the activist representatives from among the various high school graduates throughout the province (those who had answered the Party's call to go up to the mountains and down to the countryside), and naturally the Crabman was asked to be one of the representatives. Strutting about with an air of arrogance, he set out for the meeting.

It was early August, and the hoes had been put away. The team leader was in a position to help the old pensioner rebuild his house. Come to think of it, there really wasn't anything so hard about it. The four walls were still intact. In fact, after having withstood the fire, if anything, they were sturdier. All that had to be done was add a little adobe, patch up the gable, put up the reed frame for the house beams, and smooth out some straw on top. Building houses is considered technical work, not something those Shanghai students had ever been involved in. But this time, the team leader asked Four Eyes, the Professor, and Abe Lincoln to help out by passing up some straw or by handing him a spade or some such task. This may also have been a consequence of the Crabman's actions during the fire.

During that time, the team leader went to the commune once, maybe to attend a meeting for third-level cadres, maybe an enlarged meeting of the Party committee. Or could it have been a general meeting of the representatives of the peasants' associations? Anyway, it was some kind of meeting. Of course, there was no way he would leave behind that article from the *Eastern Anhui News*. We can verify that by then, his copy of the newspaper was already starting to fall apart from so much handling. It was torn at the corners, and the places that had been marked in red were nearly illegible. But what did that matter? Those particular phrases had already bored their way into the depths of the team leader's heart. No matter where you put your finger, he could recite the passage from memory. However, this does not concern us here. Instead, let's turn to several letters he picked up from the post office and brought back to the students after the meeting was over.

There was one each for the Professor and Abe Lincoln but none for Four Eyes; the letter Four Eyes was holding in his hand was for the Crabman. First, he looked at the front; then he turned it over to look at the back; next he looked again at the front. He brought it up to within two inches of his eyes and, squinting one eye, scrutinized it. Next he went outside and held the letter up to the sun and shook it slowly. From the way he was acting, you might have thought he was a bank teller examining a forged bill.

"Well, what did you find out?" asked the Professor.

"Look," said Four Eyes as he handed the letter over to the Professor. "Now for guys like us, whoever has a girlfriend in Shanghai—"

"Whether she's got a job or not?" the Professor said with an expression that reflected his doubt. "What makes you think it's a letter from her? All that's written on the envelope is 'Name and address of sender confidential.'"

"Wanna bet? Why not just open it and have a look?"

"How can we open the Crabman's personal mail? That's not right, is it?" asked the Professor.

"Hey, Four Eyes, don't you dare open it. If you do, I'll tell the Crabman," Abe Lincoln chimed in.

Have you heard the slogan Fight selfishness, repudiate revisionism? Have you ever personally experienced the complications and pain brought on by too much mental activity? Now take a look at Four Eyes. His eyes were getting bloodshot from staring so fixedly at that letter. His lower jaw was twitching nervously, his cheeks were puffed out, and sweat was pouring from his forehead. The sight he presented was that of a starving wolf tempted by a piece of bait. He was desperately struggling against his own selfish desires. Perhaps you might also feel the utter futility of his efforts. Thus you, too, would be able to breathe a sigh of relief when Four Eyes finally ended up shouting and grabbing the envelope out of the Professor's hand. "What the hell!" Four Eyes shouted. "If someone can't even be curious, then what kind of a person is he?"

Generally speaking, it's no easy matter to open an envelope without leaving a trace of its having been opened. But then again, since Four Eyes is not exactly your average individual, we can't use normal standards when we're dealing with him. According to his own conclusions, he should be categorized as a person with much baser instincts. He carefully made a small opening in a corner of the envelope and stuck a thin bamboo chopstick in the hole, then twisted it around and around until the letter was tightly wound around it. He removed the chopstick, and the letter popped out. Obviously, in a moment, he would be able to reverse the process and reinsert the letter into the envelope. In light of this, we cannot help but admit that there is nothing that cannot be accomplished as long as one has confidence, patience, a cool head, and nimble fingers.

As Four Eyes read the letter, he started to whistle. His expression was as tranquil as a calmed ocean. In fact, the tense scene he had just experienced now seemed instead to be reenacted by the Professor, who was itching for his turn. His neck was stretched so far it seemed as long as that of a wild crane. He said, "Forget it! So the Crabman will be angry. How long are you going to read it? What does it say? Hurry up and read it to us!"

"Why don't you read it yourself?" said Four Eyes.

The Professor glanced at it and shouted, "I told you you were full of shit! Right here it says, 'Dear Brother.' It's a letter from the Crabman's little sister."

"You don't understand the first thing about love letters," Four Eyes said with a trace of commiseration.

The Professor directed his full attention to the letter, mumbling all the while, "Oh! So that's how it is. . . . What does this mean? What does she mean 'Do you still care about me?' " When he reached the last paragraph, the hand holding the letter suddenly dropped. His face was covered with an expression of horror. "What? She wants to break up with the Crabman?"

"To break up with one guy one minute in favor of another in Shanghai the next—I wouldn't say she's exactly facing any great loss," Four Eyes said without changing the tone of his voice. "As I see it, it's just another vulgar love tragedy."

Abe Lincoln finally abandoned his earlier ideals and read the letter from start to finish. All three of them were in the throes of depression. They were in low spirits not just for the Crabman but also for all the "guys like us." It's quite likely that none of them slept very well that night, because the next day when they woke up, Four Eyes got on the Professor for tossing and turning all night, the Professor yelled at Abe Lincoln for having talked in his sleep, and Abe Lincoln complained that Four Eyes must have a bladder problem, since he had got up at least eight times during the night. The result of this loss of sleep was that they decided to go downtown to eat at the conference center for district-level representatives. At least then they could be sure of getting some nutritious food, which might perk them up.

That year, there was a popular saying among the high school graduates: "As long as there's a meeting, no one will starve." Most of the time when one eats at a meeting, the rice is free. But what about the meat and vegetable dishes? Well, for that you rely on meal tickets. Now for a table for ten, as long as everyone's willing, it's no problem to add a few more people. What? Are they willing, you ask? Of course they are. After all, we're all just poor wanderers on this earth.

The Crabman was delighted to see them. He started boasting about what a hit he had made at the meeting, how many girls had their eyes on him, and how the district leader had come over to shake his hand, which meant either that he wanted to send him to the province-level meeting as a representative or possibly wanted to recommend him to go to college. But let us no longer dwell on the Crabman's inflated ego nor describe the way the Professor's eyes seemed to pop out of his head when he heard the word *college*. After all, we must not forget that our main characters came here to eat, so let us allow them first to go into the dining room.

With eyes as bright as candles, Four Eyes sized up the situation, table by table. The amount of knowledge needed for scrounging for food was immense since not only did our heroes want to eat, but they wanted to eat well. After all, how else could they accomplish their goal of having a nutritious meal to perk them up? Based upon our experience, the best choice is to sit at a table occupied by female high school graduates. You know just how sophisticated those young ladies from Shanghai can be in front of their male peers. They'll eat only a small bowl of rice and occasionally, very occasionally, daintily pick up a morsel of food. Even then, they look at the food with expressions of disdain on their faces. They say they're full even though their bowls aren't empty and may raise their eyes and sigh in amazement as they say, "Really, I don't know what's wrong, but I just don't feel like eating." Of course, who are we to pass judgment on them? Maybe they would rather starve themselves than see their male classmates return home disappointed because they haven't eaten their fill. If that were really the case, then these young girls should be praised for having been blessed with the radiant, majestic glory that emanates from maternalism and love.

All roads lead to Rome. Four Eyes' choice just happened to coincide with our own. Since he understood the rules of etiquette far better than we, he appeared unwilling to accept other people's kindness without offering some sort of payment. After all, if he was going to eat somebody's stir-fried beef, he was definitely going to give them the benefit of his knowledge. Consequently, one could hear the uninterrupted sound of jokes and laughter coming from that table. You can imagine just how adorable those girls looked as they covered their mouths and giggled. Of course, they had no time to eat, which was perfectly normal and proper. The problem arose when Four Eyes brought up the subject of the Crabman's rescuing Old Chen, a topic of conversation that the Crabman did not find funny in the least. He shot a glance at Four Eyes, in which we can detect the silent suffering of a tough young man whose pride has been seriously wounded. What's more, the flavor of this suffering seemed to be doubly intense. From this episode, we can gain a profound moral lesson: never tell jokes about a man in front of a woman.

Unfortunately, Four Eyes had never learned this lesson, and there he was at the dining room table, bringing up that same old story one more time. The Crabman put down his rice bowl and dragged Four Eyes over to the corner. With a stern look on his face, he said, "A person should be a little more tactful when he speaks. Do you understand? Everything isn't just a big joke."

"Huh? Do you mean the part about saving the portrait?" Four Eyes still hadn't begun to take it seriously. "Don't tell me you're starting to believe the newspaper report?"

"The fact that there wasn't a portrait of Chairman Mao in the room isn't my fault. Hadn't I already risked my life by rushing in there? Can you blame me because Old Chen didn't hang up a picture? If he'd wanted to hang one up, don't you think I'd have helped him? In the ordinary course of events, every house should have a picture of Chairman Mao, so it follows that logically speaking, the newspaper report was accurate."

Four Eyes shook his head so hard his glasses nearly crashed to the floor; then he just stood there for a minute as if in a daze. You could see that he was trembling inside. Then he walked away. But he had only gone about two paces when he turned around, took the letter out of his pocket, and flung it at the Crabman. Then he stalked off, making it clear that he wasn't returning to the table. The Professor and Abe Lincoln exchanged glances. Finally, Abe Lincoln trailed after Four Eyes while the Professor stayed behind with the Crabman. At this point, it's hard to say whose loss was greater. There might have been another goal to this outing for the three of them (that is, apart from the idea of eating well to perk them up). But now that Four Eyes was gone, it's hard to gauge what the chances were of actualizing the goal.

We don't know how the Crabman felt after reading the letter. I heard about what happened later from the Professor. That night, the Crabman ignored the Professor's advice against going to the restaurant in town. Neither did he listen when the Professor tried to dissuade him from drinking so much. At the table next to them were several other young high school graduates from Shanghai who worked at the commune. The Crabman started arguing with one of them over some trivial matter, which resulted in black eyes and bruised faces all around. In the process, they managed to break several bowls and plates. The man who ran the restaurant was neither sympathetic nor amused. He called in the police, who took both sides into custody. Since the Crabman was an activist representative, he was handed over to the head of high school graduates in the district, who subjected him to a half-hour lecture. Luckily for him, this brought the incident to a close. However, from then on, there was no further mention of going to a province-wide meeting or being recommended to go to college or anything of the sort.

Can you actually say you don't feel sorry for the Crabman? Don't you think that he let things get a little out of hand? When you consider what a glorious future he had as a potential college student chosen from among all the activists in the province who answered the Party's call to go up to the mountains and down to the countryside (and getting into college then was certainly more difficult than it is now), it's hard to understand how he could throw everything away because of a girl. With all that going for him, could he possibly have been worried about not finding another girlfriend? Although your questions are perfectly reasonable from both the emotional and logical points of view, somehow the Crabman was unable to get this into his head. So we can only conclude that it must have been caused by the hand of Fate. Otherwise, as Four Eyes said, everything is predetermined by one's personality. In fact, it was that night, when the Crabman returned home so crestfallen, that Four Eyes delivered his famous lecture on how personality types are predetermined.

"Humans fall into three basic personality types," he announced. "Let me give you an example. The first type is called the prude, the second type is the womanizer, and the third is the pervert. That's to say, human desires can be elevated to the theoretical level. Now I'm a true pervert, so I'm not interested in taking any action unless that action is going to confirm my theories. Crabman, you're a womanizer, and that's why you drink and get into a fight over some trivial incident. The Professor is a prude, which is why he won't get involved in things like this. You see, the entire outcome of a person's life is predetermined by his personality type."

"You didn't mention Abe Lincoln. What type is he?" asked the Professor.

"I'm not exactly sure; he's so defensive it's hard to tell. I'd guess he's either a prude or a wild rapist."

The Crabman was seething. He said, "How the hell can he be a wild rapist when I'm just a womanizer?"

"A wild rapist is simply one type of womanizer. Most men are perverts of one kind or another. It's like class distinctions. There are a few at the two extremes, with the vast majority falling somewhere in between," Four Eyes was quick to explain.

* * *

The next day was another scorcher. Even the early-morning sun was so hot that everyone was panting from the heat. By the time the sun came out, the air was so suffocating that the ground seemed to tremble and the straw on the roofs softened into clumps. The two factors needed for combustion to occur were once again present; a single spark from a chimney might produce another story that would move you to song and tears. It was at this point that Abe Lincoln displayed a sign of that "wild" quality in keeping with his personality type (we really don't have the courage to repeat the particular indelicate term used earlier). He ran into the team leader's house, insisting that he immediately send someone to repair the leak in the chimney. "Otherwise, if a fire starts," he said, pointing to the roof, "I can promise you that as sure as two times two is four, it's going to be *your* house that goes up in flames next!" The team leader, who had been sitting on his heels by the doorstep, proceeded to give Abe Lincoln a sound dressing-down. "To talk like that in a farming village is counterrevolutionary. Why, it's even more reactionary than being counterrevolutionary!" Nonetheless, after lunch, he went over to Old Chen's and rounded up a couple of workers to replace the stovepipe for the students.

Since it was such a hot day, they didn't go to work until quite late in the afternoon. When Four Eyes woke up, sunlight had flooded the room. One particular patch of light was already boring its way into the door across from him. Two mud walls away, the team leader gave an earth-shattering yawn.

Four Eyes said, "Now for guys like us, whoever has a girlfriend, whether or not she's—"

The Crabman interrupted him: "I swear on that sacred portrait that I struggled so long and hard over that if anyone ever says that again, I'll smash his face in. I'm giving you fair warning, so don't anybody accuse me of turning against a friend."

"That reminds me of a poem," the Professor said as he sat up in bed.

"If you're planning to recite from a book or something, please spare us," said Abe Lincoln.

"It's nothing like that; it's not from a book. Listen: 'On such a calm and peaceful day, how sweet it is to play hooky.' "

The sound of the team leader's whistle split the long silence.

When a story begins to repeat itself, it's time to end it. But don't be in such a hurry, be patient for a couple of minutes longer, for we still have a short epilogue. That afternoon, the final touches were put on Old Chen's house. The last thing the team leader did was plaster the mud on the ridge of the roof and, for effect, place two gray bricks at an angle on the very top. After he came down from the roof, Old Chen began to set off firecrackers and gleefully passed out cigarettes. The house turned out pretty well. The straw was smoothed out flat and even, the hay for the eaves was clipped off all nice and tidy. The newly broken-off wheat stalks shone like strands of platinum. The team leader took a look inside the house and nodded his head in satisfaction. "It looks OK, doesn't it?" he said. "It's just lacking one thing." He unbuttoned his tunic and took out a sacred portrait of Chairman Mao that had been tucked away close to his heart. As he placed the portrait in the Crabman's hands, he said in a voice full of compassion, "Go hang it up. It was you who rescued it; now it should be you who hangs it up again."

While the Crabman was hanging the portrait, his hands were trembling. There was a moment when he was actually on the verge of tears, but he quickly rubbed his eyes and looked up at the straw room divider, acting as if a speck of dust or something had flown into his eye. We know he must have been feeling that he had somehow lost face (it appears that for the most part, all this was predetermined by personality type). But once again, he was wrong: no one laughed at him, not even Four Eyes. In fact, quite the contrary— Four Eyes told him later that this was the single most emotional and moving scene the production team had experienced in over three years.

TRANSLATED BY MADELINE K. SPRING

# The Past and the Punishments

## Yu Hua

On a summer night in 1990 in his muggy apartment, the stranger opened and read a telegram of unknown origin. Then he sank into deep reverie. The telegram consisted of just two words—RETURN QUICKLY—and indicated neither the name nor the address of the sender. The stranger, filing through the mists of several decades of memory, saw an intricate network of roads begin to unfold before him. And in this intricate network, only one road could bring the slightest of smiles to the stranger's lips. Early the next morning, the lacquer-black shadow of the stranger began to glide down that serpentine road like an earthworm.

Clearly, in the intricacy of the network that constituted the stranger's past, one memory, as fine as a strand of hair, had remained extraordinarily clear. March 5, 1965. A simple string of digits, arrayed in a specific and suggestive order, had determined the direction in which the stranger had begun to move. But in reality, at the same time that the stranger had decided upon his course, he had also failed to discover that his forward motion was blocked by yet another group of recollections. And because he had been standing at a remove from the bright mirror on his wall, he had been unaware of the ambiguity that had plagued his faint smile in the moments after he had deciphered the telegram. Instead, he had felt only stubborn self-confidence. It was precisely because of this excessive faith in himself that the procedural error that was to occur later on became unavoidable.

Several days later, the stranger arrived at a small town called Mist. It was here that the procedural error became apparent. The error was revealed to him by the punishment expert.

Imagine for a moment the stranger's face and posture as he walked through Mist. Besieged by several different strata of memory, he had been left virtually incapable of perceiving his immediate surroundings with any sort of clarity or accuracy. When the punishment specialist caught sight of the stranger for the first time, his heart cried out like a trumpet. The stranger entered the punishment specialist's field of vision like a lost child.

When the stranger walked past a gray, two-story building, the punishment specialist blocked his forward movement with an exaggerated grin. "You've come."

The punishment expert's tone sent a shock through the stranger's body. Although the stranger could hardly credit his own suspicions, it certainly seemed as if this man were hinting at the existence of a certain memory as he stood before him, his white hair gleaming.

The punishment expert continued, "I've waited for a long time."

This statement did nothing to help the stranger determine what role the man might have played in his past, if any at all. Perhaps he was simply a mote of dust floating across the vast expanse of his memory. The stranger sidestepped past the old man and continued on his way toward March 5, 1965.

Just as the punishment expert had hoped, however, the stranger failed to continue on toward March 5, 1965. Instead, a short and simple dialogue took place between the two men. And because of the punishment expert's warning—which was issued casually and without premeditation—the stranger began to understand his predicament. He discovered that his present course would not lead him to the desired destination. And thus he turned in the opposite direction. But the fact of the matter was that March 5, 1965, was receding farther and farther from him.

This was also the first time the stranger had thought back to the humid night when he had received the mysterious telegram.

For days, his mind had circled around the moment in which March 5, 1965, had emerged in his mind. Now his focus shifted. He began to ponder several other dates, other memories that had continued to disturb him even as they lay abandoned at the back of his mind. These memories were January 9, 1958, December 1, 1967, August 7, 1960, and September 20, 1971, respectively. And with this realization, the stranger began to understand why he was unable to move toward March 5, 1965. The telegram's message might have been just as relevant to these four dates as to March 5, 1965. Indeed, it was precisely these memories that had blocked his way to March 5, 1965. And each of these four events represented roads that ran in entirely different directions without ever intersecting with the other. So even if the stranger abandoned his search for March 5, 1965, he would be unable to find either January 9, 1958, or any one of the other three remaining dates.

This realization took place at dusk, when the stranger, thrown into a quandary by his procedural error, began to ponder how to escape his predicament. That was also when he began to devote his attention to the enigma represented by the punishment expert. He began to sense that the old man was a kind of elusive link to his past. This is why he had come to feel that their meeting had been arranged in advance.

As the sky darkened, the punishment specialist's intense excitement did not detract from a sense that he was in control of himself and of the flow of events around him. The stranger unsuspectingly yielded to some kind of preordination and followed the punishment specialist into the gray apartment building.

The living room walls were painted black. Here the stranger sat down without a word. The punishment expert switched on a little white electric lamp. The stranger began to search his mind for a link between the mysterious telegram and the room that surrounded him. He found something entirely different. He found that the path he had followed on his way to Mist had been crooked.

Almost as soon as the stranger and the punishment expert had sat down to talk, a remarkable affinity grew up between them. It was as if they had spent their lives huddled together in deep conversation, as if they were as familiar to each other as they were to the palms of their own hands.

The first topic of conversation, unsurprisingly, was broached by the stranger's host. He said, "Actually, we always live in the past. The past is forever. The present and the future are just little tricks the past plays on us."

The stranger acknowledged the force of the punishment expert's argument, but it was his own present that remained uppermost in his mind. "But sometimes you can be cut off from the past. Right now, something is tearing me away from my past." The stranger, rethinking his failure to approach March 5, 1965, was beginning to wonder if perhaps some other force besides that of the other four dates might be responsible.

But the punishment expert said, "You're not cut off from your past. Quite the contrary."

It wasn't simply that the stranger had failed to move in the direction of March 5, 1965. Instead, March 5, 1965, and the other four dates were receding farther and farther into the distance.

The punishment expert continued, "The fact is that you've always been deeply immersed in your past. You may feel cut off from the past from time to time, but that's merely an illusion, a superficial phenomenon, a phenomenon that at a deeper level indicates that you're really that much closer."

"I still can't help thinking that there's some force cutting me off from my past."

The punishment expert smiled helplessly, for he had sensed the difficulty of trying to overcome the stranger with language.

The stranger continued to move along his train of thought—at the very moment that he had left his past far behind him, the punishment expert had appeared before him with a strange smile and the cryptic assurance that "I've been waiting for you for a long time."

The stranger concluded, "You are that force."

The punishment expert was unwilling to accept the substance

of the stranger's accusation. Although he obviously found it tiresome, he patiently attempted to explain the situation to the stranger once again: "I haven't cut you off from your past. On the contrary, I have brought you into intimate conjunction with it. In other words, I am your past."

As the punishment expert spat out this last sentence, the tone of his voice made the stranger feel that the conversation might not continue very much longer. He nonetheless continued, "I find it hard to explain the fact that you were waiting for me."

"It would help if you could set aside the notion of necessity," the punishment expert continued, "and realize that I was waiting for a coincidence."

"That makes more sense," the stranger agreed.

The punishment expert, content, continued, "I'm very happy we are of one mind concerning this question. I'm sure we both understand just how very dull necessity really is. Necessity plods blindly and inexorably ahead on its accustomed track. But chance is altogether different. Chance is powerful. Wherever coincidences occur, brand-new histories are born."

The stranger, while concurring with the thrust of the punishment expert's theory, was preoccupied with an entirely different sort of question: "Why were you waiting for me?"

The punishment expert smiled. "I knew that question would come up sooner or later. I may as well explain now. I need someone to help me, someone endowed with the necessary spirit of self-sacrifice. I believe that you are just that sort of person."

"What kind of help?"

"You'll learn everything tomorrow. For now, I'll be happy to discuss my work with you. My calling is to compile a summation of all human wisdom. And the essence of human wisdom is the art of punishment. This is what I'd like to discuss with you."

The punishment expert clearly had an excellent grasp of his field. He was well versed in each and every one of the various punishments employed by mankind throughout its history. He provided the stranger with a simple and straightforward explanation of each punishment. His accounts of the bodily consequences of each punishment, once it had been carried out, were, however, stirring narratives in and of themselves.

Upon the conclusion of the punishment expert's lengthy and vivid discourse, the stranger realized with a shock that the punishment expert had neglected to touch on one rather important punishment: death by hanging. A dark, complex, and mercurial reverie had descended upon him just as the punishment expert had begun his lecture. He had somehow been anticipating the appearance of that particular punishment all along. As the punishment expert spoke, the blurred contours of March 5, 1965, had once again begun to clear. Given the circumstances, the hypothesis that someone intimately connected with the stranger's past had died by hanging on March 5, 1965, began to seem not entirely far-fetched.

The stranger, in an effort to escape from the dark grip of these memories, decided to point out the punishment expert's mistake. In doing so, he hoped to elicit another stirring discourse on this particular punishment and thus escape its grip.

His question served only to throw the punishment expert into a rage. It was not that he had overlooked a punishment, he shouted. He had just been ashamed to mention it at all. The dignity of that particular punishment, he proclaimed, had been trampled on by its indiscriminate and vulgar use by suicidal miscreants. He bellowed, "They were unworthy of such a punishment."

The punishment expert's unexpected rage released the stranger from the memories by which he had been besieged a moment before. After a taking a long breath, he directed another question to the punishment expert, who sat livid across the room: "Have you tried performing any of the punishments yourself?"

The punishment expert's rage was immediately extinguished by the query. Instead of replying, the punishment expert sank into a deep and boundlessly pleasurable reverie. Crows of memory flew across his features. He counted his inventory of punishments like a stack of bills. He told the stranger that of all the experiments he had carried out, the most moving had involved January 9, 1958, December 1, 1967, August 7, 1960, and September 20, 1971. It was clear that these dates hinted at things that went far beyond the numbers themselves. There was something of the aroma of blood about them. The punishment expert told the stranger how . . .

He had drawn and quartered January 9, 1958, tearing it into so many pieces that it had drifted through the air like a flurry of snowflakes. He had castrated December 1, 1967, cutting off its ponderous testicles so that there hadn't been a drop of sunshine on December 1, 1967, and the moonlight that evening had been as dense as overgrown weeds. Nor had August 7, 1960, been able to escape its fate, for he had used a rust-dappled saw blade to cut through its waist. But the most unforgettable was September 20, 1971. He had dug a trench in the ground, in which he had buried September 20, 1971, so that only the head was still exposed. Owing to the pressure exerted on the body by the surrounding earth, the blood of September 20, 1971, had surged up into the head. The punishment expert had proceeded to crack open its skull, from which a column of blood had immediately spurted forth. The fountain of September 20, 1971, had been incomparably brilliant.

The stranger fell into a silent, boundless despair. Each of the dates of which the punishment expert had spoken concealed a deep well of memory: January 9, 1958, December 1, 1967, August 7, 1960, and September 20, 1971. These were precisely the four events, isolated from the enormity of the stranger's past, that had been pursuing him all along.

The stranger, of course, had long been unaware of their pursuit. The four dates had become four musty breezes wafting toward him. The content that the dates concealed had hollowed, crumbled to dust and nothingness. But their aroma lingered on, and the stranger had the vague impression that if it weren't for these four dates, his strange encounter with the punishment expert would never have transpired.

The punishment expert rose from his chair and walked into his bedroom. As he moved past the white glare of the lamp, he resembled a recollection. The stranger sat motionless in his chair, tortured by a sense that March 5, 1965, was the only memory that he had left. Even March 5, 1965, was far away. It was only later, after he had already fallen asleep, that his features took on the serenity of a memory anchored firmly in the slipstream of the past.

When they resumed their conversation the next morning, there was no doubt that their affinity had grown even stronger. As soon as they began to talk, they arrived at the heart of the matter.

The punishment expert had suggested that he needed the stranger's help the night before. Now, he began to explain why: "Of all my punishments, only two have yet to be tested. One of them is reserved for you."

The stranger, in need of further explanation, was led into another black room. The room was empty save for a table in front of a window. A plate of glass covered the tabletop. The glass glittered in the sunlight pouring in through the window. Leaning against the wall was a sharpened butcher's knife.

Pointing at the glass by the window, the punishment expert said, "Look how very excited and happy it is."

The stranger walked over to the table, looking at the chaos of light playing through the glass.

Pointing at the butcher's knife leaning against the wall, the punishment expert told the stranger that he would use this knife to slice through his waist and cut him in half. Immediately thereafter, he would place the stranger's torso on the glass. His blood would continue to flow until he slowly died.

The punishment expert informed the stranger of just what it was that he would see before he bled to death on the glass. His description of the scene was compelling: "At that moment, you will feel a tranquillity you have never known before. All sounds will fade, will slowly become colors that will hover in front of your eyes. You will feel how your blood begins to flow more and more sluggishly, how it pools on the glass, and how it cascades into the dust below you like millions of strands of hair. And then finally, you will catch sight of the first dewdrop of the morning of January 9, 1958. You will see this dewdrop gazing at you from the dimness of a green leaf. You will see a bank of brilliant-colored clouds glowing in the noonday sun of December 1, 1967. You will see a mountain road. The road will wait patiently for you as the evening mist gathers overhead and night falls on August 7, 1960. You will see two fireflies dancing in the moonlight on the night of September 20, 1971, shining like a pair of distant tears."

Upon the conclusion of the punishment expert's serene narrative, the stranger sank once again into reverie. The dewdrops of January 9, 1958, the brilliant-colored clouds of December 1, 1967, the warm dusk on a mountain road on August 7, 1960, the fireflies like dancing tears in the moonlight of September 20, 1971—all these memories arrayed themselves like empty canvases before the stranger's roving eyes. He understood the punishment expert's narrative as a promise of things to come. The stranger sensed that the punishment expert had offered him the possibility of reunion with his past. A tranquil smile lit his face, one that indisputably signaled his submission to the punishment expert's wondrous designs.

The punishment expert was boundlessly excited by the stranger's expression of content. His joy, however, was contained—rather than leaping into the air like a grasshopper, the punishment expert merely nodded his head in agreement. Then he asked the stranger to take off his clothes. "It's not for me. It's just that the punishment demands that you leave the world in the same state that you entered it."

The stranger happily complied—it seemed appropriate. He began to imagine what it would be like to encounter his memories naked. His memories, he mused, were sure to be surprised.

The punishment expert stood by the wall to the left, watching as the stranger stripped off his clothes like a layer of leather, revealing skin battered and scored by the blade of time. He stood next to the glittering plate of glass, his body glowing in the sun's rays. The punishment expert emerged from the shadows by the wall, walked over to the stranger's side, and grasped the glittering butcher's knife in his hand. The sunlight danced furiously across the blade. He asked the stranger, "Are you ready?"

The stranger nodded. His eyes were incomparably tranquil. He had the look of a man awaiting the inexorable arrival of unparalled happiness.

The stranger's tranquillity filled the punishment expert with a sense of confidence and certainty. He reached out a hand to stroke the stranger's waist, only to discover that his hand was trembling. This discovery opened up new and unwelcome possibilities. He didn't know if the trembling in his hands was due to excessive excitement or whether his strength had finally deserted him. The punishment expert's strength had begun to ebb long before. And now as he held the blade, his hands began to shake uncontrollably.

The stranger had already turned to gaze out the window in silent expectation of his reunion with the past. He tried to imagine the knife slicing his body in two: a pair of wondrous, icy hands miraculously tearing a blank sheet of paper neatly in half. But the punishment expert's gasps forced their way into his consciousness. When the stranger turned to look, the punishment expert, sighing at his own humiliation, directed the stranger's attention to his trembling fingers. At the same time, he explained that it would be impossible for him to sever his body in two with one stroke of the blade.

The stranger reassured him, "I don't mind if it takes two."

"But," the punishment expert said, "the punishment allows for only a single stroke."

The stranger told the punishment expert he didn't understand why he insisted on being so fussy.

"Because it would defile the integrity of the punishment," he explained.

"On the contrary," the stranger asserted; "you might actually contribute to the development of the punishment."

"But," the punishment expert quietly explained to the stranger, "if we proceed with the experiment, your own experience would be ruined. I would hack your waist to mincemeat. Your stomach, your intestines, and your liver would just tumble to the ground like overripe apples. I wouldn't be able to put you on the glass. You would fall over instead. And all you would see as you approached the end would be a mess of wriggling earthworms and lumpy toad skin. And worse."

The punishment expert delivered his judgment with incontestable authority. There was no longer any doubt that events would begin to move in an entirely different direction. The stranger began to put his clothes back on. He had thought he would never need them again. His pants felt like oil paint as they smeared up his legs. His eyes were hooded and dark with disappointment. Through them, he could see the dark figure of the punishment expert standing by him like a distant memory.

The stranger could no longer avoid the realization: the punishment expert was powerless; the punishment expert could not reunite him with his past. And though the stranger was baffled and angered by the way in which the punishment expert had so beautifully laid waste his four dates, he was not without compassion for the punishment expert's predicament. The punishment expert suffered because he could no longer muster the strength to carry out his marvelous experiment. His own pain came as a result of being unable to reunite with his past. But they were bound together by their common suffering.

The silence that ensued was as heavy as night. It was only after they returned to the living room that they were finally able to dispel the oppressive silence that had enveloped them following the failure of the experiment. They had moved to the living room after standing motionless, enveloped by the glitter of the glass that suffused the little room. Having arrived in the living room, however, they were able once more to take up something resembling a conversation.

Soon after they had begun, the punishment expert's voice began to grow hoarse with passion. As they spoke, the punishment expert rapidly recovered his composure, despite the gravity of his defeat. For his final punishment was the best of all. His final punishment was his life's work, his masterpiece, his crowning glory. He told the stranger, "It is my own creation."

The punishment expert began to tell the stranger another story: "There is a man, strictly speaking, a scholar—a true scholar, the kind of scholar that simply doesn't exist anymore in the twentieth century. He wakes up one morning and finds several men in gray suits standing around his bed. These men lead him out of his house and push him into a car. The scholar, mystified, repeatedly asks the men where they are going. His questions are met with stony silence. He begins to grow uneasy. He stares out the car window, trying desperately to determine what is going to happen next. He watches as they pass through familiar streets, drive by a familiar stream, and finally move into uncharted territory. Soon they arrive at a grand public square. The square is big enough for twenty thousand people. In fact, there are already twenty thousand people gathered in the square. From afar, they look like so many ants. When they pull up to the edge of the square, he's pushed through the crowd and onto a platform set up at one end of the square. He gazes down at the crowd. The square looks as if it's choked with weeds. A few soldiers with rifles stand with him on the platform. They aim the muzzles of their rifles directly at his head. The scholar is terrified. But a moment later, they lower their guns. They had forgotten to load them. The scholar watches bullets glinting in the sunlight. One by one, the bullets are stuffed into the rifles' magazines. Then the rifles are leveled once more at his head. At this point, a man who looks like some kind of judge climbs up onto the platform. This man tells the scholar that he has been sentenced to death. The scholar, unaware of having committed any offense, is dumbfounded. The judge, seeing the shock ripple across his face, adds, 'Just look at the blood dripping from your hands.'

"The scholar looks down at his hands but can't find the slightest trace of blood. He extends his hands toward the judge to protest his innocence. But the judge simply moves to the side of the platform without even noticing the gesture. The scholar watches as people in the crowd stream up to the edge of the platform to give their testimony. One by one, they relate how he bequeathed his punishments to their loved ones and relatives. At first, the scholar argues passionately with those who have come forward to condemn him. He tries to make them understand that one must sacrifice everything in the name of science. He tells them that their relatives have been sacrificed in the name of science. As the procession of plaintiffs continues to stream toward the platform, however, he finally begins to realize the gravity of his predicament. His predicament is this: in a few moments, a hail of bullets will fly in the direction of his head. His head will shatter like a piece of tile. He sinks into a despair as vast as the crowd that unceasingly streams toward the platform to air its grievances. The denunciations continue for ten hours. And for ten hours, the soldiers keep their rifles trained on the scholar's head."

The punishment expert paused at this point in his narrative and commented with an enigmatic air, "The scholar, of course, is me."

He proceeded to tell the stranger that it had taken him a whole year to perfect each and every detail of the ten hours on the platform. "In the ten hours immediately following the scholar's realization that he has been sentenced to death, he falls victim to terrible psychological torment. In those ten hours, his mind becomes a whirlwind of emotion, careening from one spiritual state to another, passing through lifetimes of feeling in mere moments. One moment, he is awash in terror and abject cowardice. The next moment floods him with bravery, resolve, and indomitable courage. Seconds later, he feels a stream of urine trickling down his legs. Just as soon as he has begun to welcome the prospect of death, he starts to realize just how beautiful it is to be alive. And through the turbulent hours, each of these moments is felt just as sharply as a knife piercing his flesh."

It was clear to the stranger that this punishment was almost perfect. When the punishment expert brought his narrative to a conclusion, he clearly and unmistakably proclaimed to the stranger that "this punishment is reserved for myself."

He told the stranger that this punishment represented ten years of blood, sweat, and tears. He told the stranger that he couldn't possibly give the product of such laborious years of toil to someone else. By someone else, he was clearly indicating the stranger himself.

The stranger smiled. It was a noble smile. It was a smile that successfully hid from the punishment expert's view the doubts he harbored concerning the punishment. For he sensed that the punishment was not nearly as perfect, or as complete, as the punishment expert would have liked to think. There seemed to be a flaw that the punishment expert had overlooked.

The punishment expert rose from his seat and told the stranger that he would carry out the experiment that very evening. He hoped that the stranger would appear by his bedside in twelve hours, because by then "you'll still be able to see me, but I won't be able to see you anymore."

After the punishment expert retired to his bedroom, the stranger sat for a long time in the living room, mulling over the fact that he himself was far less confident as to the outcome of the experiment than the punishment expert himself. And later, when he got up to go to his own bedroom, he was certain that when he stood by the punishment expert's bedside the following morning, the old man would still be able to see him. He had discovered the flaw that lay beneath the polished surface of the punishment, a flaw so crucial as to virtually ensure the failure of the punishment expert's experiment.

The scene the next morning confirmed the stranger's suspicions. The punishment expert lay atop his bed, face pallid with fatigue, and told the stranger that everything had gone smoothly the night before. But just as he had approached the end, he had awoken. With a tragic sweep of his hand, he threw aside his quilt to show the stranger what had happened: "I was so scared I wet the bed."

The bed was sopping wet. The stranger estimated that the punishment expert must have urinated at least ten times over the course of the night. He gazed at the punishment expert panting on the bed. He was satisfied. He didn't want the punishment expert to succeed. For his four dates, his memories, were in this frail old man's hands. The old man's death would spell eternal separation from his own past. And this was precisely why the stranger was unwilling to point out the nature and position of the flaw in the punishment that had led to his failure the night before. Thus when the punishment expert invited him to come again at the same time the following day, he merely smiled and carefully made his way out of the bedroom.

The scene on the second morning was much the way it had been on the first. The punishment expert lay prone upon his bed, staring anxiously toward the stranger as he pushed open the door to the bedroom. In order to hide his sense of shame and humiliation, the punishment expert once again pushed aside his quilt to reveal that he had not only wet the bed but had also soiled it with a pile of his own shit. But the experiment had progressed in much the same manner as the night before—he had woken up at the last moment. In a voice tinged with sorrow, he said, "Come back tomorrow. I promise that I'll be dead by tomorrow."

The stranger failed to give these parting words his full attention. He gazed with pity upon the punishment expert, feeling as if he should tell him about the flaw. The flaw was simply this: after ten hours, a bullet should appear, a bullet that would shatter the punishment expert's head. The punishment expert had spent ten years perfecting the ten-hour process that would lead to his own death but had neglected to include the bullet with which the episode must inevitably culminate. At the same time, however, the stranger was all too aware of the danger of such a revelation. His past would die along with the punishment expert. And he sensed that as long as he was with the punishment expert, his past was never far away. He left the room without having revealed his secret, secure in the knowledge that the flaw would ensure that his past was not lost.

On the third morning, however, the stranger found an entirely different scene when he pushed open the door to the punishment expert's bedroom. The old man had fulfilled his promise of the day before: the punishment expert was dead. He hadn't died on the bed. Instead, his body hung from a rope about a yard away from the bed.

Confronted by this reality, the stranger felt a withered clump of weeds begin to entangle his heart. The punishment expert's death forever precluded the possibility of any kind of connection with the four memories he had once sought. To gaze upon the punishment expert now was to see the lynching of his own past. He distantly recalled March 5, 1965. And at that very same moment, he remembered the punishment expert's fury when he had spoken of death by hanging. The punishment expert had finally chosen to take his own life by means of a degraded punishment.

It wasn't until he left the room much later that he discovered a note written on the back of the door:

I HAVE REDEEMED THIS PUNISHMENT.

The punishment expert had clearly been lucid and sober as he wrote this message, for he had concluded by carefully noting the date: "March 5, 1965."

TRANSLATED BY ANDREW F. JONES

# The Cure

## Mo Yan

That afternoon, the armed work detachment posted a notice on the whitewashed wall of Ma Kuisan's home, which faced the street; it announced the following morning's executions at the usual place: the southern bridgehead of the Jiao River. All able-bodied villagers were to turn out for educational purposes. There were so many executions that year that people had lost interest in them, and the only way to draw a crowd was to make attendance mandatory.

The room was still pitch-black when Father got up to light the bean-oil lamp. After putting on his lined jacket, he woke me up and tried to get me out of bed, but it was so cold all I wanted to do was stay under the warm covers—which Father finally pulled back. "Get up," he said. "The armed work detachment likes to get their business over with early. If we're late, we'll miss our chance."

I followed Father out the gate. The eastern sky was growing light. The streets were icy cold and deserted; winds from the northwest had swept the dust clean during the night; and the gray roadway was clearly visible. My fingers and toes were so cold it felt as if they were being chewed by a cat. As we passed the Ma family compound, where the armed work detachment was quartered, we noticed a light in the window and heard the sound of a bellows. Father said softly, "Step it up. The work detachment is getting breakfast."

Father dragged me up to the top of the riverbank; from there, we could see the dark outline of the stone bridge and patches of ice in the hollows of the riverbed. I asked, "Where are we going to hide, Father?"

"Under the bridge."

It was deserted under the bridge and pitch-black, not to mention freezing cold. My scalp tingled, so I asked Father, "How come my scalp is tingling?"

"Mine, too," he said. "They've shot so many people here that the ghosts of the wronged are everywhere."

I detected the movement of furry creatures in the darkness under the bridge. "There they are!" I shouted.

"Those aren't wronged ghosts," Father said. "They're dogs that feed on the dead."

I shrank back until I bumped into the bone-chilling cold of a bridge piling. All I could think about was Grandma, whose eyes were so clouded over with cataracts she was all but blind. The sky would be completely light once the cold glare from the three western stars slanted into the space under the bridge. Father lit his pipe; the fragrant smell of tobacco quickly enveloped us. My lips were turning numb. "Father, can I go out and run around? I'm freezing."

Father's reply was "Grate your teeth. The armed work detachment shoots their prisoners when the morning sun is still red."

"Who are they shooting this morning, Father?"

"I don't know," Father said. "But we'll find out soon enough. I hope they shoot some young ones."

"Why?"

"Young people have young bodies. Better results."

There was more I wanted to ask, but Father was already losing his patience. "No more questions. Everything we say down here can be heard up there."

While we were talking, the sky turned fish-belly white. The village dogs had formed a pack and were barking loudly, but they couldn't drown out the wailing sounds of women. Father emerged from our hiding spot and stood for a moment in the riverbed, cock-ing his ear in the direction of the village. Now I was really getting nervous. The scavenger dogs prowling the space under the bridge were glaring at me as if they wanted to tear me limb from limb. I don't know what kept me from getting out of there as fast as I could. Father returned at a crouch. I saw his lips quiver in the dim light of dawn but couldn't tell if he was cold or scared. "Did you hear anything?" I asked.

"Keep quiet," Father whispered. "They'll be here soon. I could hear them tying up the condemned."

I moved up close to Father and sat down on a clump of weeds. By listening carefully, I could hear a gong in the village, mixed in with a man's raspy voice: "Villagers—go to the southern bridge-head to watch the execution—shoot the tyrannical landlord Ma Kuisan—his wife—puppet village head Luan Fengshan—orders of armed work detachment Chief Zhang—those who don't go will be punished as collaborators."

I heard Father grumble softly, "Why are they doing this to Ma Kuisan? Why shoot him? He's the last person they should shoot."

I wanted to ask Father why they shouldn't shoot Ma Kuisan, but before I could open my mouth, I heard the crack of a rifle, and a bullet went whizzing far off, way up into the sky somewhere. Then came the sound of horsehoofs heading our way, all the way up to the bridgehead; when they hit the flooring, they clattered like a passing whirlwind. Father and I shrank back and looked at the slivers of sunlight filtering down through cracks between the stones; we were both frightened and not quite sure just what was happening. After about half the time it takes to smoke a pipeful, we heard people coming toward us, shouting and clamoring. They stopped. I heard a man whose voice sounded like a duck's quack: "Let him go, damn it. We'll never catch him."

Whoever it was fired a couple of shots in the direction of the hoofbeats. The sound echoed off the walls where we were hiding; my ears rang, and there was a strong smell of gunpowder.

Again the quack: "What the fuck are you shooting at? By now, he's in the next county."

"I never thought he'd do anything like that," someone else said. "Chief Zhang, he must be a farmhand."

"He's a paid running dog of the landlord class, if you ask me," the duck quacked.

Someone walked to the railing and started pissing over the side of the bridge. The smell was rank and overpowering.

"Come on, let's head back," the duck quacked. "We've got an execution to attend to."

Father whispered to me that the man who sounded like a duck was the chief of the armed work detachment, given the added responsibility by the district government of rooting out traitors to the Party; he was referred to as Chief Zhang.

The sky was starting to turn pink on the eastern horizon, where thin, low-hanging clouds slowly came into view; before long, they, too, were pink. Now it was light enough to make out some frozen dog turds on the ground of our hiding place, that and some shredded clothing, clumps of hair, and a chewed-up human skull. It was so repulsive I had to look away. The riverbed was as dry as a bone except for an ice-covered puddle here and there; clumps of dew-specked weeds stood on the sloped edges. The northern winds had died out; trees on the embankments stood stiff and still in the freezing air. I turned to look at Father; I could see his breath. Time seemed to stand still. Then Father said, "Here they come."

The arrival of the execution party at the bridgehead was announced by the frantic beating of a gong and muted footsteps. Then a booming voice rang out: "Chief Zhang, Chief Zhang, I've been a good man all my life . . ."

Father whispered, "That's Ma Kuisan."

Another voice, this one flat and cracking with emotion: "Chief Zhang, be merciful. . . . We drew lots to see who would be village head; I didn't want the job. . . . We drew lots; I got the short straw—my bad luck. . . . Chief Zhang, be merciful, and spare my dog life. . . . I've got an eighty-year-old mother at home I have to take care of . . ."

Father whispered, "That's Luan Fengshan."

After that, a high-pitched voice said, "Chief Zhang, when you moved into our home, I fed you well and gave you the best wine we had. I even let our eighteen-year-old daughter look after your needs. Chief Zhang, you don't have a heart of steel, do you?"

Father said, "That's Ma Kuisan's wife."

Finally, I heard a woman bellow "Wu—la—ah—ya—"

Father whispered, "That's Luan Fengshan's wife, the mute."

In a calm, casual tone, Chief Zhang said, "We're going to shoot you whether you make a fuss or not, so you might as well stop all that shouting. Everybody has to die sometime. You might as well get it over with early so you can come back as somebody else."

That's when Ma Kuisan announced loudly to the crowd, "All you folks, young and old, I, Ma Kuisan, have never done you any harm. Now I'm asking you to speak up for me . . ."

Several people fell noisily to their knees and began to plead in desperation, "Be merciful, Chief Zhang. Let them live. They're honest folk, all of them . . ."

A youthful male voice shouted above the noise, "Chief Zhang, I say we make these four dog bastards get down on their hands right here on the bridge and kowtow to us a hundred times. Then we give them back their dog lives. What do you say?"

"That's some idea you've got there, Gao Renshan!" Chief Zhang replied menacingly. "Are you suggesting that I, Zhang Qude, am some sort of avenging monster? It sounds to me like you've been head of the militia long enough! Now get up, fellow villagers. It's too cold to be kneeling like that. The policy is clear. Nobody can save them now, so everybody get up."

"Fellow villagers, speak up for me—" Ma Kuisan pleaded.

"No more dawdling," Chief Zhang cut him short. "It's time."

"Clear out, make some room!" Several young men at the bridgehead, almost certainly members of the armed work detachment, were clearing the bridge of the kneeling citizens.

Then Ma Kuisan sent his pleas heavenward: "Old man in the sky, are you blind? Am I, Ma Kuisan, being repaid for a lifetime of good with a bullet in the head? Zhang Qude, you son of a bitch, you will not die in bed, count on it. You son of a bitch—"

"Get on with it!" Chief Zhang bellowed. "Or do you like to hear him spout his poison?"

Running footsteps crossed the bridge above us. Through cracks between the stones, I caught glimpses of the people.

"Kneel!" someone on the southern edge of the bridge demanded.

"Clear the way, everybody" came a shout from the northern edge.

*Pow—pow—pow*—three shots rang out.

The explosions bored into my eardrums and made them throb until I thought I'd gone deaf. By then, the sun had climbed above the eastern horizon, rimmed by a blood-red halo that spread to clouds looking like canopies of gigantic fir trees. A large, bulky human form came tumbling slowly down from the bridge above, cloudlike in its shifting movements; then when it hit the icy ground below, it regained its natural heft and thudded to a stop. Crystalline threads of blood oozed from the head.

Panic and confusion at the northern bridgehead—it sounded to me like the frantic dispersal of villagers who had been forcibly mobilized as witnesses to the executions. It didn't sound as if the armed work detachment took out after the deserters.

Once again, footsteps rushed across the bridge from north to south, followed by the shout of "Kneel" at the southern bridgehead and "Clear the way" at the northern. Then three more shots—the body of Luan Fengshan, hatless and wearing a ragged padded coat, tumbled head over heels down the riverbank, first bumping into Ma Kuisan, then rolling off to the side.

After that, things were simplified considerably. A volley of shots preceded the sound and sight of two disheveled female corpses tumbling down, arms and legs flying, and crashing into the bodies of their menfolk.

I held tightly onto Father's arm, feeling something warm and wet up against my padded trousers.

At least a half dozen people were standing on the bridge directly overhead, and it seemed to me that their weight was pushing the rock flooring down on top of us. Their thunderous shouts were nearly deafening: "Shall we check out the bodies, Chief?"

"What the hell for? Their brains are splattered all over the place. If the Jade Emperor himself came down now, he couldn't save them."

"Let's go! Old Guo's wife has fermented-bean-curd-and-oil fritters waiting for us."

They crossed the bridge, heading north, their footsteps sounding like an avalanche. The rock flooring, creaking and shifting, could have come crashing down at any moment. Or so it seemed to me.

The quiet returned.

Father nudged me. "Don't stand there like an idiot. Let's do it."

I looked around me, but nothing made sense. Even my own father seemed familiar, but I couldn't place him.

"Huh?" I'm sure that's all I managed to say: "Huh?"

"Have you forgotten?" Father said. "We're here to get a cure for your grandmother. We have to move fast, before the body snatchers show up."

The words were still echoing in my ears when I spotted seven or eight wild dogs, of a variety of colors, dragging their long shadows up off the riverbed in our direction; they were baying at us. All I could think of was how they had turned and fled at the first gunshot, accompanied by their own terrified barks.

I watched Father kick loose several bricks and fling them at the approaching dogs. They scurried out of the way. Then he took a carving knife out from under his coat and waved it in the air to threaten the dogs. Beautiful silvery arcs of light flashed around Father's dark silhouette. The dogs kept their distance for the time being. Father tightened the cord around his waist and rolled up his sleeves. "Keep an eye out for me," he said.

Like an eagle pouncing on its prey, Father dragged the women's bodies away, then rolled Ma Kuisan over so he was facing up. Then he fell to his knees and kowtowed to the body. "Second Master Ma," he intoned softly, "loyalty and filiality have their limits. I hate to do this to you."

I watched Ma Kuisan reach up and wipe his bloody face. "Zhang Qude," he had said with the trace of a smile, "you will not die in bed."

Father tried to unbutton Ma Kuisan's leather coat with one hand but was shaking too much to manage. "Hey, Second Son," I heard him say, "hold the knife for me."

I recall reaching out to take the knife from him, but he was already holding it in his mouth as he struggled with the yellow buttons down Ma Kuisan's chest. Round, golden yellow, and as big as mung beans, they were nearly impossible to separate from the cloth loops encircling them. Growing increasingly impatient, Father ripped them loose and jerked the coat open, revealing a white kidskin lining. A satin vestlike garment had the same kind of buttons, so Father ripped them loose, too. After the vest came a red silk stomacher. I heard Father snort angrily. I have to admit that I was surprised when I saw the strangely alluring clothing the fat old man—he was over fifty—wore under his regular clothes. But Father seemed absolutely irate; he ripped the thing off the body and flung it to one side. Now at last, Ma Kuisan's rounded belly and flat chest were out in the open. Father reached out his hand but then jumped to his feet, his face the color of gold. "Second Son," he said, "tell me if he's got a heartbeat."

I recall bending over and laying my hand on the chest. It was no stronger than a rabbit's, but that heart was still beating.

"Second Master Ma," my father said, "your brains have spilled out on the ground, and even the Jade Emperor couldn't save you now, so help me be a filial son, won't you?"

Father took the knife from between his teeth and moved it up and down the chest area, trying to find the right place to cut. I saw him press down, but the skin sprang back undamaged, like a rubber tire. He pressed down again with the same result. Father fell to his knees. "Second Master Ma, I know you didn't deserve to die, but if you've got a bone to pick, it's with Chief Zhang, not me. I'm just trying to be a filial son."

Father had pressed down with the knife only twice, but already his forehead was all sweaty, the stubble on his chin white with icy moisture. The damned wild dogs were inching closer and closer to us—their eyes were red as hot coals, the fur on their necks was standing straight up, like porcupine quills, and their razor-sharp fangs were bared. I turned to Father. "Hurry, the dogs are coming."

He stood up, waved the knife above his head, and charged the wild dogs like a madman, driving them back about half the distance an arrow flies. Then he ran back, breathless, and said loudly, "Second Master, if I don't cut you open, the dogs will do it with their teeth. I think you'd rather it be me than them."

Father's jaw set, his eyes bulged. With a sense of determination, he brought his hand down; the knife cut into Ma Kuisan's chest with a slurping sound, all the way to the hilt. He jerked the knife to the side, releasing a stream of blackish blood, but the rib cage stopped his motion. "I lost my head," he said as he pulled the knife out, wiped the blade on Ma Kuisan's leather coat, gripped the handle tightly, and opened Ma Kuisan's chest.

I heard a gurgling noise and watched the knife slice through the fatty tissue beneath the skin and release the squirming, yellowish intestines into the opening, like a snake, like a mass of eels; there was a hot, fetid smell.

Fishing out the intestines by the handful, Father looked like a very agitated man: he pulled, and he tugged; he cursed, and he swore; and finally, he ran out of intestines, leaving Ma Kuisan with a hollow abdomen.

"What are you looking for, Father?" I recall asking him anxiously.

"The gall bladder. Where the hell is his gall bladder?"

Father cut through the diaphragm and fished around until he had his hand around the heart—still nice and red. Then he dug out the lungs. Finally, alongside the liver, he discovered the egg-sized gall bladder. Very carefully, he separated it from the liver with the tip of his knife, then held it in the palm of his hand to examine it. The thing was moist and slippery and, in the sunlight, had a sheen. Sort of like a piece of fine purple jade.

Father handed me the gall bladder. "Hold this carefully while I take out Luan Fengshan's gall bladder."

This time, Father performed like an experienced surgeon: deft, quick, exact. First, he cut away the hemp cord that was all Luan Fengshan could afford for a belt. Then he opened the front of his ragged coat and held the scrawny, bony chest still with his foot as he made four or five swift cuts. After that, he cleared away all the obstructions, stuck in his hand, and, as if it were the pit of an apricot, removed Luan's gall bladder.

"Let's get out of here," Father said.

We ran up the riverbank, where the dogs were fighting over the coils of intestines. Only a trace of red remained on the edges of the sun; its blinding rays fell on all exposed objects, large and small.

Grandma had advanced cataracts, according to Luo Dashan, the miracle worker. The source of her illness was heat rising from her three visceral cavities. The cure would have to be something very cold and very bitter. The physician lifted up the hem of his floor-length coat and was heading out the door when Father begged him to prescribe something.

"Hm, prescribe something . . ." Miracle worker Luo told Father to get a pig's gall bladder and have his mother take the squeezings, which should clear her eyes a little.

"How about a goat's gall bladder?" Father asked.

"Goats are fine," the physician said; "so are bears. Now if you could get your hands on a human gall bladder . . . ha, ha . . . well, I wouldn't be surprised if your mother's eyesight returned to normal."

TRANSLATED BY HOWARD GOLDBLATT

# Green Earth Mother

## AI BEI

Earth Mother, a mythical, benevolent Buddhist saint, is the central icon in the Potala Palace. She is said to have seven eyes, with which She can see into people's hearts. Her right leg is stretched out in symbolic suppression of anger and realization of mercy. Earth Mothers come in five colors—white, red, blue, yellow, and green—of which green is the most basic. A powerful roc with golden wings is perched atop the green Earth Mother's head; it is Her protector.

Night once again deceived people's eyes. The wind relentlessly toyed with the overripe berries. In the orange morning light, Mimi pushed open the double cedar doors. The earth was blotted with the reddish brown juice of crushed berries—already rotten, they hid a hope brighter than the eyes of birds in their hearts: now that winter had passed, who could stop the multicolored seeds from sprouting green buds? Mimi asked him about the ancient division of the seasons. Spring is spring winter is winter flowers bloom in the summertime fruit ripens on autumn days once you enter that time mountains rivers flowers trees wind clouds thunder lightning snow rain frost fog all things fuse or multiply even the excretions of men and women and boys and girls increase or decrease. He said it all in one breath.

Why?

People are powerless against the mysteries of heaven and earth. He put on a pair of greasy blue shorts and walked toward the inner room, his skin a snowy white. Mimi's heart floated softly along on two hairless, spindly legs. For days, Mimi had been longing for a snowfall that would cover the land, freezing heaven and earth, solidifying the people in their places to keep their corrupt souls from fluttering all over the streets, even if her own heart were also frozen into a lump of ice. Mimi wanted to stick out her scalding tongue—I'll kiss you, kiss every pore on your body, suck in all the hidden flavors. Her tongue was already frozen. Ice and snow fused heaven and earth, embracing withered branches and dead leaves, wastelands and abandoned slopes, the bare stems of shriveled petals and the ancient forest far from the bustling city, its ruined, rust-blotched trees, and those aged, green-skinned people hobbling all over the world. The aged people wore an overcoat of snow as they seduced the young by singing the praises of parental love. Spring came, the snow slunk away to reveal the ravaged land in all its ugliness. Beneath the sun's rays, it shed tears as it related a tale of short-lived purity and a false love it should never have known.

Kiss me. Why are you afraid of Her?

It just isn't right.

It's not fair. Just look at Her wrinkled old mouth that has been stamped by hundreds, thousands of full-blooded lips, a once rosy color that has peeled away completely from countless scrapings. A kiss, you have to kiss me in front of Her.

It's as out of place as wearing a bathing suit on the street. The sound of his voice shriveled into a lump; the words ran together.

It's as ridiculous as wearing a mandarin gown in a swimming pool.

Blasphemous, sacred motherly love!

I want what's mine, it's got nothing to do with Her!

OK, tonight we'll go to some deserted spot . . .

No, I don't want any more stolen kisses in the dark.

Mimi got up out of the bathtub, every pore on her bright, pink body spreading open willfully, steam obscuring the reflection of her tender fresh naked female body in the dressing mirror. She pressed her face against the cold silvery surface. Not a single wrinkle anywhere, especially on her pink forehead. In twenty-five years, nine thousand days and nights, those delicate lips had never tasted a bright shining kiss! What appeared to be an invisible dark hand in the mirror was thrust into Mimi's small narrow chest, where it stroked a weakly beating heart that was covered by a thick, heavy layer of dust. Two streams of hot tears gouged out two pale scars. In the darkness, Mimi was hopelessly entwined by pity.

If She opened her eyes, a lover's kiss would immediately become a sinful intrigue.

If in a world of respect for one's elders, there's no room for a kiss in broad daylight, I'd rather have languished in my mother's womb and never have opened my eyes.

Not so loud. Mother will hear. He was breathing hard, his every word chiseled on Mimi's heart.

Mimi composed herself and gazed at the pale tiny tightly closed mouth in the dressing mirror. Her pink body was cooling off, turning as pale as wax. A delicate hand glided down it from top to bottom as she mused, Maybe this doesn't belong to me. No . . . but maybe. . . . Love knotted in her heart, spun a thread that circled the earth three times, maybe more. Mimi was sure that sooner or later, the world would be destroyed—by love.

Are you crying? Are you. . . . The words stuck in his throat and simply wouldn't come out. He put a towel printed with cats' eyes— red, yellow, blue, white—over Mimi's shoulders. She shook her head, raining tears onto the back of his hand. When Mimi was little, Mama had said she was born under a crying star, that she had come into this world with tears in her eyes. Granny believed she was an unlucky child, so on snowy days she secretly fed her snowballs. Mimi's mouth was frozen open like a trumpet as she sang and sang and sang, never stopping. All Mama could do was buy a set of imported earplugs.

Are you crying again? His hand was lily-white and supple, so soft it seemed boneless. He wiped away the tears on her cheeks, then carried her back to the bathtub and the hot water. He rubbed her back, massaged her shoulders, then let his supple hands rest on her trembling breasts. Beads of water dripped through his fingers.

Ribbons of orange light filtered in through a dark-green bamboo grove. The ribbons, like spirit threads, tied up her tender little heart as they swayed back and forth. Pricked by sharp leaves, her heart settled like a fine powder over her childhood dream world, with all its colored lamps. The colored lamps congealed into a swarm of moths. The moths greedily sucked up the orange-colored light, which shone through their transparent wings. Mimi had been afraid of the moon's orange rays ever since she was little.

*Knock-knock.* She was at the door.

I'm taking a bath. What do you want?

Is he in there?

He. . . . Before she could get it out, he covered Mimi's lips with his boneless hand.

Say I'm not here. His mouth was boring into Mimi's ear.

Why?

I shouldn't be here while you're taking a bath.

I'm your wife, I share your bed. What's wrong with a bath?

Blasphemous. . . . Blasphemous, sacred motherly love.

Ptui! Pettiness is the true blasphemous love! Mimi kicked the tub over. A pair of purple slippers floated toward the door on the spilled water.

Ai! A heavy sigh from the other side of the door splintered Mimi's heart. She hadn't left. Instead, She cupped a brilliant excuse in Her hands. I bought you a *Moonlight* Sonata tape. Come out here, and we'll listen to it together.

Ma—he was embarrassed beyond belief. A snow-white back slipped through the cedar doors.

It's my chest, the same old problem. The moans of a sick cat outside the door.

Ma—I'll massage it for you.

Mimi stood barefoot next to the window. She tumbled into a sea of mist, floated off toward a deep canyon—compressed into a breathless speck of dust, her bloodless lips parted, she gazed up at the creases squirming in the sky. A ruined face like a piece of rotting wood appeared in the tattered vault of heaven. Mimi rubbed her wildly beating heart. What is it I still want? she asked herself. Why hasn't my heart ossified? In spite of herself, Mimi looked down into the courtyard. That knifelike face spread out across a hairless, snow-white chest. Mimi was thinking, The flowers in Her eyes are blooming at an angle, the clouds are drifting at an angle, people are walking at an angle. Her happiness spilled out of Her crisscrossing creases. Like the new bloom of a withered flower, Her face came back to life. Four spindly legs intertwined; two bodies folded together. As though she were watching a centipede, Mimi hid, trembling, behind the curtain. Soap bubbles kept popping; water spread silently in all directions. . . . A pair of tiny feet, made plump by soap bubbles, stepped on the scarlet gravel. A shout— Mama—the orbs of her buttocks arched as she walked, arched and quivered as though restless animals were hiding in them. Arms thrust out in front of her, Mimi ran toward the churning white foam stretching out before her, leaving behind a trail of happy birds' nests with her feet. A pile of bubbles was created in a second; a drab blueness required countless millennia. She ran into it, a fleshy red butterfly toying with a boundless expanse of waves. As she swam ahead, the fleshy red became white, the blue became a deep green.

Oh, Mama, the ocean isn't blue! Mimi raised her pudgy arms, threw them around Mama's youthful long neck, and floated lightly upward, the weight of twelve years seemingly as light as a feather. Mama scooped little Mimi out of the water, cupping her like a living heart. Watery eyes spread open, a rose. You're twelve years old today. Taking you swimming in the ocean is Mama's present to you, because you never enjoyed the love of a father . . .

Mama! Two wet faces pressed together; a childish heart grew suddenly solemn. A ferocious wave crashed over them. Mimi swallowed a mouthful of seawater, brackish and salty. Mama staggered back to the beach, cradling Mimi in her arms. She looked at the stunned expression on Mama's face and felt resentment, sadness. She never swam in the ocean again.

The first time Mimi saw him was on her second trip to the seashore. She was sitting alone on the beach, staring up at the moon, a sheet of red paper stuck onto the canopy of heaven above the sea. She was laden with sorrow. He walked up and sat down beside her. The beach was deserted, the sand unbearably cold and cheerless. He spoke to Mimi in a disbelieving voice. You look just like Her, the same sadness, the same purity. She loves the moon, the early morning sun, Beethoven, Spinoza . . .

A poet?

No, unemployed. Gets by by doing odd jobs. She published a story when She was eighteen; at twenty, She had a solo vocal recital, as a coloratura. But like ordinary women, She gleaned scraps of coal and carried manure buckets, all for the sake of Her son. . . . His voice quickly faded out. Mimi's heart leaped into her mouth. The sea was unbelievably calm; all she could hear were the softly lapping waves and the violent beating of her heart.

Do you love Her?

I adore Her. My only goal in life is to make Her happy.

Mimi's heart crawled; her narrow chest began to swell. The broad expanse of the beach was nearly unbearable. She headed over to a shaded path that led to the shore. The thick branches of the towering kola-nut trees were intertwined, their thick shade forming a dark umbrella over Mimi's head. He followed quietly behind her, as still as a shadow.

Who is She?

My mother.

Thunder roared; the moon was gone. In the pitch-darkness, he grabbed Mimi's hand and drew up next to her, purring like a cat. Her suspended heart settled back down, dissolving into millions of pearls of tribute. The "motherhood" memorial arch screened out the last traces of jealousy. All the emotions in the world could be written with only the word *affection* or *filiality;* otherwise, it would be blasphemy. A bolt of lightning flashed between them; two twisted faces drew together. In the space of a minute, countless driven raindrops crashed into two bodies and two hearts consumed by flames at the base of an ancient tree. They saw nothing, they heard nothing. There was only the driven rain and the mud and an inextinguishable fireball. Tens of thousands of years ago, the heavens had opened up angrily, just like tonight, and a pair of lovers had died for love beneath the branches of this ancient tree. After tens of thousands of springs, tens of thousands of summers, two carnal-colored seeds had formed deep beneath the roots of this gnarled, ancient tree. Maybe the vows would be answered on this rainy night, and the two love seeds would finally germinate and sprout forth. As the rain fell, they exchanged their burning hearts, which sizzled with each raindrop. A chill wind brushed past, whipping up flames of joy. Thunder roared angrily; the gigantic canopy of the tree rose into the air, then crashed to the ground. Their souls flew out of their bodies. The fire was out, but gray smoke continued to curl upward. The wind died down, the rain stopped, a cluster of rice-colored stars was set free to cleanse the canopy of heaven. They stared silently at each other like a pair of clay statues, gazing into each other's expression, all genuine feelings now lost.

Come to my place, and change into some dry clothes.

No, Mother's waiting anxiously for me to come home.

They held hands tightly in the darkness, then let go. No words of comfort, no good-byes as they parted.

He knew it had been an extraordinary rainy night and that he'd given her an even more extraordinary love. Mimi knew it had been a soul-stirring rainy night and that she'd relinquished soul-stirring emotions to the rainy night. The rainy night had incurred a heavy debt. What they'd taken from the rainy night could never be easily abandoned. Love had turned their hearts into a scorched mass, but they remained fused together to avoid the pain of being ripped apart.

Mother wants to meet you.

Why?

She has to give Her permission for me to marry. I know She'll like you.

On Sunday, he climbed the Great Wall, Mimi holding his left hand, Mother holding his right. He used up a roll of color film beside the North Sea, his left arm around Mimi's shoulder, his right hand gripping Mother's arm. Mimi let him hold the parasol; She handed him her feather-light handbag. Mimi took off her jacket and put it over his shoulders; She put her half-eaten Popsicle up to his mouth. Mimi could see resentment in Her eyes; She could see superfluousness in Mimi's face. He tried to please Mimi by buying a Popsicle; he tried to please Her by buying a soft drink, all the time panting like a cat in heat.

At dusk, Mimi's first glance took in Her thick black hair, oppressive, impenetrable. Three pink moles at the corner of Her mouth were so close together they were almost one. From then on, unlucky omens began to appear in Mimi's dreams. Bright red, meaty growths appeared. Countless pink eyes hidden in Her thick black hair, shedding tears like blood. . . . Mimi often woke from her dreams in terror; in the surrounding blackness, she refreshed her image of him by looking through photographs.

How about this one?

No, you can't see Ma's disposition in it. This one's no good, either. You can't see Mother's grace in it. Um-um, these are even worse . . .

This one's pretty good.

Her hair isn't dyed.

Gray hair's a sign of kindness.

No, She looks too old. Mimi, under no circumstances are you to let Mother see this photo!

Why?

If She sees Herself looking so old, She'll be upset. From now on, you're not to call Her an old lady to Her face. His words were strings of waterdrops that seeped into Mimi's heart like poison. Mimi's nerves felt raw; she was trembling. She walked out of the house and wandered aimlessly. She walked up to a shop where people were selling all kinds of diapers; countless wrinkled, chapped feet stepped over pudgy babies lying on the ground as they fought over the colorful diapers. Mimi reached out. Four huge cats' eyes bit down painfully. She pulled her hand back and realized that her face was still pressed up against the icy window. She stared at the orange moon as it scurried in and out of a jumbled mass of clouds. Another daydream! Mimi dragged her stiffened legs out the door. What was this, a blanket of stars in the sky above and on the ground below? Heaven and earth, everything was all jumbled up! Her face was soaked; water filled her eyes. She stepped in a puddle, shattering it as an orange moon landed on her instep. She kicked it away and walked up to the room, stepping in one puddle after another. Mimi stood in the doorway, oblivious to the passage of time. His broad, heavy back blocked her view of the reclining chair. They couldn't see Mimi, but Mimi could see his limp, boneless hand massaging a mound of withered, yellowed wrinkles. Amid the wrinkles, countless stringy mammary glands converged to form two dark-purple nipples, like overripe squishy grapes.

The pain in my chest started when I was pregnant with you. Her voice seemed to float up from the depths of a dying well, then sank slowly back down. Mimi could see Her parted lips, Her half-closed eyes, the three pink moles quivering in a red tide.

Ma, it feels better when I massage You, doesn't it?

Much better. Your head was so big it was a very hard delivery. For two days and three nights, that wretched father of yours never showed his face at the delivery-room door. I was so angry I couldn't eat. My stomach ached from hunger . . .

Ma. Grief and indignation caused the big pale boneless hands to dig in too hard. The overripe purple grapes oozed two drops of pus-colored liquid. They hung there on the verge of falling off, quivering drops of muddy yellow, like a secret mixture of splendor and decay fighting off death. Mimi suddenly saw in the glass her own ghostly image.

Ai, you're all grown up. But I still remember what you were like as a child. You nursed at my breast every night and listened to me read "Snow White." You didn't blink. Remember? I spanked you once because you stole Leilei's hanky, and you curled up in my lap and cried half the night. Pretty soon, I started crying, too. Ai . . . words gradually gave way to soft moans.

Ma—the two mounds of withered yellow wrinkled skin were

getting hot from the rubbing, turning red. His hands hesitated; they began to tremble. Terrified, he stared at the overripe, oozing purple grapes . . .

Mimi threw the towel over her shoulders, burst into the room, and stood there ramrod straight, beads of water streaming down her body.

You! The big pale boneless hands froze above Her chest. All rubbing motions stopped for a full two minutes.

Reluctantly, She opened her eyes. After a momentary fright, She calmed Herself down.

What's wrong with you? He quickly picked up the sheet to cover up Mimi's naked body. As though awakened from a dream, Mimi cast a flustered look at her own dripping body, knocked his hand away, and recoiled to the side.

I told you long ago she's got emotional problems. Look at her, the poor thing. You stay here; I'll take her to the hospital. A look of great compassion on Her face.

No. Mimi huddled next to him and gripped his hand tightly.

Mimi, go to the hospital with Mother, and let them see what's wrong, OK?

Mimi looked at him for a moment as though he were a stranger, before jerking her hand free and throwing off the sheet that covered her. She ran to her own room, stepping on the rays of starlight. The bed was swirling. She buried her head in the fluffy pillow, her eyes were tightly shut. He held Mimi in his arms. He could feel her trembling but couldn't hear the sobs stuck in her throat. His body was racked by a cold shudder that stabbed into his heart. Her long damp hair gave off steam that encircled the two faces. A sharp pain in his heart as he dug his fingernails into Mimi's flesh. Mimi shrank into his embrace; for a long, long time, her terrified eyes were glued to those fleshy big pale boneless hands. He peeled the wet strands of hair off her cheeks, touched her full lips. His muscles tensed as he nervously reached for her hand. Two limpid drops of water oozed out from under her tightly shut eyelids. Don't open your eyes, hold my hand. Let's find our way out of this dark-green grove together. Pointed leaves cradled strings of last night's dewdrops, emitting light-yellow rays. Don't reach out. Every dewdrop knocked to the ground is one more shattered heart. Pressed tightly together, they walked forward, hand in hand. Stillness reigned, broken only by the even sounds of their labored breathing. As he raised his head, his face was imprinted with golden splotches of light filtering through cracks in the dark-green canopy above. So was Mimi's snowy-white blouse. Creeping forward cautiously, their shoulders bent, they made their way through the dark-green grove, a pair of intertwining silk ribbons gliding back and forth like an empty emotion being poured into an empty heart.

Kiss me. In the translucent light of the sun, a pair of feet like those of a tiny animal rose up on their tiptoes. The pointed leaves rustled interminably, sending light-yellow dewdrops cascading to the ground, shattered. His back blocked out the sunlight; a wall of darkness suddenly spread out before Mimi's eyes, probably because the lamp at the head of the bed was smashed. In a flash, two naked bodies formed a scarlet forest. Mimi's mouth opened wide, fingernails dug into his back. No, don't stop. . . . Don't stop. Mimi wanted to push him away, but she dug her fingers deeply into flesh that could have been his or could have been hers. Two vibrant lives formed a bright rainbow. Four eyes were tightly shut, blood-filled lips fused together, heaven and earth were about to explode, the ark was capsizing. . . . Don't move! I hear something. Footsteps on broken glass, hobbling back and forth beyond the door. A swarm of ants gently raised up a berry; several little stars silently leaped onto the wet window ledge. Rain dripping from the eaves turned into fine drops, falling freely to the ground in threads. The berries were completely smashed, oozing crimson earth. Already rotten, they hid a hope in their hearts brighter than the eyes of birds; now that winter had passed, who could stop the multicolored seeds from sprouting green buds? The scarlet forest began to fade, gradually becoming a gloomy violet. Mimi's verdant heart suddenly withered and cracked; springtime fled without a trace.

Is she better? Her voice was soft and supple, like a rope twisted out of rubber.

Much better, Ma. He was desperate to convince Her that nothing had happened a moment ago.

Is she asleep?

She fell asleep long ago, Ma. Still desperate to convince Her, he turned on the light and opened the door. An icy hand descended on Mimi's forehead. Oh! She's feverish. Mimi raised her eyelids, which were nearly stuck shut. She saw a knifelike old face leaning over her, a glinting cold light like the dead grasses covering a winter pasture in whose roots were hidden the hope of rebirth for snakes and scorpions, ants and bugs. Mimi was like a spring that had been stretched too far, its tension completely lost. The channels in her heart slowed down, twisted; last night, so transparent, would decompose where it stuck. She tossed down a green stone. The echo from the bottom of her heart reverberated, was still reverberating. I'm not sick! I'm not. Mimi sensed that she was an emotional, kindhearted sparrow silently keeping watch over a nonexistent snake track in the darkness of a vast forest. Deep autumn, when the birds fly south, and Mimi no longer had the strength to cross the single-file bridge of his heart. Profound sorrow wrapped itself around her. All Mimi could do was cry.

Mimi, you're sick.

There are yardsticks all over the world, but not a speck of land for me anywhere. Take my measure with your yardstick, take your measure with mine.

What nonsense is that? Mimi. You really are sick.

She has no husband, I have no father. None of us has a father.

Mimi, snap out of it. I love you, Mother loves you, too. . . . She loves . . .

She loves acting high and mighty the foreign superstition of not going outside on Friday the thirteenth eating sausage sandwiches even if they taste funny drinking coffee without sugar destroying nerves that are already too fragile . . .

Why do you insist on making this relationship impossible!

The relationship is cruel enough already. At first, I was confident in my youth and my good looks, confident that no one could replace the love of a wife. Heh-heh, I was wrong. You'll never have the courage to cut the umbilical cord, and, of course, that's what She's counting on. It's not enough just to be your wife. . . .

Goddamn that Freud and his theories!

No, it's more than that. It's castration. Most Chinese men are swallowed up by maternal love. There's nothing left. I want nothing. I'm leaving.

What nonsense is that? You're sick. Where do you think you're going?

. . . Mimi walked into the gray misty dusk empty-handed.

You can't leave. He reached out but grabbed only the empty dusk air, like an infant who's lost the nipple and stares into a great void.

Let her go and walk it off. She's just tired. She walked over abruptly and stood in his way, Her face suffused with the innocence of an eighteen-year-old girl.

Ma—she's still got a fever. She's talking nonsense. Now that he'd found an excuse, he was as excited as a drowning man reaching out to grasp a straw, someone who'd found the hope to go on living.

Take it easy. Nothing will happen. Her voice was thinner than paper.

Ma. He felt like crying, but he didn't, though his eyes were burning.

An ancient ugly dying forest way off in the corner of the dark-green sky. Decrepit forked branches, so rusted they looked as if they'd never borne flowers or brought forth tender new buds—ancient trees forced to bear the stigma of not having seen the color of green in thousands of years. Flocks of birds perching densely on the shaky forked branches were exchanging curses that birds have known since antiquity. Pair after pair of bulging eyes looked down on Mimi's life and her lives to come. Mimi was frightened out of her wits. She wouldn't choose this decaying den of spies as the place to end her life. She emerged from the forest and lay down on a desolate slope covered with years of loneliness. The grass around her was restless; the desolate slope lifted her up until she was floating in the air. Snakes and scorpions, bugs and ants lazily raised their heads, eyes heavy with sleep. Mimi was so tired she couldn't keep her eyes open. An icy softness kept brushing past her hands. There was a tautness in her belly, a weightiness, painful cramps. She undid her underwear and held her bulging belly with both hands, letting the first flakes of snow moisten the tiny new life. A momentary throbbing reminded her that the child would be born under the sign of the serpent. Why is there so much movement during a period of hibernation? A smile spread across Mimi's face as tranquillity settled upon her once again.

It's snowing hard now, and Mimi still isn't home. I'll find her and bring her back to talk some sense into her. His reproach was filled with anxiety.

I won't allow you to talk sense into her. Let her calm down first. Who knows, maybe she went to her mother's home. Mother held his arm. Her withered, yellowing body blocked the huge cedar doors.

Ma, let me bring her back and give her a good talking to. He tried to wrench his arm free from Her grip, but She held on for dear life.

I won't allow you to frighten her! She shouted anxiously.

Ma. He pushed Her hand away and burst through the door.

Stop right there! She ran out after him, stumbled, nearly fell. He had no choice but to rush back and steady Her. Her mouth was open wide; She was gasping. She couldn't speak.

Ma—

I won't allow you to be rough with Mimi. It's cold out there. I'll go with you to find her. Suddenly calm again, She looked at him tenderly. He lowered his head to avoid Her eyes. His voice was so low he seemed to be talking to himself. She's still got a fever.

Mimi raised her leg—it was stiff from the cold. She didn't have the heart to stamp a footprint onto the translucent surface, though maybe that was the way for her to experience the pleasure of destroying purity. White sky. White snow. White night. Tender snowflakes translucent in the boundless translucence. Not a breath of wind. The flakes seemed to be floating in their prescribed spots, a scene of chaos, nihilism. This was Mimi's cherished hope— heaven and earth a single color. As she stood in the snow, she could no longer see herself. Fossilized bones glistened so brightly they dazzled her eyes; her terrified, trembling heart had petrified, had been transformed into a heart-shaped green agate tossed onto the boundless snow all by itself. Don't open the door, people; give the world a chance to hold on to this pale, powerless purity! Hide under the snowbound roof to cry alone over your own death. Look, the sky is responding to human misery by sending down its symbol of filial piety—snow that covers the ground. In the snow-covered wilderness, only the emerald-green agate awaits rebirth—maybe the tragedy of these two legs will be replayed somewhere else in the universe. Mimi was overcome by sorrow, but she was at peace. In-advertently, she discovered a long piece of light-purple silk rolling back and forth across the earth's crust with a soft tearing sound, leaving behind an eternal silence. Mimi had no sense of her own being, not even as a tiny snowflake. As she slumped slowly to the snow-covered ground, she saw the bright, snowy red of the ancient grove with its rusted trees. Flowers in full bloom were like huge tongues stretching up into the vault of heaven, sucking dry all the blood vessels, turning the anemic heaven and earth paler than ever. The delicate and beautiful ancient forest trembled in the dazzling snow, sending skyward a cloud of red mist . . .

He picked Mimi up, his face as dark as the earth. He gazed in stupefaction at Mother's silvery new teeth. A confused look on his face, the twin expressions of laughter and crying.

**TRANSLATED BY HOWARD GOLDBLATT**

# When I Think of You Late at Night, There's Nothing I Can Do: Five Tales of the Wen Clan Cave Dwellers

## Cao Naiqian

### In-Law

The early-morning stillness is broken by the braying of a donkey. Blackie says, "That fucking in-law has come for you."

The woman says, "Stall him while I put on my pants."

"Shit," Blackie says, "what difference does it make?"

The woman blushes. "Just say I'm sick and I can't go. It's that time of the month anyway."

"I can't do that," Blackie says. "Chinese don't go back on their word."

Blackie walks outside to greet his in-law, who is tethering his donkey at the gate. Blackie turns and shouts into the cave, "Go fetch a chicken. I'll get some liquor from the commune."

"In-Law," Blackie's counterpart says, "I brought a bottle since we always drink yours."

"When did we start worrying about yours and mine, anyway?"

Blackie's woman walks into the yard and, without a glance at either man, heads for the chicken coop.

"No need, no need for that. A cow fell and died last night at our village," the in-law says to Blackie's woman. "I borrowed this donkey from the brigade leader, and the son of a bitch was cooking a pot of beef." He takes a leather bag from around the donkey's neck. "Here, take it. You might need to cook it a bit longer."

Head lowered, Blackie's woman takes the bag and goes into the cave without a glance at either man.

While they are drinking, Blackie says, "It's that time of the month. Day before yesterday. Want to wait till it's past?"

"Fine with me."

"On the other hand, the brigade leader might deduct work points for keeping his donkey. You can take her now. Just wait till she's finished before she does it."

"Fine with me."

"Bring her back next month. I can't borrow a donkey."

"Fine with me."

After they finish drinking, Blackie says to his woman, "Put on those clean clothes. I don't want people in the other village laughing at me."

"No need. The commune's on the way. I'll buy her a jacket and trousers there."

Blackie sees his woman and in-law on their way, across one ravine after another and over a series of ridges.

"Go on back," the in-law says. "Here's the mountain."

Blackie says, "You go on up the mountain. I'll head back." He hesitates, then turns back. The in-law smacks the donkey's rump with his large fist; the animal starts clip-clopping down the road.

Shit. Go on, go ahead. A thousand yuan less would be the same as handing me his own daughter. Shit. Go on, go ahead. It's only one month a year. And Chinese don't go back on their word. These are his thoughts as he walks.

Blackie takes another look behind him and sees his woman's turniplike feet dangling alongside the donkey's haunches, swinging back and forth.

Blackie's heart, too, is swinging back and forth.

## Woman

Wen Hai finally got a wife, which made the villagers very happy. But people listening at the door that night said she wouldn't let him do it. She refused to loosen the knot in her red sash and spent the whole night crying.

Later on, they said that not only would she not take off her trousers for him, but she even refused to work in the fields. And when Wen Hai came in from a hard day's work, instead of cooking for him, she did nothing but cry; she kept it up all day long.

Before long, the village was in an uproar. Not taking her trousers off for him is one thing, but refusing to work the fields and not cooking are things he should not tolerate.

"The founder of the Wen clan cave dwellers would not have tolerated this," they told Wen Hai.

"What should I do?"

"Beat her till she comes around."

"Can I do that?"

"Go ask your mother," said a man whose face was creased and pitted like a newly plowed hillside and on whose chin grew a wispy goatee like partially chewed grass on a grave site.

Wen Hai went and asked his mother, who told him, "Trees need to be pounded if they are to grow straight. Women are the same."

So Wen Hai went home and, taking his mother's advice, beat his wife black and blue.

People listening at the door reported, "It worked. Wen Hai is doing it to his wife right now, and he keeps saying, 'Fuck your old lady. You think I'm screwing you? No, I'm screwing that two thousand yuan. Fuck your old lady. You think I'm screwing you? No, I'm screwing that two thousand yuan!'"

"That's exactly what Wen Hai's daddy did to his mother back then," someone said.

Not long afterward, Wen Hai's wife started cooking for him.

After that, Wen Hai's wife was seen following him out into the fields, keeping her distance, a hoe over her shoulder.

"My, my, black-and-blue."

"My, my, black-and-blue."

The women in the fields scrunched up their mouths, blinked their eyes, and shook their heads.


## Leng Two's Madness

No one knew why Leng Two went mad after being just fine for so long or why, after being mad for so long, he got better again.

Leng Two's father suffered from shortness of breath, and since herbal medicine had no effect, he thought about going to the mines to get some ephedrine from Leng One.

"Go on," his wife said. "He hasn't sent us any money for at least half a year. And bring some burlap bags back home with you."

So Leng Two's father climbed unsteadily onto a manure cart heading to the mines. The day after his father left, Leng Two went mad. The same thing happened as before; he kept shouting over and over, "Murder! Murder!"

Leng Two lay face up on the kang, slapping it with his big, swarthy hands, making it resound like a threshing ground. When he tired of that, he pressed the back of his head against the hard brick sleeping platform, arched his back, and shouted, "Murder! Murder!" When he tired of that, he recommenced slapping the kang. Not daring to leave his side, Leng Two's mother kept a vigil beside him.

We're done for if he really commits murder. He would have to be possessed to really commit murder. These were her thoughts as she stood by the stove. She wiped her eyes with her sleeve.

"So fucking poor," Leng Two said often, "that we can't even eat oatmeal bread without mixing it with wild yams."

Leng Two's mother replied, "That's to save money for you."

"How many fucking years of going without oatmeal bread will it take to save up two thousand yuan?"

This time, Leng Two's mother went ahead and made some oatmeal bread. But he wouldn't eat it. He just kept shouting "Murder" and slapping the kang until he wore holes in the grass mat, which had already been mended with burlap bags.

Villagers said that if the barefoot doctor, one of those itinerant care providers, could do no good, she ought to ask the spirit healer to look at her son. But Leng Two's mother just shook her head, for she knew from experience that neither the barefoot doctor nor the spirit healer could cure him.

We're done for if he really commits murder. He would have to be possessed to really commit murder. Again these were her thoughts.

Then one day, the villagers realized that Leng Two had stopped screaming "Murder" and slapping the kang.

Leng Two slept soundly on the kang, snoring like a pig.

"Is he cured?" someone asked Leng Two's mother as she fetched water.

"Yes, he's fine."

"How did that happen?"

"He's fine." Leng Two's mother walked off in a hurry.

Leng Two's father returned on the manure cart, reporting that their daughter-in-law would give them no money but sent him back with a few burlap bags and some ephedrine. Leng Two's mother did not tell his father that he had gone mad, for she had not told him the time before either. Leng Two's father took no notice of the sorry condition of the kang mat, either this time or the time before. He was concerned only with the ephedrine, two crystals of which would take care of his problem.

Leng Two's mother mashed some boiled yams for Leng Two to use as paste to mend the grass mat with the burlap bags.

At least he didn't commit murder. At least he's not possessed, Leng Two's mother was thinking as she stood beside the stove, watching him mend the mat. She raised her arm to wipe her eyes with her sleeve every so often.

## In the Haystack

Silence all around; the moon goddess casts her light on the ground. On the moonlit side of the haystack, he and she tamp out a nesting spot.

"You first."

"No, you first."

"We'll go in together, then."

He and she climb into the nest, bringing the hay sliding down so that it buries them both. He reaches out with his muscular arms to prop it up again.

"Don't worry, this is fine." She cuddles up in his arms. "You must hate me, Elder Brother Chou."

"I don't hate you. The coal miners have more money than me."

"I won't spend any. I'll save it up so you can find a wife."

"No, thanks."

"But I want to."

"I said, 'No, thanks.' "

"And I said, 'I want to.' "

He can tell she is on the verge of tears, so he holds his tongue.

"Elder Brother Chou," she says after a long silent moment.

"Hm?"

"Give me a kiss, Elder Brother Chou."

"Don't be like that."

"But I want to."

"I'm not in the mood today."

"But I want to."

Once again, he can tell she is on the verge of tears, so he leans over and pecks her on the cheek, gently, softly.

"Not there, here." She puckers up.

He gives her a peck on the lips, cool and wet.

"How did that taste?"

"Like oats."

"Wrong, you're wrong. Try again." She pulls his head down.

"It still tastes like oats," he says after a thoughtful pause.

"Don't be silly. I ate some hard candy a while ago. Come on, try again." Again she pulls his head down.

"Hard candy, it tastes like hard candy," he hurries to say.

Neither of them says anything for a long while.

"Elder Brother Chou."

"Hm?"

"Why don't I do this for you tonight?"

"No, no, the goddess of the moon is right outside, so you can't do that. It's not something girls of the Wen clan cave dwellers do."

"Then make it next time, when I come back."

"Um."

Once again, there is a long silence, except for the footsteps and sighs of the moon goddess.

"Elder Brother Chou."

"Hm?"

"It's fate."

"Yes, it is."

"Our rotten fate."

"Mine, maybe. Yours is OK."

"No, it isn't."

"Yes, it is."

"No, it isn't."

"Yes, it is."

"I said, 'No, it isn't.'"

He can tell she is crying now. He also feels hot tears rolling down his cheeks and splashing onto her face.

## Grandpa Pothook

Grandpa Pothook was carried back from the graveyard again.

Grandpa Pothook was from another province and had no kin in the village, but everyone still called him Grandpa. When he got drunk, he became everyone's grandpa, young and old. That is exactly what everyone called him.

Pothook was the only individual who drank every day and could afford to do it. His younger brother, Panhook, a ranking official in their native province, sent him twenty or thirty yuan every month—he spent it on drink.

Pothook was not one to eat anything with his wine, which he drank warm. He had a unique method for warming his wine: he made a little pocket in the crotch of his pants, where he tucked away the wine bottle after every couple of swigs.

Pothook liked to share his wine. "Come on, take a fucking swig for your grandpa here." He'd then suck in his breath, making a hollow in his wrinkled belly so he could reach down into his crotch to bring out the bottle. It would be nice and warm. Besides the smell of wine, the bottle carried other odors, rank enough that some refused the offer. But others, less fastidious, hoisted the bottle like a bugle and—*glug glug*—took a healthy swig. Pothook, his eyes crinkled in a smile, would cock his head to watch, his mouth opening and closing as if the liquid were pouring down his own throat.

As soon as Pothook was drunk, he staggered off toward the graveyard, muttering the same two lines from a folk song:

*When I think of you in the daytime, I climb the wall to you;*
*When I think of you late at night, there's nothing I can do.*

Once he reached the graveyard, he lay spreadeagled atop a large stone to sleep it off. Weather permitting, he would strip naked, exposing his skin to ants and an assortment of bugs.

"Go on, go down to the graveyard, and carry Grandpa Pothook back. We can't let him catch cold," one of the older generation would say to one of the younger ones, who would take four or five friends along.

When he had sobered up a bit, they would start teasing him: "Do the tiger hop for us, Grandpa Pothook!"

And he'd reply, "I'm too old for that sort of stuff."

"You're not too old," they would say as they wove a tail out of tall grass.

Pothook would hold the rope in the crack of his ass and begin hopping all over the place. Instead of falling out, the tail would smack loudly against the scrawny thing hanging between his legs. That had everybody in stitches.

Now they were carrying him back once again, but this time Grandpa Pothook uttered only a single comment before passing out for the last time: "Bury me in Widow Three's grave."

Never expecting him to say something like this, everyone who heard him stared blankly into space.

TRANSLATED BY HOWARD GOLDBLATT

# The Summons

## CAN XUE

When Old Mu Xi woke up, he found himself lying on a small wooden boat afloat on a pitch-dark river. The silent river was very dirty and so wide that he couldn't see the banks. Nor were there any other boats in sight. The setting sun declined in the extreme west like a tiny red button falling into the black waters of eternity.

Old Mu Xi sat up and stretched, remembering he once had looked forward to this day for a long time, and now it had come, yet in the interim he had managed to forget about it. He looked around and found that the river was not flowing and his little boat was motionless. Furthermore, the boat had no oar on board. Once in a while, a breath of ill wind from nowhere dusted his face as lightly as if it were both there and not there. The little boat would move some distance in the breeze before stopping again. Old Mu Xi thought to himself, Turns out there's not much going on here.

Suddenly out of nowhere, a faint call could be heard: "Old Mu . . . Xi! Old . . ."

Old Mu Xi gasped and was dumbstruck, yet the call resounded in his ear. As he heard that baleful voice, his vision began to blur, and his whole body became extremely old and feeble. He struggled, trying for the last time to pronounce a syllable: "Zhuo," he said, then dropped to the deck of the little boat like a piece of firewood, his glazed eyes turned up to the gray-black sky. He was sinking back into memory.

More than a decade before, Old Mu Xi had inherited a sum of money, which he and a friend used for investments. Together, they bought a piece of uncultivated land, where they decided to grow corn. They set to work immediately, but the heavens seemed to be against them. Four years running, they harvested almost nothing because of bad weather. Mu Xi and his friend encouraged each other and continued to work hard. Finally in the fifth year, they were rewarded with a bumper crop. Just before the harvest, Old Mu Xi's friend suddenly suggested a distribution plan, insisting he should get three-fourths of the crop. He also criticized Old Mu Xi for his lazy way of working. He even hinted that the money Mu Xi had used to buy the land came from questionable sources.

All of this struck like a lightning bolt. During the ensuing quarrel, all the villagers took the side of Mu Xi's friend. Old Mu Xi knew that the villagers sided with his partner because he himself was a widower and without family. In the countryside, a widower was an ill-fated figure. Ultimately, Old Mu Xi watched his friend claim all of the harvest and also threaten Mu Xi not to get close to this piece of land—since the harvest belonged to him, the land naturally was his also. All the villagers supported Old Mu Xi's friend.

After several sleepless nights, Old Mu Xi killed his friend with a sickle and began his prolonged life as a fugitive.

He always chose to travel on mountain paths, especially those that ran through dense, primitive forests. He was not afraid of losing his way. As a matter of fact, so much the better if he lost his way, because then nobody could find him. Over several months of rain and wind, he gradually developed a pair of iron soles and an animal's stomach—now he could survive by eating leaves. During that period, the shadow of horror forever hung over him, forcing him to flee frantically. Surprisingly, the animals in the forests never harmed him. Instead, they all went their own way and coexisted without any trouble.

One evening when he had just emerged from a forest, he vaguely heard a gong. He thought it was sounded by people trying to catch him, so he quickly hid in the bushes. The people passed him by, however, laughing and talking. They turned out to be a troupe of acrobats traveling by night.

Perhaps people had already forgotten about the murder he had committed. Perhaps nobody in the village had ever thought of either reporting or capturing him. Perhaps the mountain forest he was in at the moment was far, far away from his hometown. It could be anything. But not once had Old Mu Xi pondered these possibilities. He considered what he had done to be so serious that he didn't believe there could be any pardon. Holding such a belief, he walked hurriedly through the bushes, his body scratched bloody. This character trait was destructive, driving Old Mu Xi to hide out and separate himself from other people.

Several years of dining on the wind and drinking the morning dew passed. Long thick hair grew on Old Mu Xi's body. His clothes had been worn out for some time, and long brown hair sneaked its way out through the holes. One day when he was taking a bath in the river, he was startled to see the reflection of his body. After careful thought, he felt greatly relieved: from then on, he no longer wore clothes. When he met up with people, he didn't feel so frightened because he figured nobody could recognize him. But in his stubborn mind, he refused to accept the possibility that he might get away with his crime. By now, he had become set in this way of thinking.

Life in the forest was extremely monotonous. He couldn't get used to eating meat, particularly raw meat, so he never caught small animals. His daily task was to find tender tree leaves to eat, and he disliked staying in one place—his imagination needed constant refreshing—so he was constantly on the move, picking leaves along the way to keep up his strength. He frequently encountered people as he went; without exception, they screamed and ran away, and at that moment he would feel an unreasonable satisfaction.

Yet the nights were hard to endure, and this hardship had nothing to do with the weather. Old Mu Xi had long adjusted to wind and rain, scorching heat and freezing cold. In winter, there were fewer tender leaves, so he had to eat old ones, but his stomach had become strong. The hardship derived from his feeling of suspension.

Whenever he fell asleep, he felt clearly that he was suspended in midair. Beneath him, the villagers were busy working their fields, barefoot children ambled along the bank between the plots, chimneys gave out a light-gray smoke; yet all of that had nothing to do with him. Hanging in midair, he felt dizzy; it seemed as if his innards were flying out of his body. The nightmare would continue until he was startled awake by his extreme terror. Since fleeing into the forest, he had spent every night this way. Mornings when he arose, he would be pale, his body shivering like a typhoid victim's. Each step was agony. He would struggle to collect a large quantity of leaves to compensate for the strength he had lost during the night. Slowly, he would recover his energy, and toward afternoon he would have regained his vitality almost fully.

Old Mu Xi passed one month after another, one year after another in such a pattern. In moments of desperation, he often dreamed of finding a place that no one could think of or remember. There, one would neither hear the wind chimes echoing in the mountains nor see the leaves changing color with the seasons. The earth and sky would merge. Perhaps in such a place, he would no longer feel suspended in midair, and he wouldn't have to eat all those leaves.

After many, many years, he finally returned to his hometown. He didn't choose the way home purposely. He never chose his way. This homecoming could only be called a coincidence. Even he was surprised for a long time.

On a familiar little hill, he saw the small tile-roofed house where he had once lived, and a few of the same villagers. Like one transfixed, he stood there for a long time, thinking how awkward it had been to be among them back then, when every day had seemed as long as a year. He didn't feel like going home to have a look around, even if they pardoned him; for him, returning home was meaningless, and he could no longer participate in that way of life. Calmly, he jumped into a stream at the entrance to the village to take a bath; then he returned to the mountain.

Many people saw him, yet nobody recognized him. In fact, the incident had happened so long ago that nobody connected him with it anymore. That night, people in the village closed their doors very early and stayed inside. And the topic they discussed was the wild man. Old Mu Xi stayed for a few days in the mountains near his hometown, but he soon became bored and headed north, where the forest was denser. As he left his hometown, he heard deafening firecrackers, which the villagers, fearing the wild man, set off to boost their courage. Old Mu Xi laughed and walked quickly northward through the smell of gunpowder.

One rather strange thing was that his fellow villagers had already forgotten the murder case. They had also forgotten the position they had taken in the dispute, yet they had never forgotten Mu Xi as a person. In folk legend, he had been gradually elevated to a hero of the forest, a powerful and unconstrained hero like a heavenly steed soaring across the skies. One day, they put up posters inviting Old Mu Xi to return, to come home, to return to the people, but he had gone far away and did not see those notices. Even if he had, he would not have believed in the pardon because he was confident he had seen through the people's hearts and minds. Home would not be the place for him. He wanted to go where people had totally forgotten, a place where the sky and earth had merged.

He found that lately, his capacity for food was growing and the blood in his veins had turned green (he scratched his finger once on a thorny vine). Nights had become more and more terrifying. The clear-cut separation of sky from earth forced him to struggle desperately since he felt suspended between them. Old Mu Xi was both startled and scared.

When Old Mu Xi had begun living in the forest, he often mumbled to himself. The language he had used in society obviously was strongly rooted in him. With passing time, Old Mu Xi's desire to speak grew fainter and fainter. One day, he discovered he could not speak a single word. He tried to use the language that had served him in the past for thinking, but it had escaped him. The sound he produced after much effort turned out to resemble baby talk. Quickly, Old Mu Xi discovered the benefit of losing his linguistic memory. His throat became coarse and natural. Often, he didn't need to think to express his urges accurately and easily. Thus he roared, cried, and shouted at will day and night, feeling completely free. One day after several years in his dream world, he felt extremely lucky that he had not gone home, because he could not have endured the sounds those people made. To him, they were shrill and irritating, a completely senseless display of technique. Even little children would twist their lips strangely to make outlandish sounds. Now that he was hidden in the forest, whenever he recalled that he used to talk like that, he would blush with shame.

Although the murder had occurred years before, the image of his victim was still sharp in Old Mu Xi's mind, for he was a born bearer of grudges. Numerous times in those moments before falling asleep, he engaged his enemy in bloody battle, emitting heroic roars. Numerous times, he experienced the pride of triumph and the humiliation of defeat. In these moments of half sleep, his brief human life repeated itself. When Old Mu Xi woke up, his desire for battle had disappeared completely. He would think of the foe he had killed years before and be somewhat surprised: could it be that he had not killed him? Was that forcible seizure of the cropland some kind of illusion? But regardless of the event's authenticity, it or something like it had forced his departure. Old Mu Xi was certain about that, and he felt himself very fortunate indeed. In the same way that he refused to believe in pardons, the stubborn Mu Xi would not make peace with his enemy. In the dim night, as he floated in midair, facing his opponent across two isolated realms, his emotions were clear and unambiguous. On such occasions, he would devise all kinds of unrealistic schemes for murdering his foe, maneuvering again and again, dismissing the idea, then maneuvering again, and then dismissing the plan again in order to conceal his inner horror, to forget the feeling of being suspended in midair.

One day about half a month after he had left for the north, he saw a group of people tramping around in the grassland in the woods. They all cupped their hands in the shape of a trumpet and called into the air: "Old Mu Xi! Old Mu Xi . . ."

Old Mu Xi's jaw dropped in surprise. The sound seemed familiar, yet the memory was so distant and vague that he could not understand their cries. The people struck him as somehow strange. Their pronunciation was not as displeasing as that of ordinary people, yet it was too mechanical. Always they shouted exactly the same "Old—Mu—Xi" without variation, without rise and fall, very unsatisfyingly. From the bushes, he stared at them, restraining himself, expecting that one of them would give out some different sound.

But they didn't know what he was thinking. They appeared to be indulged in their game as they called out forcefully, "Old Mu Xi! Old—Mu—Xi!" Amid the sound were children's loud voices.

Old Mu Xi flew into a rage. Without thinking, he jumped out from his hiding place, ran into the middle of their circle, and shouted, "Ha! Hahaha! Ah! Guaguagua!"

Seeing the longhaired wild man and hearing his piercing cries echo through mountain and forest, everybody fled madly down the slopes, losing their shoes along the way.

Old Mu Xi watched their backs with contempt, emitting one drawn-out syllable: "Zhuo!" The sound stirred up a frenzy in his heart.

Old Mu Xi was still troubled by his shadowy memories, which revealed themselves in dreams at night; his dreams were endless torture. Old Mu Xi's experiences removed the fear of being suspended in midair. What he really feared was the feeling that he was confronting the shadowy human world like a criminal facing execution. There emerged in his vague, groundless memory, for no specific reason, the image of a river. He recalled that its water could completely cut off people's memories of the world. With this vague thought taking hold in his mind, Old Mu Xi set out to find that river.

\* \* \*

Many years passed, quite a few, actually. Old Mu Xi had crossed innumerable mountains. Whenever he arrived at a mountain, he would climb to the top to look around. He had seen all kinds of rivers, each one different. Yet none was the one he was looking for, not at all. From the riverbanks came the faint call: "Old Mu Xi! Old Mu Xi . . ." More and more, the sound revealed its ominous meaning and seemed to hang in the air forever. Old Mu Xi wrinkled his brow and felt discouraged. He hated that sound.

He didn't know when he began to realize that his health was deteriorating. His appetite was decreasing. Sometimes he wouldn't eat a single leaf all day long, yet he walked without pause, looking more and more determined. His weakened condition lasted for a long time. Then one day, he saw his reflection in a forest creek. It looked like a ghost. The part below his skull had nearly disappeared, leaving only a few thin sticks, a rectangular box, and something lumpy. Long hair grew over the thin sticks, the box, and the lumps. He closed his eyes, not wanting to see more clearly. Obviously, his constitution could no longer stand the enormous exhaustion of his nights. He was disappearing. Then he heard shouting from far outside the forest. For him, the ominous shouts were full of foreboding. He couldn't endure it, so he covered his ears.

That morning when the frost settled over the forest, Old Mu Xi lay down inside a hole in a tree. He plugged his ears with his fingers because the unbearable sound came from afar on the wind. He lay wide-eyed in the darkness, which smelled of decayed wood. He gurgled softly as if groaning, as if complaining. He rolled over and looked out at the white frost on the ground and at little animals searching for food.

It was broad daylight. A beam of light entered the hole. Old Mu Xi could see his own body. It was about to disappear completely. His fingers and toes had become thin as matchsticks and black as the tree's moldy bark.

He began to question whether there really was a river that could erase memories, because his memory of the river was itself unreliable. Finally, he truly felt there wouldn't be any miracle. He closed his eyes and waited in terror for that final emptiness to arrive. He did not forget to plug his ears with his matchstick fingers; in fact, he couldn't forget anything at all. For the first time in his life, he fell asleep in broad daylight. In his dream, he hummed. Outside the hole, there blew a gust of frosty wind.

Old Mu Xi entered the dreamland mentioned earlier. And that dreamland led to all that was written afterward.

TRANSLATED BY JIAN ZHANG AND RONALD R. JANSSEN

# The Ancestor

## Bi Feiyu

Standing quietly at the far end of time, Great-Grandmother has transcended the meaning of life. Her life encompasses an entire century of history. She is silent year-round. During that weak and quiet century, my grandfather's generation all passed away, leaving only the old lady to look down from across the generation gap at her grandchildren and great-grandchildren. Her eyes are white with cataracts, which allow her to look down, beyond all human limits, shrinking the vastness and boundlessness of the universe while displaying the same immemorial and profound qualities of matter itself. To this day, Great-Grandmother has maintained the customs and attitudes of the Late Qing dynasty. Great-Grandmother does not bathe. All year-round, the smells of a coffin and coffin nails hover over her. Great-Grandmother does not brush her teeth. Great-Grandmother does not believe in airplanes. Great-Grandmother does not watch television. Great-Grandmother understands nothing but her hometown dialect, not even the Mandarin radio broadcasts.

Great-Grandmother spends every morning at her toilet. She has begun every morning for the last hundred years with the same ritual—fixing her hair in the Qing-dynasty style. Afterward, she sits up straight without saying a word, spending hours measuring up whatever she first lays eyes on. The old woman's way of sizing up things is like philosophical speculation—she looks but does not see, what appears true is false, and any historical conclusion is always shrouded in the mists of ambiguity. Each winter, Great-Grandmother sits in the sunshine, which seems incapable of penetrating her and instead merely casts a shadow behind her. That is the image—carved in wood—I had of my great-grandmother from ten years ago. Ten years ago, on the morning I left to study in Beijing, I looked back at Great-Grandmother's garret. She was already up and standing at her window, time covering her cheeks with a network of wrinkles. She stood as tranquilly as a piece of antique porcelain, all the tiny cracks displaying an archaeological significance. I knew she couldn't see, but I waved to her anyway. I suspected I would never see her again, and I felt very sad. Ten years later, she was still there, as tranquil as an antique, standing at the window. This time, I was the father of a son, and I could see the ravages wrought by those ten years. Great-Grandmother didn't move, as if the only thing that had happened in the last ten years were that another layer of dust was added to the antique porcelain.

I returned home with my wife and son after receiving Father's urgent telegram. My home is situated at the far end of a long, dark alleyway in a dusty gray town. To get there, you must make five turns and pass by ten thresholds. There is a dark, dank passageway, above which sits the wooden garret where my great-grandmother lives.

The space inside Great-Grandmother's garret forms a separate universe, a dark, enigmatic corner of my home. No one is permitted to enter. I remember hearing Great-Grandmother say when I was small, "Don't even think about coming in, not unless I'm dead." In those days, my father would say, "What's all this talk of death? We won't come in; nobody is thinking of entering."

Returning home this time, I noticed a number of major changes. The place was a mess and in decay; things had been torn down and removed from the house. After making only the third turn, I saw that the neighbor on the other side of our western wall had cleared out; the only remaining traces were some bricks and a few pieces of wood. And those ancient remains formed a very modern flat composition. To one side, Great-Grandmother's garret stood all alone, looking forlorn and helpless, making one think of a wooden coffin hanging on a precipice.

In the evening when the maid was helping her down the stairs to dinner, I walked up and called loudly to her, "Great-Grandmother."

Her eyes fixed on me, and after a long pause she said, "I heard your footsteps this afternoon."

I let my wife greet Great-Grandmother. Clutching our son, she stood nervously, if not fearfully, before Great-Grandmother. For a moment, I didn't know what my son should call my great-grandmother. Since he could not speak yet, I could address her for him only as Old Ancestor. Great-Grandmother stood in front of my son for a long time. She felt around inside his diaper, then she smiled. When she smiled, it was like an irregular chink that had opened in parched ground. I knew she must have touched his little penis. She drew back her hands, spit on her fingers, and pressed them between my son's eyebrows. My son cried. Irrelevantly, Great-Grandmother shouted "Old Ancestor" at him. I thought she had made a mistake, but I was incapable of deciphering the mystery and the profundity of her universe.

Great-Grandmother said, "They've all left us." I knew she was referring to our neighbors of old. "Your great-grandfather told me that our days as neighbors were limited," she said. When Great-Grandmother spoke, her perfect mouthful of teeth shone like fossils. "When this house was built, the Chong Zhen emperor had not yet ascended the throne." When she finished speaking, she heaved a long sigh and said nothing more for the rest of the night. Piercing my ears and her silence, that long sigh was like the light of a comet falling back across the ages to the Ming dynasty.

I saw our house moving in the fluid of time, and the shore upon which the arcing waves broke was Great-Grandmother's teeth. That's really weird.

After seeing Great-Grandmother back to her garret, Father

said, "You've been on the road all day, better go to bed early. If there is anything to do, it can wait till tomorrow. You two sleep in your mother's and my bed." When he finished speaking, Father opened the lattice door to the east wing. I remembered that Great-Grandmother's coffin had always been stored there and that every year Father applied another coat of black lacquer tinged with red. For decades, the coffin had calmly followed the revolutions of the earth around the sun with Great-Grandmother, both exchanging positions of responsibility, looking forward to each other. They had a mutual understanding that each would give the other its or her significance and eternal ending.

"Where are you going to sleep?" I asked Father.

"In your great-grandmother's coffin," said Father.

My wife gave me a nervous look. Unsure, she refrained from talking. Father quietly closed the door, and the east wing quickly became black as the giant pupil of an eye.

Once in bed, my wife said, "Why does he sleep in a coffin?"

"It doesn't matter, we're all one family. Dead or alive, we're all together."

"The living can't live with the dead, no matter what," said my wife.

To comfort her, I said, "That's the way our family does things. There's nothing unusual about sleeping in a coffin; sometimes we even fight over who gets to sleep in it. I had an older brother and an older sister who died young. Great-Grandmother wouldn't permit them to be buried outside, so we buried them under the bed."

My wife sat up immediately. "Where?"

"Under the bed." I tapped on the wooden planks of the bed with my foot, making a hollow sound. "Right under this board."

My wife's eyes shone with fear. She clutched my arm and said, "Why did your family do that?"

"It's not just our family," I said. "Every family is the same."

My wife held me tightly by the waist. "I'm scared," she said. "I'm scared to death."

\* \* \*

I called you home for Great-Grandmother's sake."

"Is she going to die soon?" I asked.

Silently, Father shook his head. "If only that were the case," said Father. "I don't care what anyone says, all I wish is for the old lady to die."

I asked him what was the matter and how he could say such a thing.

Father lowered his head and said nothing. Father's silence reminded me of Great-Grandmother at another time.

"In another ten days or so, your great-grandmother will be one hundred years old," said Father. It looked as though Great-Grandmother had become a wooden cangue on him. Father lifted his head, looked at me, and asked, "Did you see her mouthful of teeth?"

I didn't understand Father. I couldn't figure out what he was driving at.

Father tugged at the cuff of my Western-style suit and, lowering his voice, said, "If a person lives to a hundred and still has all her teeth, she'll become a demon after she dies."

"How can that be?" I asked.

"Why shouldn't it?" asked my father.

"Who ever saw anyone become a demon?"

"Did anyone ever *not* see a person become a demon?"

How could that be possible? I asked myself. My back seemed to go numb and felt all prickly. I saw in Father's eyes the same look I had seen in my wife's. She was afraid of death, but my father was afraid of life.

Explosions were heard all around our house. Several dynasties were reduced to rubble and dust in the strong smell of dynamite. The state of relative rest between buildings and debris is what the history books call a dynasty. The workers had done their utmost to ensure that a building would last. Later, people would complain, "What's the point of making it so solid? Dynasties are like buildings and teeth—they grow, and they crumble." The smell of dynamite is like incense in a Buddhist country—it alters the mystery present in the redeemer's posture.

My son walked haltingly around the courtyard. Holding on to the same small redwood stool that I had held on to when I was a child, he played by himself in a corner of the courtyard. He was absorbed in playing with a bamboo chopstick. After two hours, he was drooling and humming a hymn only God could understand. Great-Grandmother stood in another corner of the courtyard, eyeing my son and listening to him sing. It must have been because of him that she hadn't gone upstairs. Great-Grandmother approached my son, and they conversed with a natural affinity in a language not understood by other human beings. On their faces played an essential correspondence given to man by Nature, echoing each other like sunrise and sunset, relying on each other's heartbeats to transmit spring, summer, fall, and winter, making of humanity the most wonderful quintessence of the universe. They talked. There was no interpreter. It was the way the wind understood the sound of the leaves, or the way water guessed the direction of the waves, or the way light saw the mirror, or the way one pupil could contain another.

"They seem to be having fun. What are they playing?" my wife asked.

Great-Grandmother turned and said to me, "When I die, take a piece of cloth from your son, wrap some of his hair in it, and sew it into the cuff of my sleeve."

"What is all this talk about death? You're still young."

"Don't forget," said Great-Grandmother.

"All right," I replied.

"It doesn't matter how long you live—as soon as you open your eyes, it's time to close them," Great-Grandmother said, smiling. "If you talk about long life, then it will be among the shadows. Remember—a piece of cloth. Don't forget."

Great-Grandmother's hundredth birthday was slowly drawing

nearer. My house was shrouded in fear like the dust that silently covered the table and porcelain.

That night, Father's twelve brothers gathered at our house. I sat to one side. In my imagination, Great-Grandmother's teeth emitted a sound like breaking ice. The men smoked quietly. In their preoccupation was the solemn atmosphere of having arrived at a juncture in history. No one spoke. At a silent juncture in history, the first conclusion is the direct equivalent to the outcome of history. This is our accustomed way of doing things. At that moment, a rumble was heard outside. The sound reminded me that the road home had sent me back to the Ming dynasty, which caused me to tremble even more.

Finally, Father lifted his head in the smoke and said firmly, "Pull them." He turned to look at me. His look made me feel that I couldn't bear the weight of history. I smiled. But even I didn't know what I was smiling about. On many important occasions, I wore a foolish smile, my heart empty as the wind. I suspect that many of those present saw my foolish smile.

After things had quieted down, my wife complained, "Why are things such a mess? Why is your family such a mess? The boy's hands are always twitching."

"He'll be fine soon," I said. "He'll be fine in a couple of days. He'll calm down soon."

"I can't find the boy's shoes," my wife said.

"How could they disappear? Who'd want such little shoes?" I asked.

My wife said she couldn't find his red shoes. I looked everywhere. A little impatiently, I said, "If they're gone, they're gone. Just buy another pair tomorrow."

"That's ridiculous," said my wife. "Yesterday you lost a pair of Nikes, and today the boy's are gone. Ridiculous."

"Why make such a fuss over it?" I asked. "If Mother heard you, there'd really be trouble."

\* \* \*

Pulling Great-Grandmother's teeth constituted a unique page in the history of my life. A drizzle was blowing that morning. You really couldn't call it rain—it was like rain and like mist but also like wind. The sky secreted a viscous historical atmosphere. The plot in our house got quickly under way. Only Great-Grandmother, who was the object of the plot, was left in the dark. We were prepared, nobody said a word. There was a sense of taking fate in our hands and of participating in the excitement of a historical mission, and there was the exhilaration of committing a crime. This is the way humanity commonly approaches history. Great-Grandmother was sitting at her window, easy as a dream, like an uneventful period in a historical record. All around her, we were motionless and silent, waiting for the signal to stand up and cast the shadow of ambush onto the ground.

Around noon, Fifth Uncle came to the house. He looked nervous and worried. Fifth Uncle called for Father. Standing under the eaves and facing Father, he said, "We can't get any anesthetic; it's too tightly controlled by the hospital."

Father's face darkened, looking like the moss on an ancient brick.

"Are we going to pull them or not?" asked Fifth Uncle.

Father said nothing. Facing Great-Grandmother's little garret, Father lowered his head and said, "Grandmother, you will just have to suffer."

It was damp everywhere. The accumulated dust swelled. For a long time, I was unable to wipe away the gray streaks from this part of my memory. All afternoon, my uncles sat in the central room, drinking. The table full of wine had been prepared for Great-Grandmother, so the old lady came downstairs especially early. She was all smiles. She couldn't see well, her eyes hidden behind an inauspicious shroud. Normally, her face wore a somewhat confused expression. As soon as Great-Grandmother sat down, my uncles toasted her. My father said, "Grandmother, you will be one hundred soon. May you outlast South Mountain and be more prosperous than the Eastern Sea."

Great-Grandmother laughed. "I can't live much longer," she said happily, holding her glass. "If I live much longer, I'll become a demon." Then she drank down the wine.

The faces of my uncles darkened, looking perplexed and alarmed. The wine glasses in their hands appeared heavy; they hesitated. Fortunately, Great-Grandmother couldn't see.

I have no recollection about the moment of silence that followed. Perhaps it was just a few minutes, or perhaps another layer of dust had settled on Great-Grandmother's shoulders—it has never been clear to me. At the end of that moment of silence, Father and his twelve brothers got up from their seats and knelt before Great-Grandmother. Her lips were slightly parted, and every tooth seemed to smile. Great-Grandmother said, "Get up, get up, my darlings, we haven't observed that custom in ages." The dark shapes of her darlings stood up. Fifth Uncle held a rope, Ninth Uncle gripped a pair of pliers, and Seventh Uncle held a redwood tray. They pounced on her and held her fast. In a few minutes, Great-Grandmother's teeth were all lying on the tray; the roots of her teeth were covered with bloody shreds of flesh. I stared at Great-Grandmother's teeth; in them, I saw humanity's direct intuition of time. It is our fear of time that makes us draw a link between teeth and their loss. Seventh Uncle handed the redwood tray to me. The thought vanished, and I can't remember much. Later, I was unable to recall what I was thinking at that time. All I remember is the swift, violent, harsh, and painful psychological experience. Later, I smelled the dynamite—the odor of the dynamite burned like ice. I was bitten by the odor.

Tenth Uncle said, "Elder Brother, I can't stop the bleeding. Should we take her to the hospital?"

Father said, "We can't. The doctor will know what happened as soon as he sees her."

Great-Grandmother had collapsed on the brick floor, her lips deeply sunken. Teeth are funny things. When they are there, they can't be seen, but as soon as they are gone, the face changes beyond recognition. Great-Grandmother's hundred-year-old blood spread around her lips and flowed more disorderedly than time. Great-Grandmother lay on the floor, breathing heavily. Her throat gurgled and creaked like oars. Her skin was slowly losing color and resembled traditional rice paper.

Ninth Uncle said, "She's fading fast."

Fifth Uncle said, "Get her some water. What are you doing standing around?"

Seventh Uncle tried several times; he lifted her head and shook it several times. It was no good, the water wouldn't go down.

At that moment, my son started crying in the west wing. I ran over and asked my wife, "What's going on? Can't you even take care of the child?"

My wife said, "If he wants to cry, what can I do? What's all that racket in there?"

I said, "It's none of your business. You are not to come out unless I call you."

While coaxing our son, my wife said, "Being in your house is like being in the eighteenth level of hell. One can barely breathe here."

I frowned and asked, "Are you finished?"

Father said, "Take down a door; the floor is too cold."

A bunch of old men scrambled to lay the very old lady on the door. I walked over and lifted her eyelids. The world of Great-Grandmother's life lay shrouded in darkness behind her cataracts. Softly, I called, "Old Ancestor, Old Ancestor." Her head slid from my elbows to my hands.

Her thirteen grandchildren all knelt at the same time. Their bowed backs made their kneeling look pious.

Great-Grandmother was laid out on the lid of her coffin. The coffin was at least thirty years old. Many familiar and unfamiliar people came to offer their condolences. They walked down the dark, dank passageway to bring funeral money and to eat a mouthful of the noodles prepared to celebrate Great-Grandmother's birthday. My father and his twelve brothers as well as the thirty-seven male members of my generation took turns burning funeral money. The ashes floated all around my house, and the smell of death from the money swirled around the people who walked through the house. The smell of death was so alive. Even the rats came out of their holes and skittered away, seeing that no one was paying attention.

Kneeling before Great-Grandmother, I felt my heart go numb. Being the son of her eldest grandson, I caught a relieved look in the eyes of my father's generation. They buried Great-Grandmother's teeth separately, eliminating the chances of her becoming a demon after death. I tried to imagine what Great-Grandmother would look like as a demon, but my imagination could not break through conventional human patterns and styles, and that left me disappointed. Several times, the flames from the burning funeral money painfully licked my fingertips. I knew that money from the underworld could burn the fingers just as the money from this world was ice-cold and thus not easily touched. Father cooked the noodles, one pot after another. Everyone from the village was there—not sure of what he or she wanted to see. Many of the people removed the paper from Great-Grandmother's face. Her mouth was ghastly looking. Death always fixes the mouth of the dead at the worst moment, making death seem hideous. People came and went, each one about the same. They came, striding over the threshold into our Ming-dynasty house; leaving, they strode over the threshold and down the ancient alleyway to leave the Ming dynasty. Everyone should have had this hallucination from the moral point of view, against which the powerful explosions were powerless.

Putting Great-Grandmother into the coffin a little early was a clear expression of how flustered my father and uncles were. The coffin housed my great-grandmother. A coffin is like a classic text that records the mysteries of life and death. My father said to us, "Hold a three-day wake for Grandmother's soul." When Father pronounced the word *wake* he touched the coffin. My heart jumped when I heard the word. What is a wake? In my imagination, a soul is more alive than life itself. This way of thinking left me worried, but I couldn't say it out loud, for that would spell disaster. The strip of yellow cloth from my son's clothes became a banner fluttering before my great-grandmother's soul. She relied on that vigorously waving banner to make her way with ease through the underworld, where ghosts, big and small, could do nothing.

Father said, "Great-Grandmother's bad luck can be turned to good." Father was better at dealing with the affairs of the underworld than with those of this one. All members of the older generation are like that.

The most shocking event occurred at midnight. On that blue night filled with the odor of dynamite, my house fell into an utter life-and-death confusion. We held a wake according to Father's orders. Great-Grandmother's coffin was placed in the central hall on two supports. I slept under the coffin; a soy-oil lamp flickered weakly in front of the coffin all night. A number of white candles dozed amid long coils of incense. Uncooked noodles, steamed bread, and cubes of tofu and bean jelly were covered with lead-colored ash. The sound of a pile driver could be heard outside, vigorous as a cow but a little breathless. My ancient home seemed in decline, filled with an atmosphere of death. Just after midnight, nearly everyone holding the wake fell asleep. A few of my uncles were sitting around a small square table, their eyes shining with a green light. They were playing mah-jongg. Each piece they placed on the table sounded as heavy as a coffin.

"Two."

"Eight ten-thousands."

"Match."

My ears were filled with the shouting that followed as they played. Dreams like bats fluttered at dusk, their bodies flitting nervously. I don't know if I slept or not. I'm not sure. Those days when I slept, I seemed to be awake, and when I was awake, I seemed to be asleep. And the dreams I dreamed—half the time I couldn't tell what was real and what wasn't. I heard Seventh Uncle say, "Last game. After we finish this hand, let them take over." Then came the sound of shuffling mah-jongg tiles like a summer rain falling on Lake Taihu stones. Hearing these sounds, I was as if in a trance, but I clearly heard the sounds that followed. Betokened by the gods, I heard a sharp sound coming strangely from the edge of heaven. I propped myself up and barely missed hitting my head on the bottom of the coffin. I smelled the strange odor of the coffin and heard the sound of fingernails on the wood. I shook my head. It was completely quiet. Apparently, they heard something. We exchanged a look of terror. We clearly heard the sounds coming from the coffin, which functioned like a bass drum, amplifying the criticism and dissatisfaction of Great-Grandmother's fingernails against the coffin. My hands went slack, a number of my uncles looked at me, and their eyes shone to their biological limits. The scratching of her fingernails on the coffin was weak but frenzied, like the sharp, doomed cries of a rat in the mouth of a cat. Full of death's fervor, Great-Grandmother must have opened her cataract-covered eyes in the darkness and, at the same time, opened her toothless mouth. Great-Grandmother longed for light and space. Great-Grandmother's tiny three-inch bound feet—her golden lotuses—must have burst with energy as they kicked out twice, decisively opening a crack behind us as a cold wind blew in from eight hundred miles around.

Fifth Uncle said, "Open it up. Hurry! Open it up." Actually, Fifth Uncle didn't express himself in such a clear manner—his tongue was stiff as salted meat.

At first, Third Uncle didn't utter a word. Then he said, "Why weren't her fingernails clipped?"

We suddenly remembered Great-Grandmother's pointed gray nails. This threatening material became the most frightening part of a future countryside legend. We all held our breath, all our energy focused on listening. The sounds grew weaker and weaker, the pauses longer and longer. Finally, dead silence. To this day, I still believe that Great-Grandmother's left index finger was sticking up. We all knew she had her reasons for not prying with her nails, but we still waited a long time.

After the funeral procession, Great-Grandmother's descendants strode over the torches. In the field, the torches formed a wall between life and death. No, that's not accurate. After you've stepped past the torches, you've crossed over the screen between life and death. Flames blazed between each person's legs, and purplish smoke fled into the sky, where it formed a variety of hieroglyphs, like difficult-to-decipher prophecies left by the ancients. All I know is that half were written on sheepskin, the other half in the sky.

Entering the passageway at home, we just had to pause. I said, "Let's take a look at Great-Grandmother's garret."

Father said, "Everyone else stay put. He and I will go up alone."

We opened the door, and a cold wind from the last century spread its long hair and long nails toward us. Her garret was devoid of furniture, save for a bed and a dressing table. Father and I were at a loss. Our curiosity was like a free-falling body in reality.

Father said, "Shoes. Your son's little red shoes." I stepped forward. My son's red shoes were under her bed, toes pointing toward the bed plank. I also saw my old, beat-up Nikes. Behind my Nikes, arranged in order of age, were a pair of green army shoes, a pair of cotton shoes, a pair of cotton slippers, and a pair of wooden clogs. I noticed that the shoes, which were laid out in a spiral, seemed to gaze at one another with a light-footed expression. Confident yet ridiculous. It was at that moment that the illusion occurred. I saw the arrival of the ranks of my clan in a long spiral procession. They greeted me in our local dialect and the inherited manner of our clan. Like time, they were toothless, their eyes clouded with cataracts.

Father said, "What's this? What's going on here?"

I was on the point of asking my father the same question. But hearing his voice, I held my tongue.

TRANSLATED BY JOHN BALCOM

# Moonlight over the Field of Ghosts

## YANG ZHENGGUANG

Dou Bao was awakened by a full bladder. Throwing off his ripped and torn quilt, he sat bare bottomed on the edge of the kang, two spindly legs feeling the ground for his sandals. When he found them, he shoved his feet in and shuffled out the door of the cave. Dou Bao never bothered to bring a chamber pot to bed at night, not even in the winter. He just relieved himself as soon as he cleared the doorway. Since it was summer, he walked a little farther, until he was standing in front of the levee. The moon was bare bottomed, too. He raised his head, and in the quiet of the night he heard his piss flow in a rivulet down the side of the levee.

He shuddered, then shook himself. As he turned around, he spotted someone sitting on the rock in front of the cave. In the bright light of the bare-bottomed moon, he could see that it was his daughter, Dou Gua. She sat there so silently, resting her head in her hands, that her body seemed to have grown out of the rock. Dou Bao's face twitched.

He shuffled past his daughter. He lit the oil lamp, then climbed back onto the kang to put on his clothes. He reached for his pipe on the stovetop connected to the kang and settled back with his legs crossed. He knocked the bowl of his pipe against the stove twice, and his daughter entered the room.

Dou Gua rested her backside on the edge of the kang but didn't look at Dou Bao. Puffing away on his pipe, Dou Bao soon finished a bowl of tobacco, and still Dou Gua hadn't spoken. He refilled his pipe, the long stem tilting stiffly upward, as if to say, Fine, go ahead and just sit there. Sit until dawn if you want. But . . .

"He's dead," Dou Gua announced.

Dou Bao's face twitched a second time. The stem of his pipe seemed to go limp, almost drop off, but quickly tilted upward again.

"He followed me to the Field of Ghosts. I hit him with a rock. It caught him on the forehead, and he went down. He must be dead," she said. "He was still on the ground when I left. I killed him."

Dou Gua thought she heard a swish. The whip that Dou Bao used to herd sheep hung behind the door, its thong snaking quietly down the mud wall. She knew by experience that that was how it sounded when it skimmed past her ear; she felt a muscle on her back jump. Actually, nothing moved. The oil lamp had crackled, sending off a spark and causing the shadow of the whip on the wall to flicker.

Not a hint of expression on Dou Bao's face.

Earlier, when Dou Gua had returned from the town of Shaping, it was already dark. She hadn't got anything done in town. She'd run into Teacher Chai as soon as she got there, and his brief conversation with her had left her feeling bad. She'd sat down where the stream wound toward the irrigation ditch and watched the market goers pass by, one after the other, until they had all disappeared, leaving only a parched brown road. Then she had turned and come back home.

Mangmang was waiting for her in their cave. His arms swiftly closed around her, drawing her toward the kang. When she spat in his face, Mangmang loosened his hold to wipe the spit off with the back of his hand. He looked at her, smiled a secret smile, and climbed onto the kang. Stripping off his clothes, he slipped naked beneath the quilt.

She felt miserable and spat on him.

Afterward, she had come here.

Everyone called this place the Field of Ghosts. No one ever came here, least of all at night. This piece of land had never yielded a single crop, not a single blade of grass. It was only an expanse of red soil, while everywhere else the earth was brown. And because there was only this unvarying red soil, it was called the Field of Ghosts.

She came here often, always at night.

Tonight the Field of Ghosts was shrouded in a layer of moonlight. The red, red soil was shrouded in moonlight. She sat at the edge of the field, all by herself, without even a blade of grass around.

"Lanying!" Teacher Chai had called out to her in town as he approached from the other side.

Lanying was the name she'd used in school.

"Lanying, so you've come, too," he said.

"Teacher Chai," she greeted him.

"How have you been, Lanying?"

She remembered that she'd produced a smile.

"Quanmao's come back," continued Teacher Chai. "You remember him, don't you? Last year, he passed the exam and got accepted to high school, and now he's back for summer vacation. Why don't you go see him? He came by to see me and asked about you. You two were the top students in my class. . . . Quanmao is the first one from this town . . ."

She remembered that she'd produced a smile.

The smile she had to produce for Teacher Chai made her feel so miserable that she just turned around and headed back. She sat down where the stream wound toward the irrigation ditch and watched the market goers disappear, one after the other, until only a parched brown road remained. It was such a very long road.

She began walking, too. She walked and walked and became the girl of the pancake stall. She walked and walked and became Mangmang's woman.

Since it was Sunday and there was no school, she was tending the pancake stall in front of the house. A crew from Qiao Family Gully on their way to mend the terraced paddies walked by, their heads swiveling around to look in her direction.

"That's some tender young cabbage," one of them remarked.

"Belongs to Dou Bao," said another.

"If anyone on the way asks who we are, you just say we're man and wife. . . ." Someone started a bawdy song.

She was a little frightened. She wanted to go to the latrine, but she didn't dare get up until all the men were gone.

The latrine was located west of the levee, screened by corn-stalks. She had just crouched down when she heard someone laughing above her.

It was Mangmang. He was laughing. Then he laughed some more, his head tilted to one side so he could see her thighs.

To think that there could be such a shameless man on this earth! She wept. She locked herself in the cave and wept until Dou Bao came back from herding sheep.

Dou Bao already knew. His face livid with anger, he called for her to come out. She heard the swish of the whip as it skimmed past her ear and felt a sharp pain on her back as if she had been slashed with a knife.

That evening, Dou Bao went to Qiao Family Gully to look up Mangmang's father.

"Your Mangmang has laid eyes on my daughter's body. Fork over a few coppers, and take her into your house. It's a fucking bargain for the lot of you!"

She was sixteen then and never set foot in school again.

Mangmang was a bull. When he wasn't working, he was sleeping. His hands were rough as winnowing fans, his toes like the fangs of a tiger. As soon as he walked in the door, he threw his arms around Dou Gua.

The tender young cabbage was plucked three times that night.

"Mangmang, please go easy on me," she begged.

He just looked at her and laughed.

"Mangmang, can't you do something else?"

"Like what?" he replied. "This is what everyone does."

As soon as dusk fell, the village became silent as a graveyard. Not a sound to be heard, not a soul to be seen. All the men had their arms around their women. After all, what else was there to do at night? It was only at this time that the men, exhausted by a day of hard labor, could shift their weariness onto the bosoms of their women, then stretch out beside them, and fall into a deathlike sleep that even a jab with an awl couldn't disturb.

While Mangmang slept in oblivion, Dou Gua wept softly. He couldn't hear her sobs. He needed a good night's sleep; he had to go up the mountain in the morning.

Before Mangmang left for the mountain, he made himself a packet of Dou Gua's pancakes. Then, for rolling tobacco, he tore off sheets of paper from the head of the kang, pages from Dou Gua's schoolbooks.

And so the tender young cabbage was plucked by Mangmang.

Three years had passed, and still no offspring.

"Dou Gua, don't you want to spend your life with me?" asked Mangmang as he straddled her. Not understanding what he was trying to say, Dou Gua could only stare into his face.

"You won't give me a son," said Mangmang.

"You want to run off with some other man, don't you?" Mangmang accused her.

Mangmang became a real bull because he thought the problem could be solved by exerting more force. The tears on Dou Gua's face flowed in rivulets.

"Pa, I can't live with Mangmang. I can't stand it. I can't stand it anymore." Dou Gua was on her knees in front of Dou Bao.

A crowd gathered on the levee, above the cave, looking at Dou Bao. Nobody knew what he would do.

His face livid with anger, Dou Bao strode into the cave, then emerged with his shepherd's whip. The onlookers watched as he raised it high.

*Swish!* Dou Gua heard a noise close by her ear. As the tip of the whip trailed across her back, she felt it cut into her flesh. Too weak to pick herself up, she rested her face against the ground, trembling all over.

Dou Bao didn't utter a word and went back inside.

"Serves her right! We should all do like Dou Bao. Women! Pah!" someone commented.

"I hear she even keeps books on the kang!"

"What does she have against Mangmang?"

"I'll bet you she's got someone else on her mind . . ."

One by one, the crowd dispersed. From their remarks, Dou Gua could tell that the single lash of the whip had cost her father his reputation.

When there was no one left, Dou Gua pushed herself to her feet and returned to Qiao Family Gully. She stripped naked and stretched out on the kang.

"Come on, Mangmang," she said. "You can do whatever you like.

"Mangmang, you've ruined my life," she wept.

She hadn't visited her father Dou Bao since that time.

But she became a frequent visitor to the Field of Ghosts.

An expanse of red soil, nothing else—not even a blade of grass. Yet she loved to go there.

At this moment, the Field of Ghosts was shrouded in a layer of moonlight that drifted here and there like mist. The lenses of Teacher Chai's glasses, too, seemed to have been covered with a layer of drifting mist.

Then there was the road; it, too, drifted about. She walked and walked and became the girl of the pancake stall, became Mangmang's woman.

She heard somebody walking toward the Field of Ghosts. She knew it had to be Mangmang. Worried that she was meeting another man, he had come looking for her.

Mangmang, you've ruined my life, she thought to herself. With that, she picked up a rock that lay close by and struck him on the forehead. Mangmang sank to the ground without a murmur.

The sound made by the rock was not very loud, but it traveled far, startling the moonlight on the Field of Ghosts into flight, wings fluttering, like a swarm of white butterflies.

She glanced at Mangmang. His eyes were opened wide as if to ask her what had happened.

And that was the only thing that Dou Gua did.

Now Dou Gua was in her father's cave, her backside resting on the edge of the kang; she was confessing to him. There was no movement inside the cave. Dou Bao's shepherd's whip hung behind the door, its thong snaking quietly down the wall. Even the shadow of the whip remained quiet and still.

The bare-bottomed moon shone bright and clear. Dou Gua remembered the moonlight on the Field of Ghosts, wings fluttering like a swarm of white butterflies. She had gone there so many times, but only tonight was the moonlight like white butterflies. And that she would never forget.

TRANSLATED BY ELLEN LAI-SHAN YEUNG

# Remembering Mr. Wu You

## Ge Fei

### 1

Not until the two middle-aged policemen in white uniforms and their young skirt-clad female partner showed up did the villagers reluctantly recall Mr. Wu You.* That bygone episode, like a maiden's lost chastity, stirred the people's emotions. And since their recollections were triggered by the introduction into their lives of the three outsiders, village elders were quick to tell youngsters eager to revisit the painful past, "Time erases all memories."

Thanks to the three uniformed guests, the villagers learned of such things as handcuffs and, so they were told, alarm sirens. A sense of security accrued from the presence of the outsiders, even though they were not above putting on airs at times. One of their favorite pastimes was getting farmers to stop work, either out in the woods or in the shade of high walls, to relate obscure details regarding Mr. Wu You. They failed to get the answers they sought, not because the people were uninformed but because they were so blasé. Nothing excited the people of this village. I, on the other hand, was eager to work with the outsiders. I still recalled how the condemned man was shot that morning.

Mother reacted to the news that I was going to watch them shoot Mr. Wu You at a spot five miles from where we lived by slapping me across the face. "Killing a man is the same as killing a

---

*Pronounced WOO-YO.

236

chicken," she said. So I went out back to watch my younger brother do just that. Old K, who was still little then, held the chicken by its neck in one tiny hand and a small penknife in the other. As I walked up to him, he asked me to help. "Killing a chicken is the same as killing a man," I said.

"They're the same thing," Old K replied.

Suddenly, the bird broke loose and flapped its way across a block of stone before soaring over the wall. Old K stood there holding his blood-streaked penknife, mesmerized by the sight of chicken feathers floating above us. I grabbed his hand and dragged him out the gate, telling him we were going to watch them actually kill a man. He was standing beside me when they shot Mr. Wu You. His mouth hung slack, and he was a different boy from the one who was trying to kill the chicken. On the way home, he muttered the only thing he would say for three whole days: "Killing a man is a lot easier than killing a chicken."

I divulged this to the three outsiders, who wouldn't dignify it with a response, would not even jot it down. But when I told them I was a distant relative of Mr. Wu You's, they smiled and turned real friendly, urging me to go on with my story. My ears rang with official jargon in a singsong twang that made my skin crawl. I said Mr. Wu You was shot on the day of the dragon-boat festival.

"That's perfect!" the skirt-clad young woman said.

It really was the day of the dragon-boat festival. Women, some of whom had stayed up all night, went down to the stream to pick leaves, which they floated home on bamboo rafts, in sampans, even in washbasins as wrappings for their glutinous holiday treats. A gossamer mist hung in the early-morning air like evanescent steam, heavy with the subtle fragrance of water reeds. Men were washing rice in large sieves. Children played behind their parents as they worked, splashing stream water with stripped willow switches. Just then one of the younger wives took off running from one end of the village to the other, shouting the whole way. And that is how people learned that Mr. Wu You was going to be shot later that day. Everyone watched her run, except for a smattering of young fellows who had no idea what was going on, since they were too busy staring at the fleshy mounds jiggling beneath her pink chemise to worry about what she was shouting. Much later, whenever they discussed the affairs of that morning, they admitted it was the first time they had ever seen a woman run like that, and for them all other living objects hung in a state of suspended animation.

## 2

As soon as they heard the clanking noise, the villagers knew that the police were out for a stroll: all manner of brass contraptions in all sizes hung from their uniform belts. Encountering a middle-aged woman out on the street, they decided to question her. One of them casually slipped a brass hoop off his belt and fitted it over the woman's head, telling her it was a high-frequency lie-detector ring, the most advanced of its kind in the world. It shrieks every time you tell a lie. So she clammed up while the hoop was in place. But as soon as it was removed, words gushed from her mouth. Their technology had met its match.

Apparently feeling tension in the air for the first time since their arrival, the outsiders asked me to show them Mr. Wu You's living quarters, in an old, dilapidated, and boxy little ancestral hall. His room had been sealed on the day of his death, and no one had entered it since. Prying open the rusty latch was hard work. When we finally got the door open, we were greeted by a thick cloud of dust. It was stifling inside, and we were sweat soaked in no time. The room was just as its occupant had left it, as if awaiting his return. A coat of fine white dust had accumulated on a pencil sketch tacked to the wall: a black sun sinking into the reedy bank of a black river inhabited by a pair of egrets with crossed beaks. The sketch had been done for him by an itinerant artist. Appearance was important to Mr. Wu You, who could not abide dirt or slovenliness. He shaved with a finely honed straight razor and wore a black oilcloth apron when doing the dishes. Years later, whenever his name came up in conversation, the villagers invariably remarked, "Just like a woman!"

While finding nothing germane to their reinvestigation of the Mr. Wu You case, the police did note that his bookcases were empty. Mr. Wu You had been a lover of books. On the day the village headman ordered the people to move Mr. Wu You's books outside and burn them, it took more than five hours for the flames to consume the whole pile. Villagers watched the curling ashes of all that paper get sucked up a chimney as their faces were turned blood-red by the blaze. Only Apricot wept. A frequent guest at Mr. Wu You's ancestral hall, where she enjoyed his books, she was the only person he ever taught to read, and it did not take her long to learn a hundred and one ways to cure measles.

Unanimity has not been reached on what actually led to the fiery episode: some say the headman was drunk at the time, but they are refuted by others who say he drank very little that day.

## 3

The villagers found Mr. Wu You's behavior that day shocking, to say the least. Armed with his seven-inch straight razor, he confronted the village headman in the area's largest public square, and people who saw how jumpy he was knew he had been waiting there for some time. The headman stripped to the waist and hung his shirt in the crotch of a nearby tree, exposing a muscular chest tanned the color of bark. Brandishing his razor, Mr. Wu You charged like a crazed jackass, but the headman stepped nimbly out of the way, clenched his fists, and launched a ferocious counter-attack. The first blow landed squarely on Mr. Wu You's nose, spraying blood all over the place, as if a rotten tomato had splattered on his face. The second one caught him on the back of the head, and he teetered briefly before thudding to the ground—just as I opened our attic window, which gave me a ringside view of the mayhem. Surrounded by spectators filling the square, Mr. Wu You staggered to his feet, drying clots of blood clinging to his face, and took a few wobbly steps, like a circus clown trying for a few laughs. Then with a slight churning motion, he hit the ground again.

The three outsiders danced a jig when this incident was related to them by an old man who guarded the woods. The skirt-clad young woman shocked him by planting a kiss on his whiskered cheek. It was he who had lugged Mr. Wu You home afterward, only to incur the wrath of his wife—that day and every day thereafter—for bloodstains on his shirt that wouldn't wash out no matter what she did. Even now, traces of those badges of glory remain on the back of his yellowed undershirt. After the old watchman laid Mr. Wu You on his bed, Apricot opened the door and strode in, obviously having got wind of the fight. As she approached Mr. Wu You's bed, he spat a mouthful of bloody phlegm in her direction; but she merely removed her apron, leaned over, and gingerly wiped the blood from the corners of Mr. Wu You's mouth. The watchman gets all choked up even now when he recalls that incident. "I've never seen a more fetching girl," he says. "Like a pixie."

Mr. Wu You was just another villager, no one special, even taking into consideration the fact that he had once owned a roomful of books. Then some village children came down with what everyone called the sweats, for which the only known treatment was pillowing their heads on oven-dried river gunk. Mr. Wu You tried to convince them that a certain wild herb could cure their children, but no one listened. Nothing could win over the zealous disciples of the pillow treatment until he employed an argument they could understand: bulls seldom get sick because they graze on wild grasses. The villagers decided to give Mr. Wu You's treatment a chance. It worked, and overnight his ancestral hall became the local clinic.

# 4

The burning of Mr. Wu You's books shook the people's confidence in his healing arts. But he had committed an astonishing quantity of the incinerated books to memory; it was an extraordinary gift that not only saved the clinic but simultaneously invested him with mystical airs. By then, Mr. Wu You and Apricot had become nearly inseparable, a development that sparked mixed reactions in the villagers. To some, the relationship seemed shady at best, since she hardly ever left the boxy ancestral hall until late at night, in the company of Mr. Wu You. Over time, they wore a path through the woods between his home and hers, luminous and white. Gradually, the villagers warmed to Apricot. For by then, they nearly worshiped Mr. Wu You, and rather than concern themselves with the rectitude of the relationship, they convinced themselves that an atmosphere of harmony and sanctity prevailed. Naturally, the village headman was never far from their thoughts, since he had secured his position as headman not by grasping the essentials of forest-fire prevention or by practicing the art of divination but by virtue of a robust, muscular body and a broad, menacing forehead. He was a mighty lion, or so the village women said. Later, after the headman had been carried off by dysentery, a village old-timer told me, "The women were moved to tears even when they knew the headman was feeding them a line."

One day, an outsider came to the village. He swept a spot of ground clean of snow and set up a performing-monkey show. Mr. Wu You and Apricot, who were in the audience that day, looked over at the smirking headman, who said deliberately and in full voice, "I'm going to kill you two." People close by were laughing so hard at the performer's antics they didn't hear the headman. But my brother Old K heard him, and he streaked home as fast as his legs would carry him. Long after the incident, he told me he ran like the wind that day, flung open the door, and fell flat on his face. Yet even before he could clamber to his feet, he was shouting, "The headman's going to kill Apricot and Mr. Wu You . . ."

Like so many village women, Mother was off in some lovely dreamland as she stitched soles for cloth shoes, so she may not have heard what Old K was saying. Which is probably why she merely grunted in response.

Many days passed. Green buds popped from willow branches growing wild above crumbling walls at the village entrance; if you looked past the reeds on the riverbank, way off into the distance, you could see new grass in the mountain hollows. Suddenly, the village buzzed with talk that Mr. Wu You had killed Apricot. No one doubted the truth of the story, since he had confessed to the crime. A couple of forensic interns were invited to the village for what would be their first autopsy. They began by laying Apricot's body out on a three-legged Ping-Pong table, then stood on either side of her, butcher knives at the ready. She looked just as she had when she was swimming in the river in midsummer, the way people had so often seen her: ruddy faced and full of life. Not knowing exactly what to do, the two interns commenced cutting and kept at it all day, until it was impossible to tell what was what. Winding up with seven separate pieces of unequal size, they concluded that Apricot had been strangled after being raped.

# 5

The three visiting police officers really knew their business: the skirt-clad young woman filled every page of her thirty-by-forty-centimeter notebook. One day, she and the others spoke to the person who actually shot Mr. Wu You, a lad named Kangkang. On the eve of the dragon-boat festival, after the magistrate informed him he would be Mr. Wu You's executioner, he decided to make some repairs on his double-barreled shotgun, a family heirloom that hung on the wall of his mother's room. A one-time paralytic whom Mr. Wu You had cured, she had just got out of bed when her son came in to take down the shotgun, which had gathered dust for thirty years or more. "Going after wild boar?" she asked. He walked out without a backward glance.

Kangkang painstakingly wiped down the shotgun three times before taking it to the blacksmith to straighten out the barrel, which was thirty degrees off center. Then he loaded it, went down to the river, took aim at a billy goat, and fired, creating a dark hole the size of a man's thigh in the animal's belly. He smiled contentedly.

The next morning after Old K and I sneaked out to watch Mr. Wu You's execution, we encountered a woman with bound feet, moving as fast as those tiny feet would allow, sort of like bouncing along on stilts. A month or so after Mr. Wu You's execution, we

learned the facts of the murder from her lips: her husband had suffered a terrible headache that night, so she took some spirit money
into the woods to burn at the family grave site. There she saw the
headman force Apricot, who had been walking home alone, to the
ground. She was no more than twenty paces from them at the time.
The night was absolutely still, she said, and the subtle fragrance of
reeds along the riverbank drifted over on gentle winds. It was an
intoxicating setting, with a milky miasma that hung over the woods
and a lovely halo girding the moon. She declared that the sight of
the headman ripping off Apricot's clothes and white underpants
had moved her to tears.

For more than a month following Apricot's death, she was in
the grips of dementia, her eyes vacant and clouded, until she knew
she must do something to keep from going stark raving mad. So on
the morning the young wife ran shouting from one end of the village to the other, the bound-foot woman, knowing she could keep
the truth bottled up inside her no longer, decided to reveal what
had happened that night. She ran like a woman possessed to the execution ground.

The onlookers grew impatient as a light rain fell. Kangkang
took aim at Mr. Wu You on a signal from the magistrate, who held
a red three-cornered flag in his raised hand. He dropped his arm,
and Kangkang pulled the trigger. *Blam!* The shotgun misfired,
blackening the front of Kangkang's white shirt. He spat angrily
and reloaded. There was fear in Mr. Wu You's eyes. He strained to
open his mouth, but his tongue had been cut out a month earlier.
He was gesturing frantically when Kangkang's double-barreled
shotgun roared one last time.

By the time the woman with bound feet hobbled up to the execution ground, mud-spattered from head to toe, Mr. Wu You was
already in the ground. A few bloodstains and some bristly hairs
were all that remained. A fine rain was still falling as way off in the
distance a wedding party of men decked out in reds and greens was
on its way to fetch a bride, their horns blaring, their drums banging. They disappeared from view on the opposite bank of the river.

TRANSLATED BY HOWARD GOLDBLATT

# Footsteps on the Roof

## Chen Cun

### 1

As you all know, I live in the Huangpu East district of Shanghai. There is nothing wrong with the place, except that it is a bit of a pain to get anywhere from here. A tunnel under the Huangpu River, completed some ten years ago, links the district to downtown. The air quality in the tunnel is awful. Often, hundreds of idling vehicles sit inside unable to move an inch, each emitting its own fumes. What always strike me are the walls, through which water oozes, leaving behind grimy rings. The light is very dim. Every time my bus crawls out of the tunnel, even if it is raining outside, I feel that I am back in the sunlight again. Because of all this, I tell people of only passing acquaintance not to come see me at my place. Whatever business they might have, they can just tell me over the phone. When they do come, I have to make apologies for the tunnel. Such apologies pile up. It's no fun.

For a while, I enjoyed passing through the tunnel at night. At night, it is better lit than the streets, making it easier to recall its virtues. Sometimes you might not encounter another oncoming vehicle for the whole two miles. Those water rings still hang on the walls, like paintings by gods or ghosts. Occasionally, you see a deep crack. The Huangpu River is right above you, and a thousand-ton liner might be passing overhead. The tunnel is a rectangle, yet it meanders along. There is no light at the end. The road appears to hang in front of you, so quiet that all you can hear is your own engine. Not another soul for the whole two miles. The single eyes of the cameras on the walls stare at you coldly, one after another, as in a relay. Once my bus stopped in the middle of the tunnel, and all was deadly silent. There I was, on a bus with eight men and three women, every one of them sitting quietly as though waiting for some sort of visitation.

## 2

From my window above, I can see the tunnel exit on this side. Often when I have nothing else to do, I look to see if there is a traffic jam in the tunnel, if there are a couple of hundred cars stuck on the street. Whatever the season, beneath my window there is always the noise of cars and, occasionally, of tractors.

I live on the sixth floor, the top floor.

On my floor, there are four apartments, two on either side of the stairway. Once inside the cast-iron gate, you pass number 602 to reach my apartment, 601. There is rarely anybody living in number 602. It is a rather large two-room apartment, furnished only with a bed, a table, a couple of chairs, and some cooking utensils. The owner, who also has a nice apartment in the Huangpu West district, often lends this one to people passing through Shanghai, such as honeymooners.

Owing to the might of the cast-iron gate, I hardly ever run into 603 or 604. What we see of one another is the laundry we hang out to dry.

I rarely go out. Except to get a newspaper or to take out the garbage, I don't even go downstairs much. I live alone, a very quiet life. Sometimes the doorbell rings, and the door opens to old friends. Then I am happy. Sometimes the telephone rings; I am also happy then.

I have two rooms. There are some books in the study, and a full-length mirror in the bedroom. I rarely stand in front of the mirror, except when I shave. Beyond the bedroom is the balcony. Late at night, there is always a strong wind that makes spooky noises.

That's why I keep a knife by my pillow. When I wake up in the middle of the night and see the knife, my heart calms down, and I can go back to sleep.

## 3

I moved here half a year ago.

The day before I moved, I met someone at a friend's home who claimed he could tell fortunes. As soon as he saw me, he congratulated me on my pending move. I smiled. It was no big secret. Then I asked casually if there was anything else to congratulate me for. He held my hand for a careful examination and said he saw a peach blossom, which meant lucky in love. After that, he stared intently at my palm for a long while.

"This romantic good fortune of yours is really peculiar. Look here, it lies hidden in the lines of your palm." He stroked my palm with his index finger. "Also, there is major yin influence."

"Any harm in that?" I asked.

"Can't tell."

This amateur fortune-teller was the first honest man I had met, someone who would actually admit that he couldn't tell. Which must have meant that he *could* tell about the other stuff.

The next day, I moved.

I should make it clear that even after finishing the move, I didn't have any luck that was even remotely peachy.

A chrysanthemum I had planted in a flowerpot was blooming—yellow petals, the kind the woman poet Li Qingzhao liked to write about. The mums made my empty balcony look like a small cemetery.

Now back to my move. The building was finished only a few years before, yet I was already the third owner of this apartment. The day I moved in was dark and cloudy. Our truck was stuck in the tunnel for a whole hour, until we were all seeing stars. By the time we emerged, a storm had come and gone. But the sky remained gloomy. On the porch in front of my building was a stain, a light-brown one. At first, I didn't take any notice of it—until I stepped on it and slipped. I was puzzling over it when my friends started to carry my stuff upstairs. So I pulled myself together and followed them up.

The move was completed, and not a single neighbor had come out to watch the show.

It was dark by the time I saw my friends off. Standing at the curb, I looked at the building. Only a few lights were on, including my own two. Weeds grew amid heaps of construction material abandoned at the curb. The streetlight was broken, and there was darkness all around.

It was a bit of an effort to walk all the way up to the sixth floor. I opened the cast-iron gate and realized that someone was standing in the corridor, leaning over the banister to look down.

I cleared my throat.

"Are you the new tenant?" It was a woman with a very soft voice. Her door was half-open, and the light from inside lit up the tip of her nose. Some music wafted out, the kind with poor sound quality.

"Are you the owner of six-oh-two?" I asked.

"Oh, no. I used to live here, in six-oh-one. Just here to take a peek. No, I'm not the owner."

I couldn't very well pursue the matter, so after exchanging some pleasantries, I went back to my own apartment.

Inside the new place, even the four walls felt cold. I didn't plan to stay here for long, so I decided not to paint the walls. The noise from the tunnel drifted up. I stood on the balcony and looked around for a while; then I moved the chrysanthemum to the windowsill. The blossoms were no longer fresh.

I started to gather together some odds and ends, tripping all over myself. Just to boost my spirits a bit, I turned on all the lights in the apartment. Still, it didn't feel bright. The walls were beige, painted by the previous owner. There were drawings by a childish hand, friendly like. And a faint footprint. A couple of mosquito corpses. At this point, the doorbell rang.

As I strolled over to the door, I tried to guess who it might be.

The door opened, and there was the neighbor I had met just a minute ago. I asked if anything was the matter.

She answered, beaming a bright smile, "If you have any questions, or if there's anything you don't know, just come and ask me."

"All right. I won't hold back."

Under the light, her face seemed pale, her lips painted a bright red. She had a pretty neck. Her hand rested casually against the doorframe, a young-looking hand. We were standing so close that I didn't look at her figure. She had a sort of baby face, but there were tiny wrinkles in the corners of her eyes.

"This place is different from Huangpu West," she said. "You hardly ever see anybody, and it might take some getting used to."

She gave me another smile and went back to her own apartment.

At this point, I remembered the fortune-teller's peach blossom. When the mums were fading, would a peach come into bloom?

Alongside the beige walls, I resumed my unpacking, starting to feel very lonely. My stereo system was still packed away, so not a sound could be coaxed from it. I dropped what I was doing and walked over to the wall. I pressed my ear against the wall but couldn't hear anything. I opened the door—the corridor was pitch-black. The cast-iron gate was shut, the iron bars glistening under the faint light.

I smoked a cigarette in the corridor and went back inside, leaving my door open.

Then I sat down in a chair and lit up another cigarette, keeping my eyes on the open door.

# 4

She didn't close the door when she came in but walked straight to the study and, without saying anything, started putting my books into the bookcase. Her waist was like a young girl's, a nice figure. I watched her upper body as it rose and fell, and when she bent down, her buttocks, wrapped tight in jeans, looked like a twisted face wanting to speak. She had long limbs and elegant wrists. Her breasts were not prominent, barely discernible, and when she raised her arms to put the books into the bookcase, they were no longer even that.

I finished my cigarette. Still, I didn't move.

When she had filled two bookcases, she stopped, sat down in an armchair, and took a cigarette from the coffee table. I lit it for her. "Want something to drink?"

She nodded.

I went to the refrigerator for a beer and poured it into two glasses. "Cheers."

"Cheers." She downed half a glass in one gulp.

Then I finished mine. The beer was tepid.

"More?"

I nodded.

She came back with more beer, refilled mine, topped off her own. "Let's go outside."

I followed her out and leaned against the balcony. The cars had thinned, ducking into the tunnel or popping out. I thought of the tunnel walls, with their water rings.

"Huangpu East is like an island," I said. "And this building is an islet surrounded by an island."

Without looking up, she said she was a little cold. So we went back inside. The lights were bright.

"My bed, it used to be here, too," she stated out of the blue. "A bed is like an island. Or maybe a pool of water. When I lie on the bed, my body becomes a boat."

I understood that when she talked about the bed, it was just a metaphor, with no undertones of seduction. We continued with our beer.

"You've got a lot of books."

"Do you like to read?"

"No. I don't read much."

She looked like an educated woman—although even educated women nowadays, once they leave school, don't tend to read much. It's the same with men.

"The books I do read a lot are medical books," she said. "Every chapter is intriguing. Having an illness is like an art. Bacteria and viruses are the artists, the human body is the canvas, or the clay for sculpting." She continued, "I like to imagine myself living through one disease after another. I have now lived through every possible kind of disease. Every one has been painful but artistic."

I said, "I don't like being sick."

"Me neither. But I like to imagine myself being sick. I can really get into it."

"I don't even like to imagine it."

She said, "You and I are not the same kind of people."

I wanted to find a medical book in the bookcase for her. But by the time I found one, I realized she had already walked to the door. She noticed I was looking at her, gave me a smile, and vanished.

Slowly, I walked over and closed the door.

## 5

In the time immediately following, I sat in the armchair she had sat in and drank down the beer she hadn't finished. It was lukewarm, slightly bitter. I held the glass until I finished the last drop. Then I turned off the lights.

There was a noise on the balcony—*shashasha*—like footsteps. When I went to have a look, there was nothing but a rope dangling over the eaves, swinging to and fro in the breeze. It was raining outside again, a light rain. I stuck my hand out for a good while. It was barely wet.

The tunnel exit looked very faint and hazy.

I was exhausted and went to bed yet couldn't fall asleep. There was movement on the roof, as though someone were walking. I wished I could hear a cat's screech, that sort of piercing screech.

My stuff was spread all around the room, surrounding me. I remembered she said she was like a boat. Now I was a boat stranded on this island. At this point, all the boats in the world might be on an island. I wanted to make a phone call. I glanced at the clock; it was too late. I was overcome with the desire to call, the desire to listen.

"Twelve fifty-six A.M., twelve fifty-six A.M., twelve fifty-six
A.M. . . ."

I waited until "one A.M." before hanging up. The voice announcing the time was just like hers, my next-door neighbor's, very
soft. She said we were not the same kind of people. She left right
after saying that. Probably lying on her own island now, thinking
about diseases of every possible kind. She said it was an art.

I decided I'd better get up and go knock on the door of 602. I
could say I was locked out when the wind slammed the door shut.

The sound of the wind slamming the door shut was deafening.
It frightened me.

## 6

I knocked softly. No response. I knocked for a long time; I was getting desperate. I figured she had no reason to open up. Maybe she
was frightened, too. Or maybe she didn't hear it. I couldn't very
well pound on the door. Late at night, any sound at all can be a
soul-shattering experience.

I started to feel despondent. That's when the door opened.

"It's open." She gave it a jerk. I wondered if I should follow her
into 602. "Come on in, you."

"I was locked out by the wind. I wanted to check with you to
see if there's any way to cross the river at this time of night. Also,
could you lend me some money?"

She took a look at my pajamas, shook her head, and smiled.

"Come on in." She closed the door behind me.

The light flickered on. I saw a bed, a table, and a few chairs.
The blankets were spread out on the bed. The pillow displayed the
imprint of a head.

"I'll go heat up some water."

I looked at the empty room, then moved the two chairs up to
the bed, folded the blankets against the wall, and rested the pillow
against the blankets. Then I leaned against the pillow, propped up
my feet on the chair, and waited for her.

"Do you want an ashtray?"

I said no.

"I need a cigarette, but I'm out. Do you still have some?" she asked.

She put the ashtray on top of a book and placed it on the sheet near me.

"Not on me."

"Well, how about going back and getting them?"

By the time I got the cigarettes, she was leaning against the folded blankets, her feet propped up on the other chair.

"My place isn't as nice as yours."

"It's fine."

"I often don't sleep a wink the whole night. How about you?"

"I fall asleep after midnight."

"I'm used to it by now. How about you?"

"Me, too."

She kept at her cigarette, I at mine. We shared the ashtray between us. There was something peculiar about the way she smoked. The ash grew very long until it fell off; then she suddenly remembered to tap it.

"The water's boiling. I'm going to take a bath. Make yourself at home."

After she left, I pulled the book out from under the ashtray. It was a medical book, *Internal Medicine,* quite a thick volume, written by some American and translated into Chinese. The book opened to the section on hepatitis. Since I had no interest in anything to do with the liver, I closed the book and put it back under the ashtray.

The sound of water drifted in like waves. Listening to it made me feel lonely. I walked to the bathroom and gave the door a nudge. It yielded. She was squatting in the tub, soaping herself, her back slightly bent. I took the soap and lathered her up. Then I scrubbed her back and rinsed it off. I very much wanted to rub her shoulders, so I reached out my hand.

Her skin was very white, glossy, too. She had a very attractive body; the only imperfection was an ugly navel. And the navel is a person's core.

"Do you want to take a bath, too?"

"Not really."

I gazed at her while she washed, until she put on her night-gown.

We went back to the bed and sat down.

"What's the date?" she asked.

"I can't remember. It's Sunday."

"Today even God is taking a break."

Only God was taking a break. We mortals, how could we ever take a break?

There was the sound of soft footsteps on the roof.

"Don't be afraid. It comes every day. Once you've been here a while, you'll get used to it. Don't pay it any mind."

"What is it?"

"Don't know. Maybe it's a person. Then again, maybe not."

She took away the ashtray and covered us both with a blanket. "It's late. Sleepy?"

I closed my eyes and answered that if I could fall asleep, I would do it just like this, and she shouldn't wake me up.

"You won't be able to fall asleep."

"Then talk to me. About anything at all. I'm listening."

## 7

"I'm a virgin. Believe me?"

I shook my head.

"How could I be?" She stroked her own face. "Yet sometimes I like to think I am."

I nodded. "Then you are."

"For a while, I used to think that sexual differences were very interesting. I was moved by the whole idea of sexual differences among humans. Later on, I changed my mind."

"Same here."

"You and I are not the same."

I said we were in this respect.

"I'm a woman. How could you be the same as me?" She gave me a sly smile.

"But I'm human."

She said, "This bed hasn't been sat on by two people for a long time." She said, "The last time was half a year ago. A long time."

I listened.

She said, "Before me, the last person who sat on it was also a woman."

I had seen her emerge from the bath, seen her walk out of the bathroom, and I knew she didn't have any makeup on. Yet her face looked as though it were forever enveloped in a white fog. Her neck was lovely, a delicate curve rounded to her shoulders, which were wider than most other women's, not so slanting.

"Am I pretty?"

"Yes."

"Would you like to hold me?"

I ceremoniously held her for a moment, then let go.

The cigarette was bitter, the night too long. The rain was probably still coming down. Inside this room, I couldn't hear the traffic from the streets, couldn't hear anything. Except the intermittent footsteps on the roof.

She fetched another lamp and turned the shade toward the wall.

"Do you know where I was just now?"

I shook my head.

"I took a bus to Huangpu West and then walked back through the tunnel. It was very damp." She picked up the clothes she had changed out of. They were like the walls in the tunnel, with yellow water stains. "The tunnel is huge. It took me a good half hour, walking fast."

"Is it allowed?"

"There was nobody there. Altogether, only two cars went by. It was pitch-black inside the cars. Couldn't see a thing."

"Weren't you afraid?"

"How could I be? The ground was also damp, sort of slippery."

I was reminded of the old stain on the porch downstairs.

"Like that spot downstairs, sleek like?"

She glanced at me; her face fell. And she grew silent.

## 8

"Would you like to take a walk in the tunnel?"

"I don't think so."

"Whenever I'm unhappy, I go out walking alone. The tunnel is empty, abandoned. Many of the fluorescent lights overhead are broken, so sometimes a long stretch is totally dark. Walking in the dark and looking at the light ahead is very poetic. Sometimes a light flickers on above me, blinking on and off, on and off, making it easy to think about spooky things. Sure you don't want to come along?"

"I'm sure."

"Fine, whatever."

I was used to falling asleep in the small hours and was exhausted at this point. I looked for my key, wanting to be in my own bed. Although I'd be lonely in a dream, still it would be better to have that dream. I couldn't find my key. Maybe I left it behind when I went back for the cigarettes.

"I want to sleep."

"Go ahead."

She arranged the pillow and the blankets and let me sleep on the side next to the wall. Then she turned off the light and lay down beside me. The bed was very narrow. I could feel the chill of her skin. "How would it be if I held you?"

"Go ahead," she said.

I held her loosely.

"How do you feel?" she asked.

"That you're quite young."

"That's not what I meant. Do you feel better?"

"About the same."

"At least you're honest," she said. "I used to think you always feel better with someone in your arms. When I'm alone, I often make myself think that way."

"Even now?"

"Yes." She wrapped her arms around my waist. "Want to go further?" she asked.

"No." As soon as I said that, I changed my mind. "Why not? Maybe I'll fall asleep if I tire myself out."

"Come on, then."

"I need the light on. Do you mind?"

She turned on the bedside lamp.

I removed her nightgown and took off my own clothes. Then I lay on top of her and looked into her face. She was gazing intently at a distant spot on the ceiling, looking sort of vacant. There was the sound of those footsteps on the roof again. I embraced her tightly. She smiled and turned her eyes to that distant spot again. I ceremoniously fondled her breasts, then stroked her face. I lay down beside her again.

She asked, "Finished?"

"Yes."

It was too quiet in the room. I couldn't help but listen to the sound of the footsteps. They were moving very slowly, from this end to that, back and forth, back and forth. I could hear every single step.

"Don't be afraid." She patted my back. "If it stops, *then* you should be afraid."

The footsteps stopped. I waited for them to resume, but they didn't.

She sat up, looking for the cigarettes.

"What's the matter?"

"Go to sleep. I'll just sit for a bit. I thought I'd be able to sleep with you here. But it isn't working."

"Maybe I can help."

I tossed away her cigarette and pulled her under the covers, and I began stroking her attentively. In order not to see her face and thereby spoil my mood, I even turned off the light. Every part of her I touched felt nice. It was like stroking an ivory sculpture. I'm normally easily excited. Yet strangely at this point, I was quite calm. The sensations somehow stopped at my fingertips and would not go higher.

"Enough, that's enough," she said harshly. With a jerk, she sat up. "You're just wasting your energy." She climbed out of bed and switched on the overhead light. She put on the jeans and shirt still damp with water stains. Then she put on her jacket.

"I'm not mad at you. Just a little restless. I have to go and take a walk." Her voice had become soft again. She put her hand into her pocket and pulled out a key. "Here's your key. I thought I could use it to make you stay. I've been alone for too long. I'm glad you came tonight. All I wanted was to have a good sleep for a change. You tried, but it didn't work. Not your fault."

"It's late. Want me to come with you?"

"No. I always walk alone. You've let me have my way in everything. I want to thank you for that. Just let me go take a walk alone now. You can either sleep here or at your own place, whatever."

I heard the door shut, then the cast-iron gate. The sound of footsteps resumed after a long hiatus. I turned my eyes toward the ceiling; it suddenly seemed to have become transparent. Against the pitch-black sky, I could see a pair of feet rise up and then come down. As though through a translucent glass, the feet came down, turning from murky to clear until I could even make out individual footprints.

The feet walked straight on. Following them, I returned to my own apartment.

In my imagination, I stroked the feet walking over my head. Yet the only thing I could really make out was the sound. It was like her voice, very soft, very young, yet not tempting. She was beautiful, both her body and her voice. Yet rather than tempting, she repelled. I was tempted by the repulsion. At this very point, I tried to respond to her repelling footsteps with my own spirit, not with my voice or with my body. I had already tried that. It didn't work.

I don't know how long it took, but I finally fell asleep. Even the wavelike noise of the cars below didn't wake me up. In my dream, I was trod on by the everlasting feet, every single step treading on me. Suddenly I thought, In the whole human body, only the basest things, the feet, always leave traces on the ground. The things that never leave any traces are the head and the sexual organs.

Thus I slept on in a daze until the doorbell started ringing insistently.

# 9

At the door stood a middle-aged woman. She was very friendly and very gossipy. She said she was my neighbor, the owner of 602. She happened to be in the neighborhood so dropped in to have a look.

"I don't know why, but my door was open," she said. "It's happened before."

"Did you give the key to anybody?"

"No, never."

I followed her into 602. I could smell the faint scent of cigarettes. The rooms were very neat. On the desktop, there was a thin layer of dust.

I asked, "Anything missing?"

"Nothing much is kept here. Nowadays, what thief would steal a blanket? I wanted to trade this apartment. I've looked but just haven't found the right one yet."

"Why trade it?"

"It's haunted." She glanced at me and then said mysteriously, "A young couple moved into six-oh-one, your apartment, right after the building was completed. The woman was pretty, a baby face. The man was handsome, too. He could carry a bicycle all the way up to the sixth floor without even being out of breath. Then the woman went on a long business trip to Xinjiang. The man jumped out of the upstairs window."

She led me to the corridor and pointed to a spot downstairs. From way up here, no trace was visible.

"Dead?"

"Of course he was dead. Six floors. How could he survive?"

"After that, a lonely single woman moved in. She had such white skin and a soft, gentle voice. Also a baby face. She never made a sound all the time she was here. Nobody even knew if she was in there."

"No friends ever came to see her?"

"Didn't seem to." She pointed to the tunnel. "One night, real late, a tunnel clean-up crew found her."

"Dead?"

"Dead. Hit by a car. They say she slammed into the wall. Internal bleeding. Maybe the liver was punctured. Hit-and-run."

I let out a deep sigh.

"That's why I had to move out of here. This building is unlucky. Used to be a cemetery."

I invited her in. She looked around, then said she had some business to take care of. Said she'd drop in some other time. Before she left, she remarked in a small voice, "They say that every night there's the sound of footsteps on the roof. I've never spent a night here. Did you hear anything last night?"

"I was exhausted by the move and was asleep as soon as my head hit the pillow. Didn't hear a thing."

"True enough. Moving is hard work."

"Take care."


## 10

Over the past half year, I've paid close attention to next door but have heard nothing—except for one day when the light went on. I happily went to knock on the door. Out came a young man, then a young woman from the north. They were on their honeymoon.

Whenever it rains, the stain appears on the ground in front of the door. Rain or shine, I always avoid that particular spot. I've got used to the sound of footsteps on the roof. I feel lost if I don't hear it.

Once, I climbed onto the roof to take a look. A couple of TV antennas stood there like scarecrows. Out of the blue, I snapped the ground wire: it was very brittle. There was also a Coke can and a cigarette butt. I walked back and forth on the roof. It was big enough to hold a basketball court. Below me, not far off, cars were whizzing in and out of the tunnel. They looked tiny. The wind was strong up there.

Off in the distance, in Huangpu West, stood many tall buildings. I recognized one of them as either the Hilton or the New Jinjiang.

I stood on the roof for a long time, as though I, too, were a scarecrow.

While climbing down, I lost my footing and scraped my arm. The wound was red, with pink liquid oozing out. I opened the cast-iron gate and closed it behind me. Then I opened the door to my own apartment and closed it. I opened all the doors in my apartment: bathroom, bedroom, study, pantry, even the balcony door. I also opened all the windows.

Above the balcony, the rope was still swinging gently in the wind. Sunlight slanted through, casting its swaying shadow on the wall. My potted chrysanthemum had long since withered, leaving only the bare, brittle branches. Its shadow was also cast on the wall. The shadow, too, was dead, dead still.

I glanced downstairs. All of a sudden, I felt the urge to jump. I wanted to leave my own mark on another piece of concrete. Leave it with my head.

Jump. Just that.

I returned to my room and closed all the doors and windows. Then I sat in the armchair she had once used and poured myself a glass of beer. There was a lot of foam, which didn't go away until I finished a cigarette. The foam was this deadly white, like the tunnel entrance on a rainy day, like her neck.

While drinking the beer, I thought of a metaphor. Her ugly navel was just like the tunnel, upon which I depended for my coming and going.

I sat like that until late into the night. I knew that these few days would pass uneventfully. Then on a rainy night, I would take a walk. I would walk into the tunnel to breathe the damp foul air. I would study the grimy stains on the wall. Perhaps behind me would be the sound of footsteps on the roof. I would not look back.

At this point, the doorbell rang.

**TRANSLATED BY HU YING**

# Willow Waist

## Chi Li

The late-spring plum rains fell softly, sadly, lightly, silently. Dusk encroached everywhere; the sky was dark, the earth dizzy, everything near and far was completely dreary.

A small dreary street in a big dreary city.

A small eel-like sedan drifted up slowly.

Faint streetlamps were so far apart that the shadows of the few pedestrians out on the street were stretched taut. They swayed unsteadily. The superstitious driver slithered in and out like a snake, afraid of running over someone's shadow.

"What's the problem, Tian?" asked the old man in the backseat.

A bit put out, the driver replied, "What do you mean, 'What's the problem,' Mr. Guo? Are we there yet, sir?"

"You can park just up ahead."

"Hm," said the driver, as if relieved of a heavy burden.

The old man said, "You know I won't need a car anymore after this, don't you?"

The driver was rattled, "Mr. Guo, how can you say that? I can't stand it! I'm not one of those petty, opportunistic people who burn their bridges behind them! All these years you—"

"Stop the car," said the old man.

Not waiting for the driver to open the door, the old man stepped out, slammed the door shut behind him, and walked off.

The old man turned into a small alley.

The old man purposefully wound his way down the labyrinthine alley.

The old man stopped in front of a building with dappled walls. He sized up the building, which looked like an ancient Buddhist temple, reached out to touch the green moss between the bricks, and then rang the bell above the two huge China-fir doors.

The creaky door opened a crack. The entryway was dimly lit. The old fellow who opened the door recognized the guest in the dim light, stepped aside, then closed the squeaky door after the guest. Steam began hissing from two kettles at the same time. Both kettles lay atop charcoal stoves alongside two doors. Old men standing in the doorways stopped what they were doing and stared through rheumy eyes at the visitor climbing the stairs.

The stairway seemed darker and narrower than before. The banister was cold and smooth, like a frozen snake. The old man was forced to lean his paunchy body forward as he negotiated one step at a time. The steps creaked and groaned beneath the heavy weight. The sound of the old man's footsteps echoed through the foyer like the sound of a bell in a deserted valley. A shrill voice shattered the quiet from downstairs: "Who's that? Stop that devilish clomping, or you'll bring the house down! What did those poor stairs ever do to you?"

Ignoring the woman, the old man kept climbing, one step after another.

Suddenly, the stairway was illuminated. The old man raised his head and saw her. She stood at the top of the staircase, thoughtfully shining a flashlight on the steps beneath the old man's feet.

He reached the top of the stairs. She looked up at him and remarked tenderly, "You've come."

The old man said, "Yes, I have."

The old man felt relaxed, like a bird returning to its nest, as if he came here every day.

She followed him into the room, leaving the door unlatched.

The winter warming stove hadn't yet been put away; on it sat a

steaming earthenware kettle. The dark-blue flames danced play-
fully at the base of the kettle. The small room was warmer than
early summer. The faint smell of sandalwood incense hung in the
air. A small light above the stove formed a halo of light around the
stove. The rest of the room was dark and shadowy.

In the dark shadows, she took off the once costly woolen coat
that she wore when she went out, revealing a black, narrow-sleeved
thin cotton jacket. Oh, her waist was still hourglass thin. Even at
her age.

The old man gazed at her.

She took the old man's hat and shook the fine droplets of rain
off the woolen surface, saying, "Oh, these spring rains."

Then with a dry towel, she gently dried off the old man's
clothes, from his collar to his pant legs.

She moved two faded old-fashioned armchairs up to the stove.
"Sit down," she said, "I'll make some tea."

The old man sat down. Amid the delicate fragrance of the
warm, dry heat, the old man felt completely relaxed; his joints
cracked as they loosened up.

She carried over a serving tray and removed the tea towel covering it. On the tray were an Yixing ceramic teapot, two ceramic
teacups, and a ceramic jar. After warming the teapot with hot
water, she scooped a few spoonfuls of tea leaves out of the ceramic
jar with an ivory teaspoon and put them into the teapot. She then
refilled the teapot with hot water and put the lid on tightly. After a
moment, she lifted up the water bottle and poured hot water over
the outside of the teapot. The reddish-purple color of the ceramic
tea ware and the pair of small, pale, bony hands looked like a
flower of unmatched beauty slowly blossoming. She prepared the
tea with composure, her hands and eyes in perfect accord, completely absorbed in the task.

The aroma of the tea seeped out.

After pouring a cup of tea for the old man, she took out a plate
of his favorite treats, long famous in the small alleys of the big city:
crab cakes. A habit of many years it was for the old man to enjoy
this treat only if he hadn't already eaten.

She poured herself half a cup of tea and sat down across from the old man, separated from him by the stove.

How did she know that the old man hadn't eaten?

Did she know why the old man had walked away from the dinner table?

Did she know that the old man had already retired?

Did she know that the old man had decided to move out of the small red building?

Did she know that because of all this, the old man's children had attacked him?

Did she know that his wife was prepared to fight to the death to retain the small red building?

Did she know of the looks of resentment in the eyes of the two domestics who served him his meals?

Did she know that the quiet, soft-spoken driver of many years had begun saying things to distance himself?

And even more awful things—did she know of them? That would be . . .

"I was afraid you might not have had dinner. Take the edge off your hunger with these snacks," she said. She looked at the old man, smiled, and took a sip of tea. She knew it all.

The old man felt transparent: he was a mass of agitation and anger. Was it necessary to tell every little detail?

Her knees were together, her feet side by side. Narrow shoulders, a slender waist, delicate fingers, a warm expression of quiet humility—as she sat with an air of quaint antiquity, her warm, peaceful humility flowed endlessly toward the old man.

The old man's frustration and anger gradually subsided.

Separated only by the stove, they gazed at each other in silence, using their beating hearts to read the history of each new wrinkle on each other's face.

The old man's face was crisscrossed with ravines.

The skin on her face had folds in length and breadth.

An abstruse heavenly tome that only the two of them could understand.

Suddenly, it dawned upon the old man that her hair had turned white. Puzzled, he wondered when it was that the last strand of black hair had disappeared.

Silently, she shook her head, releasing waves of silvery light.

Why should he be puzzled? The first strand of hair turns white, and so does the last one. What's so special about one's hair turning white? It would be strange if hair that had grown for so many years did not turn white; a person isn't truly old until the hair turns white. Her white hair was like snow, her face was like snow, kindly and yet noble. The dimple on her left cheek appeared as a hollow spot on the surface of that snow created by a hot teardrop. Therein lay the essence of old-fashioned feminine beauty. So why be sad over white hair?

The old man understood.

The tea mellowed on the second brewing. They sat facing each other without a word or a sound.

Oh, her waist was still hourglass thin. Even at her age.

Yes, she's old now. Time flies like an arrow; everyone grows old. What's so special about growing old? How boring life would be without change.

What is there to be sorry about? What else do you have? In the end, what does anyone have? Doesn't everyone come into the world naked and leave the same way? How pleasant that the stove is so warm tonight, the tea steeped so well, and that you and I can still drink a cup together.

She took a sip of tea.

The old man took a sip of tea.

The gloomy look on the old man's face vanished, replaced by a spreading glow. He was at peace, refreshed.

They sat, and they sat, and they sat, a hint of happiness and joy occasionally flickering across their stony faces.

The dark-blue flames were no longer dancing. The coals in the stove were completely red, burning silently. The rolling steam atop the kettle turned to white smoke and curled upward.

Was that a cat or a person outside? Tiptoeing back and forth, then stopping just outside the door for a long time before walking on.

The tea weakened considerably on the third brewing. The old man stood up and paced the floor. Each piece of furniture was where it had always been; only the colors had darkened—spotlessly clean, but already the color of death. The sandalwood incense had burned out; the ashes had fallen to the floor. The smell of mildew emerged from the four corners of the room. It was the old, rotten sort of mildew that the sun could not burn off or shine through.

The old man was reminded of something. He asked, "Did this flare up again?" He pointed to his heart.

Without turning her head to look, she answered clearly, "Twice, both times in the winter, and both times I was hospitalized."

The old man said, "I had two attacks, too, also in the winter, and I was hospitalized. We're the same." The old man laughed like a child. She smiled.

"Well, I should be going," said the old man.

She rose slowly and picked up his hat. The old man leaned forward and lowered his head; she stood on tiptoes to place the hat properly on the old man's head.

Oh, her waist was still hourglass thin.

The old man put his hands on the slender waist. "I'm no longer an official. I can finally relax."

"You should be going," she said.

The old man's grasp loosened. He was secretly ashamed. Had she not stopped him so quickly he might have broken his word.

In the dark shadows, she put on her once costly woolen coat and tied a scarf over her head. Looking like a baby in swaddling clothes, she raised her wrinkled forehead and said, "Come again if you have time."

The old man turned back and looked at the stove, at the old-fashioned armchairs, and at the two nearly empty teacups. Then he looked into her calm, quiet, humble eyes and said, "All right."

She escorted the old man to the front door, curling up inside the doorway.

The old man stopped, turned, and waved her back inside. She stayed for a moment, then retreated; the shiny black door creaked.

In the instant before the two doors met, the old man thought he saw a single teardrop ooze through the crack.

The old man hurried back to where he had been and touched the spot where the tear had emerged; it was wet. He touched his finger to the tip of his tongue and tasted it. Salty and sweet at the same time. When he touched it again, the whole door was wet. The plum rains were still falling, softly and sadly.

The fog turned the alley vast and hazy; the fog turned the street vast and hazy; the fog turned the boulevard vast and hazy. The outlines of tall buildings were blurred; dark shadows were everywhere; lights in homes were dim as starlight. The sky and the earth fused at the horizon, misty and blurred, a ball of chaos. Even if you were a good son, how could you clear away the clouds and fog and stop the wind and rain to seek a sky you yourself loved? No, let nature take its course; nature is fair, so why must we seek things by force?

Take a step back; the sea and sky are boundless.

The old man said to the driver in an unusually calm tone, "I've made you wait too long."

TRANSLATED BY SCOTT W. GALER

# The Sleeping Lion

## KONG JIESHENG

It is hot today. In this place, it is hot every day. There are no distinct seasons, so no one can ever remember what month it is. To be sure, the weeks and months bring incidents of note, but after a while even those merge and blur. In this remote corner of the world, we have forgotten even the year.

We are, in any event, dripping sweat, even a little blood. Not that a man would die here; it is only that staying alive somehow doesn't seem to be one of our major concerns.

Old Wu—Number Five—is scraping his metal pipe.

I position our homemade level.

Beads of sweat fall on the scalding trowel, hissing into steam, and the mountains quiver in the summer heat. At this latitude, the sun is eternally fierce, the day eternally long. The body's biological clock all but stops. If it weren't for the stone wall rising layer by layer, you would think today is a carbon copy of yesterday or perhaps of one day sometime last month. There are moments in this green basin when we desperately wish something would happen to dot the white expanse of time—like the night when someone who went outside to take a leak looked up to see a white spot streaking upward, receding into the heavens' canopy, finally melting into hazy silver. Presented with this rare display, we carried on for several days, pondering how these spirits augured for the future. Then when the newspaper was delivered, already many days late, we learned that our own satellite had traveled into space! Old Wu, for whom there are no mysteries, announced that the launching site was on this island of ours and that this region, being close to the equator, allowed the launch to be both swift and convenient, and on and on. We were quite proud, and our meal of dried turnips and rice seemed crunchier and tastier than ever before. All of us felt that our nation and our people had suddenly become much stronger.

The trowel taps monotonously. Under the scaffold sits a pile of sheer-white plaster. Bright, silvery clouds float overhead, effortlessly reflecting the red sun, sweeping away human shadows without a twinge of conscience. Who knows how many of these masses of steam have been wrung from our bodies?

Even men can be scorched to a crisp. I think of cursing but save my breath. With a parched throat, there is little point in swearing. Blame it all on the legendary Yi, who shot down only nine of the ten suns.

Suddenly, an explosion.

"Thunder?" I hear myself ask.

Hey, thunder god, is that you? Deafening, blinding noise.

Only then do I see the brown smoke curling slowly over the opposite ridge. What is it? "Over there," we call to one another and scramble down the wobbly scaffold.

At last, a special event to make up for the tedium. The outside laborers, having blasted open an underground tomb, are running in all directions. As if transfixed by evil magic, the men gaze from afar at the rumbling black vault with its eerie glow.

Few people take themselves less seriously than the membership of our little group. Valor wells up in me, for I have nothing to lose, and in spite of the presence of a strange, vile smell, I leap inside. There I see the sleeping lion.

It has been blown onto its side and lies among fragments of coffin planks, but I am awestruck. Heavy and icy, the brass green manifests an ageless deep sleep. The long day we once cursed has now become so short and abrupt that we lose all sense of time.

Vessels and pots are also strewn about. Neither Old Wu nor I turn them over, so completely are we seized by the simplicity and majesty of this sleeping lion.

We have stumbled into the Bronze Age!

It is all I can do to keep from shouting. The resident expert has yet to speak. He covers his nose with his hand, frowning, thinking, as history rests quietly, waiting for his verdict.

Western Xia, Yin, Shang? Spring and Autumn period, Warring States? Each fabulously distant and remarkable.

"A Han grave," Old Wu announces solemnly.

I breathe a heartfelt sigh and bend respectfully toward the sleeping brass lion, only to hear Old Wu rebuke me: "Don't touch it!"

I withdraw my hand, sobered by the singular wonder of this event.

"What does it mean?" he asks.

From deep in my pant pocket, I pull out a watch with a cracked crystal.

"Ten oh-three. Note this time." Old Wu is quite solemn.

But reality drags us back to the present.

Master mason Yellow Hair is shouting at us from the opposite slope. The Farm Headquarters boss may be on patrol, and though it puts a damper on things, we had best not linger. In any case, it is nearly quitting time. We slip back to camp.

Old Wu isn't old, nor does the five indicate that he is the fifth child. His name is Wu, and he is my age. Next to him, everyone appears a head shorter—of course, I am referring to physical stature. In terms of intelligence, I'd venture to say he surpasses us by more than a head. He is very bright—in astronomy, geography; in matters foreign or domestic. Everyone can benefit from his instruction. And those who refuse to believe him—someone like me, for instance—can never get him to change his side. In any event, here in the wilderness, where there are neither sages nor scholars, there is little harm in listening.

"How can you be so sure it's Han?" I have to ask.

"Aiiii—some ancestor of the Yellow Emperor you turn out to be! The Bronze Age did not achieve aesthetic perfection until the Han. Everything declines when it reaches its peak—" He is about to elaborate.

"Shhhh. Do you want to lose your head? There can be absolutely no casual talk about peaks."*

"Yes, yes." Ever vigilant, he agrees that his choice of words was imprudent; then, glancing about, he begins again. "After the Bronze Age, stone was the vogue, up until Wei and Jin, when stone carvings reached their, uh—you know what. The Tang had three-color glazes, as did the Song."

I earnestly accept the wisdom imparted from his lips. Still, I don't think I'm stupid, and I read a fair amount in my spare time. I cannot help being skeptical. The Han was a remarkable dynasty, but back in those days Hainan lay beyond Chinese cultural influence. Of the earlier generations who traveled to the edges of the Celestial Kingdom, I knew only of Li Deyu of the Tang, Su Dongpo of the Song, and Huang Daopo of the Yuan. And the Hainan native Hai Rui did not appear until the Ming.

"Not true," he says. "There was also the illustrious Madame Xi, the female warrior of the Northern and Southern dynasties."

Maybe so, but the distance between the Northern and Southern dynasties and the Han is the thickness of *Tales of the Three Kingdoms*—all 120 chapters' worth!

He persists in his rebuttals. "Although Emperor Han Wudi lacked for literary talent, when it came to military prowess, he lacked for naught. Under heaven, no spot was unclaimed by this emperor; from shore to shore, no prince failed to pay fealty." Observing that I refuse to alter my foolish notions, he points out with some irony the absurdity of my logic: why must I always think of history in terms of famous people? Those old bones, whether of a local tyrant or evil gentry—had to be a dull fellow. Don't hope to

---

*In the late 1960s, Lin Biao and Jiang Qing pronounced that Mao Zedong thought was the "peak" of Marxist-Leninist ideology.

find his chronicle in the annals of officialdom, published or otherwise. Number Five certainly deserves his reputation. I ponder a while longer, then relax.

This round of academic contention brings out other emotions in me. Our nation is indeed amazing. Any ancestral grave one treads upon can be traced back hundreds of generations. Take the thatched hut we live in, for example; six or seven thousand years ago, the people of Banpo village built their huts in the very same style—a civilization ancient enough to make one sigh in wonder.

The scaffolding shakes, and we are quiet. But the person who shows up turns out to be Yellow Hair. One of our own. He drops the weighted plumb line over the corner of the wall, then squints down and swears, using all his might to pry off one stone that protrudes prominently from the others.

If Yellow Hair has it in for Old Wu, it is because the latter is a loafer. And really, given half a chance to loaf, who wouldn't take it? When it's almost time for the bell to ring, there seems little point in being so diligent. It is not as if this structure will someday house people; it is going to be a meeting hall. We will continue to live in thatched huts. And while no one can dispute the fact that meetings are more important than sleep, on the other hand, there seems little danger that a column will come crashing down in the midst of a struggle session on account of a misplaced stone. This job is appropriate compensation for Old Wu, I kid him, because he has for years written political essays, beautiful works that he recites with great verve. A bit of Marx, Engels, Stalin, and Mao; of landlords, wealthy peasants, reactionaries, bad elements, and rightists—there is something in his speeches for everyone, and so naturally his audience resounds with animated shouts of support. After each meeting, he routinely crumples the perfectly crafted manuscript into a ball, which he tosses atop his mosquito netting to await appropriate use the next time he visits the pit that serves as the gentlemen's lavatory.

Old Wu has grown indignant, and in order to avoid a quarrel, I try to tell Yellow Hair that we weren't in the mood for work a moment ago, which is why the stone was not in place. Yellow Hair's eyes widen. Before I can finish my sentence, he takes hold of the rope on which the pipes are hung and slithers to the ground.

Yellow Hair is, of course, also a nickname. His hair is a yellowish brown. We have yet to learn if this is a genetic trait that has been passed down over the years or evidence that he offended his ancestors. In fact, he is of pure Chinese extraction, last in the line of several generations of master masons. Even after traveling to the South Seas, he was not able to cast off his legacy, for he became the master mason of our construction group.

The bell rings. Still no sight of Yellow Hair on the opposite slope. Strange. Then, in a moment, he arrives with a face as black as india ink and, out of the blue, begins swearing: "Are you playing games with me? Just watch me plaster your mouth shut with a bucketful of mortar!"

What has happened? We sense immediately that something is wrong. The ghost grave hasn't got a damn thing in it. Even the bones have rotted into thin air.

We look at one another for a moment, but Old Wu is quickest: "It's them!"

Them. A complete mystery.

They are from the mainland, the Leizhou Peninsula. I was there once visiting relatives: barren soil as far as the eye could see, bringing to mind the saying red earth for a thousand miles. Here the soil is rich and black, yielding bricks as light and porous as steamed yeast cakes. Fortunately, there are rock formations in the mountains with such a good grain that in cutting them out, one has only to drive in a wedge to pull out neat square blocks. On the surface, it looks easy enough, but there's a trick to it, and no one at our farm can manage it.

They are strangers here and, as strangers, have yet to communicate with anyone outside their group, although the sounds of pounding echo in our respective camps. I have never been able to get a head count, but there must be six or seven of them. To me, they all look alike: jet-black faces with no more than a few ounces of flesh, their arms nevertheless thick from wielding a sledgehammer. They have their own language. The difficulty of the Leizhou linguistic family has stymied even the linguistically gifted Wu. A clan unto themselves. Though our brigade has empty huts to spare, they insist on pitching their own camp; our brigade has an eating hall, but they prefer to choke on the smoke of their cooking fires, stubbornly preserving their self-contained society. They know only work, with one exception. When the occasional young peasant woman makes her way to the rice fields, they come to life, first staring, then talking softly, perhaps in an exchange of opinions. Though the odds of viewing educated young women, who leave like clockwork at dawn and return at dusk, are greater, the stonecutters dare not take liberties—their eyelids never budge. While phoenixes may not be as valuable as chickens here in the wilderness, surely the cutters should allow themselves to take a glance or two.

The outside laborers keep their trade secrets to themselves. Their blasts produce scarcely any reverberations, the sound waves seemingly swallowed up into deep crevices. Every year when we expand our frontiers by opening up the mountains, we try to appropriate a small quantity of dynamite to throw at fish in the river, in the hope of varying our otherwise vegetarian diet. Damnably, control is tight, one stick to a ditch, and without this stuff there is no hope of snaring even a bit of fish scale.

*They* do not use sticks of dynamite; heaven knows what alchemy they perform. Do you think you can glean their secrets? They pretend not to understand what you say and refuse to let an outsider observe them at work. Even stranger is the imported marvel called directional blasting, of which we have heard vague mention. Who would have guessed that the Leizhou natives mastered this technique long ago, for they are able to set off silent blasts that are devoid of flying chips, and they do so in seeming disregard of their own mortality. Worthy indeed to be the descendants of the men who invented gunpowder. Although this technique is primitive, the clan has passed down its secret for years, perfecting it with each successive generation.

The riddle of their existence is particularly elusive.

Even the concept of outside laborer is tarnished and suspiciously independent of the established social order. In our civilized nation, the relatively advanced notions of isms and social classes, dictatorships and party lines permeate the hearts and minds of even women and children.

What could have befallen the homeland of these nomads? Was there a restoration? A coup? Is their fee divided up according to work points, or do they split it evenly? Such a casual approach to compensation flies in the face of political economics.

Our brains are routinely washed, our tails routinely lopped off. But as we listen to nightly lessons on political struggle, we can hear in the distance the pounding of rocks, and we feel sorrowful and alone. When we aspire to conquer the mountains and rivers and then remember that we are stuck in this anthill of a meeting room, we have new regard for our comrades in the wilderness who continue the revolutionary struggle apace.

But then comes our epiphany: in a land so vast, with a population so great, some things just shouldn't be too conscientious. The people from Leizhou are capable of overturning anything and yet seek only to keep their families from starving. Their stomachs are not thinking organs. They do not concern themselves with philosophy.

And so it is as if we were living in different worlds: our philosophies conflict, our political lines differ, yet we coexist in peace.

Sleeping brass lion!

Well water and river water wage war before the ancestral graves.

"Who's in charge here?" We rush into their self-contained hut. Old Wu towers above the group, his voice ringing out, his query threatening.

No response. The scorching white rays of noon creep in to reflect detached wooden faces.

We take a look around, but of course the brass lion is nowhere in sight. We have never seen anything like this: woks on stone, bed-

ding on stone, with no cushioning pads. The bed planks shine
where sweat has polished them. The hammer handle of hard bamboo, which they replace daily, has been split into kindling and flickers and sputters as the cassava roasts.

I once thought that we were wanderers, unencumbered with
material possessions, going nakedly about our life's business. But
these fellows are the true nomads, a fact that somehow serves to
deepen my awareness of their ability to endure hardship. When I
realize that people can survive under such extreme conditions, our
own incessant complaints seem rather petty. But no matter how pa-
thetic the stonecutters look, I'll not relent, even if they begin to
chew on cassava bark. So I shout out, "Hey, we're talking to you!"

"Don't pretend you can't hear us!" Old Wu chimes in
forcefully.

It is like advancing upon a steadfast and impenetrable stone
wall, which causes the invading enemy to crumble in despair. Pity
that their knack of self-preservation does not fool us: we understand each other only too well.

Yellow Hair is furious: "Up your mother's. . . . Don't play
dumb with me. Hand over the brass lion right now!"

They respond by smoking a long bamboo water pipe, which
gurgles loudly as it is passed from one sinewy hand to the next. A
secret signal, perhaps? After one round, the black faces still do not
appear contented; on the contrary, they now seem savage.

I decide a change of tactics is in order. "Do you know what that
mound of dirt is? A national treasure! Aren't you Chinese?"
Wasted breath, playing a zither for a cow. They're Chinese, but
they're pretending not to understand Chinese. Damn them!

The cassava is done, but it could cook until it was burned to a
crisp, and we'd still be at a standoff. How could these obedient citizens have become so greedy and contemptible so suddenly? Is it
that they're too poor and they want to make some money? They
had to have heard Yellow Hair's insults and challenges, yet their
gaunt faces remain unmoved. Their bulging biceps twitch danger-
ously, signaling nervousness and anger, as if to say that no matter

what country or region they are from, they are still human beings, not beasts of burden to be abused.

Old Wu, who normally thrives on conflict, is silent.

Who is the flying dragon of strength here? We are. Who is the snake accustomed to this turf? Again, we are. It is not they who can hurt us but the other way around. Except that it would appear we can't do much. What—beat them to death and boil them for dinner? Very well, the countryfolk's stubbornness and tenacity have not gone unnoticed. Now we must come to grips with this type of warfare.

"Surely, at least one of you must have had some schooling? You must know what a historical relic is. You can't eat it, and you can't *do* anything with it, so what's the point of keeping it? Are you hoping to make a couple of yuan? I'll give it to you straight: this piece of brass is a priceless treasure; it has no price, understand? When something is so valuable that its value cannot be reckoned, you won't be able to dispose of it. If you try, the Public Security Bureau will get wind of it and will clap handcuffs on you in no time flat."

This seems to have had an effect. One of the younger members of the group looks uncomfortable, glances at his fellow workers. But as long as they continue to act dumb like this, it's still rats pulling a turtle—there's no place to get a handhold.

My remarks arouse Yellow Hair, who lets forth a barrage of patriotic invective and then announces that we have already reported the situation to Farm Headquarters and that the security section is sending someone out to guard the grave. "Know how the security section makes its living? Don't wait to see the coffin before you start crying."

Good old Yellow Hair, every word worth its weight in gold.

With this exchange, the cassava gets really burned, and the stonecutters finally open their mouths. Leizhou-style Mandarin is pretty awful, every syllable harsh and palatal, and the grammar is a mess. But their message is clear: they were the ones to blast open the unclaimed tomb, and finders are keepers.

What an infuriating band of rogues. We'll see who first discovered this national treasure. Why, if Old Wu and I hadn't come onto the scene, they would have been scared out of their wits and probably would have set off firecrackers and burned paper money to drive away the evil spirits.

"Watch what you say. Whose turf is this, anyway?" My face grows stern.

Fearless leader Yellow Hair is undaunted. "This is a case of piling earth on top of the emperor's head. What nerve! Leizhou men, go back home, and dig up your own ancestral graves!"

The situation is rapidly deteriorating. Should Yellow Hair turn and strike the bell, the army would come charging in and torch the hut.

Old Wu has been muttering to himself; he must have something up his sleeve. "All right, you don't know how to read, you're uneducated; it's not really your fault. But common folk have to obey the law, too. The law states that the land belongs to the nation, including the skeletons in the ground. Even if your great-grandfather had gold bricks and silver ingots buried with him, don't think you could touch it. This is no bluff. Nowadays the government is picking up people like caterpillars; the man with the chop that's round and not square—the man with the government chop—is the man who gets to point the finger. And if, when they look at your family history, they find one tiny bit of dirt, they'll push you into a bad social class, then walk you right past the hall of justice to where the firing squad is waiting."

Old Wu is a real hero, who approaches all matters from a position of strength. He threatens and coddles, mixing truth with fiction, his cause just and his message stern. I watch the stonecutters pale as they exchange glances. Silenced.

A psychological attack is best, and we won't stop until their number has been called. Old Wu shouts a command: "Return the brass lion to the ancient tomb, and handle it carefully!"

Total victory. Their troops withdraw.

The wicked still fear the law.

But is there really any law? I am not so sure. And if it did exist at one time, where is it now? In point of fact, it's there if you want it to be but disappears when you don't. At times of crisis, we offer it up as a sacrifice, but when the crisis has passed, we no longer think in such terms. To what higher court can one appeal? The Farm Headquarters political department? The Yanghuo County Revolutionary Committee? There are countless serious matters to seize hold of and promote; moreover, the people who have not been deprived of schooling are not necessarily more intelligent than the stonecutters. Foolish people can be taught. We are taught wherever we go, but no one will talk reason. Most frightening of all are the teachers who extract political elements out of the nonpolitical, revolutionizing the very life out of our bodies.

Back at the dormitory, the brass lion eats away at our gray matter, and we find it difficult to sleep at noontime. Old Wu pontificates about Shang wine cups, Zhou tripods, Qin and Han tiles. Yellow Hair does not aspire to such refined topics. I worry that we will be forced to let the truth be known and say that during the current "movement," we made a mess of this unidentified tomb, stirring up all sorts of spirits and unleashing the primal forces of nature.

Only now does Old Wu, our wise sage, wake up. "Since the world is the way it is, it's best not to publicize this incident. No one is able to communicate with heaven, and no one can frighten the authoritative scholars of history into action. Those who might are under house arrest or have been banished. Who has any authority these days? When academia itself founders, it's tough to be a scholar."

Should we bury the lion here for a few years, or should we make a switch and pretend it is still inside the tomb? Old Wu announces that he is up for family leave next month and that he would prefer to take the relic back to his hometown, where he can hide it in his house. Leave it to him to come up with this plan. Over the last couple of years, his home has been searched twice, and there is no guarantee that it won't be searched again. Besides, with him off in another part of the world and the road home long and arduous, what would his family do if that happened?

Who would have thought this matter would become so irksome? Without warning, a sleeping lion enters our stagnant-water lives, and suddenly towering waves crash upon us, and we are surrounded by whirlpools. The world is fraught with peril.

Yellow Hair has no plan of his own, but he is quick to agree with other ideas. "Don't scratch your ears and rub your temples like an old pedant," he says. "Do you think we have to stuff it back into the coffin and bury it for it to be at rest? Aren't you afraid of the stench? Any way you spread it, that precious relic can't leave this precious place; that would have disastrous consequences for the local geomancy."

We are agreed in principle but continue to debate until I have a brilliant idea. Aren't we about to put up the roof truss? We can add a few extra diagonal stays between the roof beam and the purlins, making an attic the size of a chicken coop that no one will ever notice, allowing the lion to continue its peaceful slumber.

Shouts of approval on all sides. Master Yellow Hair says he'll take care of the details. To think of the violent criticism and revolutionary struggles that will take place in the meeting hall while the brass lion, the emblem of royalty and imperial power, sits solemnly overhead, reigning over all—an interesting picture, indeed.

What lies in store now for the sleeping lion, already steeped in the vicissitudes of history? Will our own fate be linked to it? Maybe the sleeping lion will be our charm in days to come, and we'll be famous throughout the nation on account of this great achievement.

After a moment's reflection, I say, "That would be wonderful, of course, but in keeping the relic for individual fame and fortune, let's not forget what is ethically proper. For educated youths like us, the nation and the people come first; so as soon as an opportunity arises, we should turn the piece over to a museum." Old Wu quickly adds that when he visits his family next, he will make inquiries in the provincial capital.

The blood courses even more passionately through our veins. Although confined to a wasteland, we have not forgotten our duty to the motherland, and this, the thought of our spiritual loyalty, moves us greatly.

Who would have guessed that before long, our dream would be shattered? When we go out to work that afternoon, there is no sight of the outside laborers, and when we poke around in the chamber, we find not only that the brass lion has not been returned but that many of the broken vessels have been carted away as well. What a band of wily foxes! We run straightaway to their lair, only to find that the place is deserted.

We stomp our feet, fuming, unable to contain our venom. Yellow Hair, especially, having never had a chance to see for himself if the object is brass or iron, is so angry that his yellow hairs are all standing on end. He vows to bring the stonecutters back, even if we have to traverse the four corners of the earth. Then it occurs to me: this place cannot be compared with the mainland, for on Hainan even if you sprouted wings, you would find it difficult to escape. The only way out is to hop on a boat at Haikou. Why not travel to the county seat and seal off the bus station—someplace where the law exists, where *they* won't be allowed to act as they please. If the stonecutters try to pull something funny, we can insist on seeing these officials, who will hardly be able to pardon them.

More shouts of approval. It is resolved that we will skip half a day's work and cut over to the highway to thumb a ride. The trucks that pass are mostly from the farm. Some stop, some don't. We press our way along the dusty road to the county bus station, which we carefully comb three times, then wait in ambush until the last bus finally prepares to leave, and we have nothing to show for our efforts.

Disconsolate, we make the rounds of the town. Anger fills every pore in our bodies, but we still need to eat, which in turn necessitates that several bottles of whiskey be opened. These we drink in silence. Soon, though, we begin to curse the band of thieves and then one another, for not having acted more decisively in the first place and for expecting the roving bunch of dirty thieves to have a change of conscience. The liquor and food are gone, and I hide a couple of plates to keep the tab down. Yellow Hair reaches under the table to snatch a machete from the seat of an intoxicated

Li aborigine. A gentleman, Old Wu takes only half the toothpicks in the jar. We derive little pleasure from these pranks, however, for our setback has been too great.

On the road home, there are no trucks traveling in our direction, so before the evening sun drops below the horizon, we negotiate the mountain paths back to the work brigade in abject misery. The path is narrow and the grass tall; with our heavy hearts, we are more than a little weary. But then we think of that gang of stonecutters laden down with heavy equipment and precious cargo that may not be jostled or bumped—now won't they be huffing and puffing at a snail's pace? Apart from the highway, the only road that goes to the county seat is this steep trail.

Upon hearing this, Yellow Hair slaps his head and shouts, "You little thieves, when the road narrows, enemies shall meet!"

Old Wu ponders for a moment. "Not necessarily," he says but offers no explanation.

No matter, we become very cautious. The sound of chattering insects and birds fills the air, and the layered mountain peaks are already beginning to be wrapped in fog. A few inauspicious shadows move about the expanse of grassland that surrounds us.

I break out in a sweat. In the lead, Old Wu disappears into a clump of tall grass, perhaps to relieve himself, and then all of a sudden he is following us.

Dark evening mist is now everywhere. In my uneasiness, I reflect upon the fact that having fled in panic, the gang of outside laborers does not have one penny of what is due them as salary for crushing stone, more than a month's worth of backbreaking work. There's no turning back now. I am convinced we will run into them. I can almost smell the blood; this is a lawless place. Maybe no one will get killed, but blood will be spilled, and whoever falls in this thick grass will have to wait for days for someone to come along.

And while it is true that bloodshed increases the value of antiques, it is better when it does not flow. Big, strong Old Wu remains at the end of our little squad. I have dedicated myself to the service of my country but cannot match Yellow Hair's bravery, for he leads the way, standing tall, grasping the broad Li machete and shouting threats: "Think I'm afraid you'll fly across the ocean? If you don't fork over the brass lion this time, I'll chop off your thief claws!"

But who's going to chop whom? The more Yellow Hair shouts, the more nervous I become. What has been the loud voice of righteousness now sounds a little feeble.

Yellow Hair also seems to have seen through all of this and makes a few snide remarks to Old Wu, saying that *we* are only risking our own lives but that if *they* die, they will leave entire families without providers. This inspires us to action.

Brass lion!

People want to be buried in martyrdom in behalf of an object that was once buried alive for thousands of years. That moment has arrived! Yellow Hair fixes his eye on something, crouches like a cat, screams wildly, then leaps forward. My body is ice-cold, but since I am one who values friendship over life itself, who joins his fellow soldiers as they advance or retreat, I rush over as well. The dim light of evening reflects strange rock formations and several battered straw hats. Atop the rocks, we spot a few lumps of wet tobacco pulp.

Relentlessly, Yellow Hair searches the site, whereupon he discovers that this gang of wily men has not traveled over primitive bridges and steep trails but has blazed a path across the open grassland.

With his sharp eyes, the determined Wu spots a bundle that has dropped into the crevice of a rock. As he unfolds the crackling paper, we assume at first that the object within is a tattered remnant of the coffin lining, but it turns out to be a silk painting of some value.

Yellow Hair is not about to give up now; he is determined to track down the stonecutters. But after this most recent assault, I am no longer battle hungry. It is nearly dark. The tall grass, the height of two people, is sending off a deathlike aura. Although my life is not particularly enjoyable, it is worth more than a piece of tarnished metal from an unidentified grave. All along, I have had a vague notion that the lion wasn't really from the Han, and this feeling is even stronger now that the object is owned by other people.

Old Wu, of course, concurs with me on this matter and analyzes the situation: "If we keep going, we'll cross over into the next county anyway; those Leizhou wanderers have allies everywhere, who will certainly be lying in ambush for us. Better to wait for the danger to pass before making any plans." His commentary is thorough; his logical deduction beyond reproach.

Yellow Hair swears loudly but has no recourse but to give up the chase.

By this time, the sky is completely black.

The brass lion has escaped alive: in retrospect, how can that tattered rag ever make up for the loss of the lion? When we shake it open, it is dirty and black, and what is left is sprinkled with holes and mildew, perhaps stained by bodily fluids and muddied to such an extent that we cannot even determine what the subject of the painting is. Mountains, water, or simply a rock? If it weren't for the faint trace of a square chop, one would think it nothing but a shroud.

Our great plan to offer up a national treasure has become a pipe dream. All that remains is a topic that gets revisited again and again, bringing a strain of sadness to the tedium of the life of educated youth.

I still can't understand why those men would abandon their hard-earned salary for a brass object, cutting themselves off from the possibility of ever working in this region again. Is it worth it? They won't ever be able to cash it in to feed their families.

Although time is magnanimous to brass, fate can change people's lives in an instant. Our dreamlike era comes to a dreamlike end, and we take leave of this far corner of the world, each of us forging his own path.

Yellow Hair throws his energies into a machine-tool factory, producing blades that slice through iron as easily as if it were mud. If people slice their fingers, however, they will not bleed—a quality that suits Yellow Hair's temperament.

Old Wu's great intelligence sweeps from the imperial examination system to the philosophy department at the university, where he continues to research isms and ideologies.

As for me, I become intoxicated with literature, paint a few pictures, and taking advantage of the literary wasteland, make a name for myself, to my great surprise. And so I have continued to write. At times, I reminisce and ask if I should excavate the story of the lion but always fail to put it in writing. I have a little talent, it is true, but I am a purist, and were I to romanticize the rise and fall of the sleeping lion, I could legitimately be accused of cheap vulgarity.

But how to forget such an event? The sleeping lion was lost for a thousand years before seeing the light of a single day; then it was lost again, this time never to return.

Only gradually do I learn how difficult the discipline of art can be, and how very cruel its means of sorting talent. A person like me who has read little must rely on diligence of effort, must browse through the classics of every school of thought if he is to dream of "scholarization." One day as I skim through the pages of a book, I find something that stops me cold: people in the great Western Han dynasty were unaware that lions even existed; moreover, only during the last years of the Eastern Han did our Chinese ancestors see one of these strange creatures for themselves. It was, of course, presented to officials in the remote area that is now Xinjiang, meaning that the palace residents never knew anything about it. How could a lion have migrated to Hainan so quickly to take a long nap?

Only an amateur would say that the brass lion was from the Han; I have always had my doubts. Who knows what dynasty and what era it really belongs to? Chinese history is so long that the thought of dating the piece is daunting.

I still cannot forget it.

And then one day, I get a chance to visit the ancient capital of Xi'an, to see firsthand the stone engravings of the Han, objects sim-

cause our great and wise government decided to permit the locals to dig tunnels into the mountains, some deep and some shallow, from which black rock was extracted. Narrow, twisting asphalt roads were built, pale-faced folk from the south moved in, and that led to a surfeit of tales regarding loose behavior. Generally speaking, southerners call that black, flammable stuff coal, but in Fritter Hollow it's called charcoal; it stands to reason that the black tunnels are called charcoal pits. The discovery that the term *charcoal pits* was unacceptable is linked to Wheatie Liu, Fritter Hollow's village chief, which meant he had the responsibility of overseeing activities at the charcoal pits even though people could no longer call them that; when 1992 rolled around, Wheatie Liu was being called the mine boss. Which is also what people once called the murderer Talented Wu.

Who, then, is Talented Wu?

## A Village Tale

In order to tell this story reasonably well, it is necessary to introduce Talented Wu, the murderer. Strictly speaking, you'd be lucky to find a single person in Fritter Hollow with anything good to say about Talented Wu. The explanation is as apparent as the cobblestones in the road. Talented Wu, the murderer, led a bunch of men over to the mountain quarries west of the village, where they dug seven or eight tunnels without extracting a single lump of coal; not only that, he wound up owing the village the grand sum of 140,000 yuan. That does not take into account the two hard-luck fellows who were crushed to death, both of whom were posthumously admitted into the Party: one was Small Stuff Wu, who had incredibly small genitals—about the size of lima beans—hence the name Small Stuff, and the other was Greater Principle Zhou, about whom more later (although the randy things I'll have to say about him should probably be kept from any women present).

People familiar with the history of Fritter Hollow do not have to be reminded of the following list of village chiefs:

| Dog Killer Li | 1948–1952 |
| Nine Changes Li | 1953–1959 |
| Rich Furs Wu | 1959–1965 |
| Good Stuff Wu | 1965–1967 |
| Defend the East Liu | 1967–1976 |
| Talented Wu | 1976–1986 |
| Wheatie Liu | 1986– |

And now the rest of you know that Talented Wu was village chief for an entire decade. People who emerged from their mother's womb in 1942 are, for the most part, considered to have been born in the year of the horse, but some who arrived on the scene a little late might well be considered a sheep. Talented Wu was born in the year of the horse, making his appearance in the twelfth month. He was a soldier for a time, serving in the western province of Qinghai, where there's a whole lot of salt; Talented Wu once said he had frequent nosebleeds. From there, he went to Sichuan to repair a cavernous pit that was dark as pitch and wet as an underground spring. After that, he came home, where his ability to use a gun got him elected head of the local militia, and his subsequent experience as militia head got him chosen village chief. That, more or less, is Talented Wu's story. But it is necessary to describe him physically, his good looks, as it were: of medium height, he had an oblong face with fair skin and dark, bushy brows. He was so good-looking that he managed to bring a sloe-eyed Sichuan girl home with him. There was talk that he had got her pregnant up on the Sichuan mountain where he was working, and sure enough, not long after she arrived in Fritter Hollow, she lay down one day, and out popped a baby boy.

Everybody called the girl the Sichuan dolt. If she had been from the northeast they would have called her the Northeast dolt; if from Hunan, they would have called her the Hunan dolt; and so forth. Easier that way.

Altogether, the Sichuan dolt presented Talented Wu with two sons: Golden Oil (the elder brother) and Silver Oil (his younger one). Both inherited their father's good looks. The older boy enjoyed his share of conquests in the corn patch, including one with the wife of Greater Principle Zhou. But now both boys are tasting the bitterness of prison life. How they keep themselves busy during the day is not documented, but at night they hunt for lice. As a rule, rather than pop lice between their thumbnails, people in prison set them free to find a new home elsewhere in the cell. While in prison, Golden Oil and Silver Oil exhaustively debate the question, Do lice eat grass?

## A Tale of Murder

People familiar with the topography of Fritter Hollow and its surrounding area would never overlook the Tatar Cemetery at the western end of town. A mound of earth where nothing grows, it looks like a big steamed bun, which is why it is also called Bun Hill. It's too flat to resemble a corn muffin, which is pointier; but if you travel west from Tatar Cemetery just a little ways, you'll come across a place actually called Muffin Hill.

For generations, people have spoken of all the Tatars, they with the light-brown hair and beards, who are buried in Tatar Cemetery; this fact, it goes without saying, is not unrelated to murder. Apparently, back then, people baked great big dough figurines in which they hid weapons so sharp they glittered, although most were less than imposing: daggers, even women's scissors. The people were ruled by a truly benighted government, which decreed that in the name of security, only one kitchen knife was allowed for each ten families. The people were not happy. (If you history buffs ponder for a moment, you will recall the one regime that instituted that particular measure: the Yuan dynasty of the Mongols; that narrows the time frame for this part of my story.) So the people baked dough figurines in which they hid their weapons; as a result, many unfortunate men whose beards were not dark enough paid the price. The slaughtered Tatars were then tossed helter-skelter into a pit, like so many pigs or dogs. This is one of Fritter Hollow's tales of murder.

If there is a kernel of doubt anywhere, it is why in the year

1981, people suddenly decided to go to Tatar Cemetery and dig up the remains, then sell pile after pile of bleached bones to the county pharmacy. Small Stuff Wu, who was still alive at the time, dug up a leg bone bigger than anyone had seen before, and people wondered how their ancestors could have been so much larger than they. Had their forefathers passed on defective genes? But then somebody informed the others that it wasn't a human bone at all; strangers in spectacles came, then concluded their investigation, announcing that these were dragon bones.

That being the case, Fritter Hollow did not have a history of murder after all.

Good! Now I feel free to relate a murder that *did* happen.

## Another Tale of Murder

Most murder stories are set in the dark of night. On the twenty-eighth of March 1986, light snowflakes fell on Fritter Hollow. Local men usually settled down with a bottle on such nights, which was just fine with their womenfolk, since that meant two things: the men would stay home and, after the lamps were put out, would perform much better than usual. Fritter Hollow's birthrate during this period outstripped that of all the neighboring communities; the women stretched their midriffs to the bursting point, and the babies just kept coming. Official investigators concluded that alcohol had increased the local men's vigor, and not until much later did they admit that alcohol was not the culprit. The high birthrate was a result of nonelectrification. Precious Li of the Family Planning Commission and Talented Wu once had a discussion that would be quoted often afterward:

"How the fuck can you people have so many babies?" Precious Li asked, his face dark.

"What do you expect people to do at night when there's no electricity?" Talented Wu was smiling.

This brief exchange was reported to the higher-ups, who received it with such hilarity that the chairman of the meeting had to call for order.

It was on the night when light snowflakes fell that Talented Wu and his sons, Golden Oil and Silver Oil, forced their way into Wheatie Liu's yard. Talented Wu carried a knife that sent sheep to their maker on New Year's; Golden Oil brought a hammer with a redwood handle; and Silver Oil came armed with a spade. As they neared Wheatie Liu's gate, Golden Oil snatched the knife out of his father's hand. "I'm younger than you," he said; "I should have the knife. Nothing scares me, certainly not that motherfucker!"

Simply put, the gate wasn't bolted. When Talented Wu and his sons entered the yard, they spotted Wheatie Liu and his wife laughing loudly in the pigpen off to the left, where their sow was delivering a litter of piglets. Golden Oil leaped into the pigpen, knife in hand, and attacked Wheatie Liu, who didn't even have time to stand up. Instinctively, he raised his right arm to protect his head. The arm quickly sustained seven cuts, so he raised his left arm over his head; that arm sustained five. Silver Oil, meanwhile, raised his spade over Wheatie Liu's wife. "Don't harm my wet nurse!" Golden Oil shouted. Silver Oil lowered his arm. As a baby, Golden Oil had suckled at Wheatie Liu's wife's breast. At that moment, Wheatie Liu's daughter, Maple Leaf, heard the commotion in the yard and came charging into the pigpen. Having been in the middle of making bean dough at the time, her arms were covered with bean powder to the elbows. Seeing what was happening, she shrieked and turned to run. Talented Wu, the murderer, sneaked up behind her and attacked with his hammer. Another shriek— from pain this time—and Maple Leaf was writhing on the ground.

Golden Oil resumed the attack on Wheatie Liu, whose arms were torn and bleeding, turning his fury on the buttocks, which sustained five cuts. Then came the pigs: the sow suffered nine cuts; each member of her litter suffered one. The sky resounded with screams—human and porcine; the ground ran red with the blood of people and swine. Right about then, someone vaulted into the pigpen and reached down for Maple Leaf, who was still writhing in the muck; he wondered what that thing swinging back and forth across her cheek was. Once he had her in the house, he held her up to the lamp, where he discovered it was her eyeball.

"Cram it back in!" the old devil Kiddie Wu urged the people crowding round, but how in the world were they to do that?

Back in the pigpen, Wheatie Liu's wife had soiled herself; she could neither stand nor speak, and as she sat amid the muck and blood, she heard the shouts of someone running around the yard in a panic: "The former village chief has killed the current one!"

## Wheatie Liu

Wheatie Liu had an older brother named Millet; his younger brothers were Rice and Beans. Most place and personal names in Fritter Hollow have something to do with food. If, for instance, someone is called Hundred Cereals, pretty soon there'll be someone named Thousand Cereals, then Ten Thousand Cereals; since the people of Fritter Hollow have no concept of million, the next in the series will be Heavenly Cereals, reaching the apex—until, that is, a rival family has a newborn baby whom they promptly name Gobble Cereals! Heavenly Cereals' family accepts the challenge, and the battle is engaged—fisticuffs, brandishing lit torches, and the like; few ever go so far as to pick up a knife and actually commit murder, as Talented Wu did.

Wheatie Liu was so fit that Talented Wu's attacks did not prove fatal, surprising no one. He even continued as village chief. No problem. Or hardly any. For three days after the death of Talented Wu, Wheatie Liu fell seriously ill. He'd never been sick a day in his life prior to 1992, as nearly as anyone could recall—not even a headache or a high fever. What could this mean?

## Matters Relating to Wheatie Liu

Like most villages, Fritter Hollow boasted a school, which was located in a local temple, whose clay idols, painted or not, had long since disappeared. The school was charged with teaching the local tots how to read some basic words, such as *attend school* and *finish school, cow* and *sheep, boy* and *girl;* how to write New Year's couplets, like "The earth is our mother" and "Nature rewards hard work"; and how to make banners for house-raisings that say RAISE THE ROOF BEAM FOR ETERNAL GOOD FORTUNE. There was a time when everyone had to know how to write "Fight selfishness, repudiate revisionism" and "Serve the people," but no one studied those things anymore.

Besides the school, Fritter Hollow had a country store, also like all villages, which had once been called a purchasing co-op; but now that name had fallen out of favor, and it was simply called the country store. Behind the country store, which was situated neither too far east nor too far south, stood a scrawny old tree of medium height, covered by fat red wriggling caterpillars known as hairy worms; actually, the name doesn't fit since they never grow real hair. Some people cook them over an open fire and eat them. Like all country stores, this one boasted a counter, some wooden shelves for stock, and blackened vats filled with soy sauce and vinegar. The shelves were lined with colorful canned goods and narrow-necked liquor bottles; ready-to-eat snacks and simple cotton goods were available plus, of course, hard candies. In the past, none of this stuff would have sold, but the coal mines changed that, and now it nearly flew out the door.

Every country store must have a proprietor; Fritter Hollow's proprietor had a scar on his neck, so everyone called him Scarface; a bit wide of the mark, perhaps, but Scarneck sounded funny, so Scarface it was. A man of thirty-five, Scarface was unusually fat. When there were no customers, he could normally be found sleeping atop the store counter. But on this particular day, he was running around busily, taking care of a steady stream of customers, until finally he asked one of them what was going on and learned that Wheatie Liu had fallen ill.

The first to buy canned goods and snacks to take along when calling on Wheatie Liu were men from the mines. They drifted in, made their purchases, and drifted out. Then came the villagers, who also drifted in, made their purchases, and drifted out. They came, and they came, and by nightfall the shelves were empty.

Broad Bean, the final customer of the day, was carrying a flashlight.

"Why so damned late? I've got nothing to sell," Scarface said.

"Who all's going?" Broad Bean could have kicked himself for being so late and letting the others buy up everything.

"People these days are all fucked up," Scarface blurted out. "Smell that," he continued, sniffing the air. "The guy's been dead for days now, and nobody's doing anything about it."

"Why don't you bring it up with Wheatie Liu?" Broad Bean said, flashing his light back and forth across Scarface's face. Back and forth, then straight in his eyes, then back and forth again. "Got the nerve?" Broad Bean asked.

## A Conversation of Sorts

In twenty or thirty years' time, when members of the next generation of Fritter Hollow's inhabitants look back on their glorious history, they may well talk about the time Wheatie Liu took ill and received 500 gifts of canned food. If that's all they say, of course, the word *history* is being ill served, so I must break in with a more revealing look at what happened that time Wheatie Liu took ill.

A conversation was recorded between Broad Bean and Wheatie Liu as the latter sat on his own kang, leaning up against a colorful backrest; the sides of the brick bed were decorated with depictions of colorful pomegranates, peonies, plum blossoms, watermelons, rabbits, bananas, pears, peanuts, apricots, and of course, magpies and goldfish.

Wheatie Liu had been enjoying a leisurely smoke when Broad Bean entered; the table, the kang, and the windowsill were all but covered with canned goods and packaged treats brought by well-wishers. It was a lovely sight, but to Broad Bean the real significance was the number of visitors it represented.

"Are you sick?" Broad Bean walked up and observed Wheatie Liu, who just smiled.

Here we must be reminded that Broad Bean's full name was

Broad Bean Tian and that Wheatie Liu's wife's name was Bean Sprout Tian, which tells you all you need to know about the relationship between Wheatie Liu and Broad Bean.

"Me, sick? No fucking way!" Wheatie Liu scooted up next to Broad Bean and whispered, "I just wanted to see if people would treat my death as meaningless, like they did with that other guy."

"How could anybody compare that murderer to you?" Broad Bean stared wide-eyed.

"What about that murderer?"

"Well, maggots are starting to wriggle into his yard," Broad Bean said with a shudder.

"It's still not time." Wheatie Liu smiled again. "Let him stink," he continued as he looked at the red scars on his arms.

Broad Bean held his tongue and studied his fingernails, first the left hand, then the right.

"Count them, see how many there are." Wheatie Liu, his eyes mere slits from the broad grin, pointed to the colorful array of canned goods. "See for yourself. I told people not to come, but they came anyway, didn't they?"

Broad Bean started counting, from the table all the way to the windowsill. "Three hundred and twenty-seven," he said.

"Now count the ones inside."

Surprised that there were more in the other room, Broad Bean froze for a moment before going in to see for himself. "A hundred and seventy-three," he said as he reentered the room.

"Go tell Scarface I want to see him," Wheatie Liu said. "It's business." He tossed a cigarette to Broad Bean.

That's as far as I need to go with this conversation. While I can't comment on its broader significance, on the surface at least we have learned that Wheatie Liu wasn't sick at all; and that is the beginning of yet another story. I've thought about whether I ought to see where this story takes us. I could, for example, say:

Fritter Hollow once had a village chief named Wheatie Liu, an upright, fair-minded, and handsome individual. One day, he took ill and was visited by a steady stream of well-wishers, young and old, male and female, all bearing gifts of canned food and prepared snacks, nearly wearing out his threshold. They wished him a speedy recovery. Fritter Hollow's accountant, Broad Bean Tian, dropped by, discovering to his surprise that Wheatie Liu wasn't really sick at all. This gave rise to an intricate tale. Listen up, for this is what happened . . .

A pretty common opening, if you ask me. What do you think? I realize that my readers are concerned about why Wheatie Liu would feign illness following the death of Talented Wu. So here goes.

## Yet Another Conversation

In Fritter Hollow, July is the best month to eat corn. On one particular night, Broad Bean's wife, Jade Beauty Wu, sweat oozing from every pore in her body, was boiling a pot of corn. Broad Bean was eating fragrant kernels right off a cob, using both hands. As he munched away, he told his wife to light a coil of mosquito incense. She walked over to the kang and lit one. "That guy pocketed seven or eight hundred just by getting sick," she muttered for the umpteenth time. His patience long since worn thin, Broad Bean reached out and poked her a couple of times on one of those fleshy spots of hers. "Fuck you!" he said.

Broad Bean's wife giggled. Picking up the mosquito coil, she walked over and set it down on the windowsill, then leaned her head back to sniff the air. "What a stink! If fucking doesn't kill me, the stink will."

Broad Bean also leaned his head back, then gagged and turned to run outside; before he got there, he puked all over the floor.

"You're supposed to do that in the pigpen," his wife said. "Who do you expect to eat it in the house? Your father?"

"Fuck you! I'll feed it to your mother if I feel like it! What if somebody heard you?" Broad Bean wiped his mouth. "I think I'm going to do it again."

His wife went outside and returned with the family pig in tow to clean up Broad Bean's yellow mess, but the animal turned its nose up at it.

"Fuck you, you old sow!" Broad Bean kicked the pig. "You're more pampered than Wheatie Liu!"

"That Wheatie Liu is no one to fool with," Broad Bean's wife said from the side. "I guess everyone's scared to make a phone call to the district office."

"Not so loud. Why don't you go?" Broad Bean said. "Take a look outside, make sure there's nobody around."

## Telephone

Fritter Hollow had a telephone, but hardly anyone ever used it. Countryfolk don't need such things; if they have something to say, that's what fences are for. If the district office called, it was always to talk to someone in charge about tying off tubes or wearing diaphragms or fertilizer costs or planting trees or water conservation. So there isn't much to say about telephones. The only reason they ever came into the lives of the citizens of Fritter Hollow was because of the episode when Talented Wu cut Wheatie Liu seventeen times, an incident that resulted in the loss of one of Maple Leaf's eyes. Big Eye Liu at the district clinic later had this to say: "You didn't think of making a phone call? If you'd called the clinic, would she be blind in one eye today?" Now that caused a real stir among the people.

In the final analysis, residents of Fritter Hollow thought about many things in their day-to-day lives: plows, hoes, axes, spades, picks, baskets, hampers, creels, carrying poles, wicker ornaments, pickle vats, manure sacks, rats, insects, dogs, pigs, donkeys, cows, cats, mules, goats, sheep, peppers, aniseed, salt, vinegar, children, women, eating, sex, and more; but they never thought about telephones. Until August 2, 1992, that is. That was five days after the death of Talented Wu, and Greater Principle Zhou's younger brother, Lesser Principle, suddenly thought about the telephone. "Why doesn't somebody call the epidemic-prevention station?"

Greater Principle Zhou spread himself across the counter and said to Scarface, "Let the epidemic-prevention people come over and collect the body of that fucker Talented Wu."

"Who will make the call?" Scarface asked as he handed over the telephone. "You?"

Greater Principle Zhou clammed up at that and rolled his eyes. "You want me to offend Wheatie Liu?" He spat in disgust.

No one else advocated telephoning the district office either, even though the stench from the ripening corpse was getting to them all, and they were dabbing wine on their upper lips to counteract it. Whose idea that was no one knows, but soon everyone was doing it; even the notoriously henpecked Kiddie Wu managed to talk his wife into giving him some wine, which he then guzzled down, having suffered a long dry spell.

## How Do I Wrap This Up?

Comrade New Day Tian once said that telling a story is a bit like weaving a basket: hard to start and hard to wrap up. But my stories seem to start out all right; it's wrapping them up that I have trouble with. This story about Fritter Hollow is a case in point; I have no idea how to end it. But I'll give it a try:

Neither Broad Bean Tian nor Scarface went straight home that day, since Wheatie Liu seemed to be softening his position a bit. They talked and they cajoled until Wheatie Liu decided to go with the current; he gave the OK to bury Talented Wu and put his own vengeance to rest. Broad Bean Tian and Scarface wasted no time getting on with the preparations, heading immediately for Talented Wu's home, where they were greeted with the revolting sight of a steady stream of maggots crawling out the door . . .

Sorry, I can't do it. That ending simply doesn't work since in point of fact, it was Wheatie Liu who summoned Broad Bean Tian, and not as I have given it above. This, then, is how the tale is supposed to end:

Without warning, Wheatie Liu summoned Broad Bean to his home. Seated all nice and proper, he smiled and said, "Call the fucking epidemic-prevention station, and have them dispose of that murderer!"

Broad Bean could hardly believe his ears. "You want me to call the district?" he asked with staring eyes.

"That's right."

It was another scorcher that day, and Broad Bean's shirt was soaked through by the time he reached the country store, where several men were drinking. They were quickly let in on the news that Wheatie Liu had told Broad Bean to phone the district.

## Lime

Before I take up the matter of lime, I need to deal with the aftermath of Broad Bean's telephone call to the district. The very next day, two very ordinary individuals—one tall, the other short, but enough of that—came to the village; when they strode into Talented Wu's courtyard, they drew the attention of Fritter Hollow villagers, who followed behind them—at some distance—to see what they would do inside the house of Talented Wu, the murderer. Everyone had pretty much stayed clear of the place over the past six days, but now a few people rested against the compound wall just in time to see the two district personnel come charging out of the house, ashen faced, and run straight to the medium-sized tree outside his yard, where they emptied the contents of their stomachs.

"What are those chickens doing in the yard?" someone asked.

"Eating maggots!" one of the district personnel replied. He had been vomiting so energetically that tears clouded his eyes.

Repulsion quickly showed on the villagers' faces.

"We have to spread some lime," the man said, "and put something under our noses."

Just before dark, Fritter Hollow villagers saw the two men from the district epidemic-prevention station enter Talented Wu's house and spread lime all over the floor; it showed up very white in the fading light of dusk but was quickly marked up by chicken tracks.

That evening, villagers repeatedly chased chickens out of the yard, sending the squawking birds flying over the wall in the direction of the tree.

How about that, enough of an ending for you?

No? Then, how about this (briefly):

The day after the epidemic-prevention personnel spread lime in and around the house was yet another scorcher. The villagers, having learned that Wheatie Liu had said it was OK to put Talented Wu into the ground, rushed over to watch, turning it into a festive occasion and raising clouds of dust. There they saw Wheatie Liu, in his straw hat, walk over to the shade of the tree in the company of the two district personnel; people at the rear of the crowd were too far away to hear what was being said but not too far away to see the strangers put on rubber gloves and spread a sheet of plastic on the ground, then dip their gauze masks in strong wine.

"Hell, I'll go inside and take a look," Wheatie Liu announced out of the blue. Everyone close enough to hear him stared as he lit a cigarette, took several casual puffs followed by several deep, violent ones. He then walked in the direction of Talented Wu's house, scattering the hungry chickens as he passed through the yard; one particular rooster knocked a bedpan off the wall and onto the head of a child on the ground. The startled victim screeched in pain as blood trickled down his scalp.

Like everyone else, Broad Bean watched Wheatie Liu enter Talented Wu's house; but instead of just standing there, he felt compelled to go inside and take a look for himself. Picking up a nearby bottle, he dabbed some wine on his upper lip, then stormed into Talented Wu's yard. He had a fit of sneezing, which made him feel, if anything, worse.

Talented Wu's room was too dark for the men to see anything. So Broad Bean closed his eyes to accustom them to the dim light; when he opened them, he was in for a shock. Wheatie Liu, who had lit the lamp, was looking down into the face of the murderer Talented Wu and stabbing him over and over with a pointed stick—always where the eyes had been.

"Scooping out maggots," Wheatie Liu said as he looked up at Broad Bean. "Those damned things go straight for the eyes," he added without a pause in his violent stabbing.

Broad Bean heard a snapping sound, not particularly loud but loud enough to scare the hell out of him. Wheatie Liu was holding half a stick in his hand; the other half was buried in one of Talented Wu's eye sockets!

## The True and Final Ending

Truth be told, I really don't have anything to add to the above; force me, and I'll say the obvious, that presently they went ahead and buried Talented Wu. Closely related to this event was a trip to the county seat by Wheatie Liu and his daughter, where she was fitted for a glass eye. Not much to that either, but since the thing had to be taken out and washed on a regular basis, the following was bound to happen: one night, Maple Leaf removed the eye and placed it in a drinking glass before going to bed, and Wheatie Liu came home from drinking with some friends from the district office; feeling particularly thirsty, he picked up his daughter's glass and gulped down every last drop. You can guess the rest.

Sometime later, Wheatie Liu's stomach started acting up, and he couldn't move his bowels no matter what. He went to see the district doctors, who put him through a rigorous examination of his digestive tract. When New China Fan, a renowned internist, looked through his anoscope, he nearly keeled over. After regaining his composure, he turned to the others and said something so funny they nearly died laughing: "I've looked up a lot of assholes in my life, but this is the first time I've had one look back at me!"

\* \* \*

And that, dear reader, is the end of my tale, except to say that Maple Leaf got another glass eye, and Wheatie Liu regretted not gouging out one of Talented Wu's eyes when he was alive, and so on and so forth . . .

**TRANSLATED BY HOWARD GOLDBLATT**

# About the Authors

**Ai Bei** ("Green Earth Mother"), born in Shanghai in 1957, has been a doctor and an army writer. She now resides in the United States.

**Bi Feiyu** ("The Ancestor") was born in Jiangsu province in 1964. He graduated from college in 1987 and is currently a reporter for the *Nanjing Daily*.

**Can Xue** ("The Summons") was born in Hunan province in 1953; there she finished primary school only. She has been a "barefoot doctor," a laborer, and a tailor; she is now a professional writer.

**Cao Naiqian** ("When I Think of You Late at Night, There's Nothing I Can Do") was born in 1949 in Shanxi province. He was once a miner and now works in the Public Security Bureau of Datong City. He started writing fiction in 1986.

**Chen Cun** ("Footsteps on the Roof") was born in Shanghai in 1954. Having worked as a peasant, a laborer, and a teacher, he is now a professional writer.

**Chen Ran** ("Sunshine Between the Lips") was born in 1962 in Beijing and studied music in her childhood. She turned to literature when she was eighteen and published her first works when she was twenty. She is now an editor for the Writers Publishing House.

Chi Li ("Willow Waist"), born in Hubei province in 1957, was sent to the countryside in her teens. Afterward she worked as a primary school teacher, a doctor, and an editor. She is now a professional writer.

Duo Duo ("The Day I Got to Xi'an"), born in 1951, is known for both his stories and his poetry. He was a journalist before leaving China for the West, where he now resides.

Ge Fei ("Remembering Mr. Wu You"), born in 1964 in Jiangsu province, studied Chinese literature at East China Normal University in Shanghai and taught there after graduation. The story included here, his first work, was published in 1986.

Hong Ying ("The Field") was born in 1962 in Chongqing. She began writing poetry in 1981 and fiction in 1988. She now lives in London.

Kong Jiesheng ("The Sleeping Lion"), born in Guangzhou in 1952, worked in a steel mill for two years before being sent to the countryside during the Cultural Revolution. He was one of the earliest writers to emerge in the post-Mao period.

Li Rui ("Sham Marriage") was born in 1950 in Beijing. Sent to a village in Shanxi province, where he spent several years, he later worked in a steel mill and began publishing fiction in the 1970s. He has been an editor for *Shanxi Literature* since 1977.

Li Xiao ("Grass on the Rooftop"), the son of Ba Jin, the celebrated novelist of the 1930s, was born in 1950 and now works in a government office in Shanghai.

Mo Yan ("The Cure"), born in 1956 in Shangdong province into a peasant family, joined the army in 1976 and later taught in a cultural unit of the People's Liberation Army in Beijing. In 1981 he started his career as a writer; he is the author of *Red Sorghum*.

Shi Tiesheng ("First Person") was born in Beijing in 1951. Crippled during the Cultural Revolution, he began publishing in 1979, frequently writing about the lives of handicapped people in China.

*Su Tong* ("The Brothers Shu"), a native of Jiangsu province, was born in 1963. He studied Chinese literature at Beijing Normal University and was an editor for *Zhongshan,* a literary magazine. The author of *Raise the Red Lantern,* he is currently a professional writer.

*Wang Meng* ("A String of Choices"), was born in Beijing in 1934. A member of the Communist Party, he served as Minister of Culture but was dismissed after the June Fourth Movement in 1989. He began writing in his twenties.

*Wang Xiangfu* ("Fritter Hollow Chronicles") was born in 1958 in Shanxi province. After graduating from college, he worked as a photographer for six years and a teacher for nearly ten.

*Yang Zhengguang* ("Moonlight over the Field of Ghosts"), a native of Shanxi province, was born in 1957. Besides fiction, he also writes film scripts.

*Yu Hua* ("The Past and the Punishments"), born in Hangzhou in 1960, works in a cultural center in Haiyan county, Zhejiang province. He started publishing fiction in 1983.

# Acknowledgments

"First Person" was first published as "Diyi rencheng" in *Zhongshan* (1992): 2. Copyright © 1992 by Shi Tiesheng. Printed by permission of the author. Translation copyright © 1995 by Thomas Moran.

"The Field" was first published as "Neinian de tianye" in *Zhongshan* (1994): 1. Copyright © 1994 by Hong Ying. Printed by permission of the author. Translation copyright © 1995 by Susan McFadden.

"The Brothers Shu" was first published as "Shu Nong" in 1988. Anthologized as "Shujia xiongdi" in *Shaonian xue,* Nanjing, 1993. Copyright © 1993 by Su Tong. Printed by permission of the author. Translation copyright © 1995 by Howard Goldblatt.

"A String of Choices" was first published as "Xuanze de licheng" in 1987. Anthologized in *Qiuxing qiyu ji,* Beijing, 1990. Copyright © 1990 by Wang Meng. Printed by permission of the author. Translation copyright © 1993 by Zhu Hong. English translation reprinted by permission of *Chicago Review.*

"Sham Marriage" was first published as "Jia hun" in 1986. Anthologized in *Hou tu: Lüliangshan yinxiang,* Taipei, 1988. Copyright © 1988 by Li Rui. Printed by permission of the author. Translation copyright © 1995 by William Schaefer and Fenghua Wang.

"The Day I Got to Xi'an" was first published as "Wo daoda Xi'an neitian" in *Beijing wenxue* (1987): 2. Copyright © 1987 by Duo Duo. Printed by permission of the author. Translation copyright © 1995 by John A. Crespi.

"Sunshine Between the Lips" was first published as "Zuichun li de yangguang" in *Zuichun li de yangguang,* Wuhan, 1992. Copyright © 1992 by Chen Ran. Printed by permission of the author. Translation copyright © 1995 by Shelley Wing Chan.

"Grass on the Rooftop" was first published as "Wuding shang de qingcao" in *Zhongguo* (1986): 6. Copyright © 1986 by Li Xiao. Printed by permission of the author. Translation copyright © 1989 by Madeline K. Spring. English translation reprinted by permission of *Mānoa.*

"The Past and the Punishments" was first published as "Wangshi yu xingfa" in 1989. Anthologized in *Xiaji taifeng,* Taipei, 1993. Copyright © 1993 by Yu Hua. Printed by permission of the author. Translation copyright © 1995 by Andrew F. Jones.

"The Cure" was first published as "Ling yao" in *Shen liao,* Beijing, 1993. Copyright © 1993 by Mo Yan. Printed by permission of the author. Translation copyright © 1995 by Howard Goldblatt.

"Green Earth Mother" was first published as "Lü du mu" in 1988. Anthologized in *Nü lao,* Taipei, 1990. Copyright © 1990 by Ai Bei. Printed by permission of the author. Translation copyright © 1990 by Howard Goldblatt. English translation reprinted from *Red Ivy Green Earth Mother* by permission of Gibbs Smith.

"When I Think of You Late at Night, There's Nothing I Can Do" was first published as "Dao heiye wo xiang ni meibanfa" in *Zhongguo xiaoshuo: 1988,* Hong Kong, 1989. Copyright © 1988 by Cao Naiqian. Printed by permission of the author. Translation copyright © 1995 by Howard Goldblatt.

"The Summons" was first published as "Buxiang de huhansheng" in *Qingxiang* (1993): 1. Copyright © 1993 by Can Xue. Printed by permission of the author. Translation copyright © 1995 by Jian Zhang and Ronald R. Janssen.

"The Ancestor" was first published as "Zuzong" in *Zhongshan* (1993): 6. Copyright © 1993 by Bi Feiyu. Printed by permission of the author. Translation copyright © 1995 by John Balcom.

"Moonlight over the Field of Ghosts" was first published as "Guidi shang de yueguang" in *Zhongguo* (1986): 9. Copyright ©

1986 by Yang Zhengguang. Printed by permission of the author. Translation copyright © 1989 by Ellen Lai-Shan Yeung. English translation reprinted by permission of *Mānoa*.

"Remembering Mr. Wu You" was first published as "Zhuiyi Wu You xiansheng" in *Mi zhou,* Beijing, 1989. Copyright © 1989 by Ge Fei. Printed by permission of the author. Translation copyright © 1995 by Howard Goldblatt.

"Footsteps on the Roof" was first published as "Wuding shang de jiaobu" in 1989. Anthologized in *Wuding shang de jiaobu,* Wuhan, 1992. Copyright © 1992 by Chen Cun. Printed by permission of the author. Translation copyright © 1995 by Hu Ying.

"Willow Waist" was first published as "Xi yao" in *Taiyang chushi,* Wuhan, 1992. Copyright © 1992 by Chi Li. Printed by permission of the author. Translation copyright © 1995 by Scott W. Galer.

"The Sleeping Lion" was first published as "Shui shi" in *Zuopin,* 1985. Copyright © 1985 by Kong Jiesheng. Printed by permission of the author. Translation copyright © 1995 by Susan McFadden.

"Fritter Hollow Chronicles" was first published as "Youbingwa jishi" in *Huacheng* (1993): 6. Copyright © 1993 by Wang Xiangfu. Printed by permission of the author. Translation copyright © 1995 by Howard Goldblatt.